Death and Compassion

Death and Compassion

The Elephant in Southern African Literature

Dan Wylie

WITS UNIVERSITY PRESS

Published in South Africa by:
Wits University Press
1 Jan Smuts Avenue
Johannesburg 2001

www.witspress.co.za

First published 2018

http://dx.doi.org.10.18772/12018102187

978-1-77614-218-7 (Paperback)
978-1-77614-446-4 (Hardback)
978-1-77614-219-4 (Web PDF)
978-1-77614-220-0 (EPUB)
978-1-77614-269-9 (Mobi)

Copyeditor: Monica Seeber
Proofreader: Alison Lockhart
Cover design: Fire and Lion
Typesetter: MPS
Typeset in 11 point Simoncini Garamond

Contents

Acknowledgements

This book has been maturing over many years, and there are doubt-less many helpers and discussants along the way whose contributions I have forgotten. Mostly, I read books, but I have tried to ground the study in the real elephant world, too. I have been to numerous game parks and elephant sanctuaries, sometimes just as a visitor 'in mufti', at other times in a more probing way. All of them yielded insights, experiences and conversations that affected my views. I have read many more books, articles and pamphlets, and seen more films, than I explore or can cite in this study, but they have made their subtle and cumulative impacts. All these direct and indirect influences I am thankful for. In particular I have had the inestimable pleasure of being close to elephants in various countries and quarters, most formatively in Zimbabwe's Mana Pools in the late 1970s, and most recently in Addo Elephant Park, near which I now happen to live. I am more than thank-ful for all these opportunities. They have changed my life.

Some conversations have been deep and ongoing, others brief but influential. Sometimes just a word of encouragement or interest, or the loan of a book, has been important to me. Of those I can recall, I thank Bob Bieder of Bloomington, Indiana, who opened the door to my writing *Elephant* for Reaktion Books; Mark Bowler, former Zimbabwe National Parks ranger; Jane Carruthers; Marion Garai of the Elephant Study and Action Group; Pat Irwin; Hennie Lötter; Alan Northover; Wayne Matthews, who let me trundle around Tembe Elephant Park with one of his rangers; Michelè Pickover; the late Norman Travers of Imire, Zimbabwe; Samantha Vice; Greg Vogt of the Knysna Elephant

Park; and Wendy Woodward and her Animals Studies group at the University of the Western Cape, several members of which have been periodically supportive and intrigued.

Friends and colleagues in Grahamstown have weathered innumerable grumbles, comments and presentations about elephants over the years. I thank you one and all for being there; you know who you are. Students in the several years of my literary animals and ecology courses have helped stimulate, instruct and entertain me. The Department of English at Rhodes University has been a consistently sustaining place in which to conduct research. Rhodes University itself has for years provided funding for a project that they likely had given up as a lost cause, but I hope the result will vindicate their trust in me. Most memorable perhaps was being able to deliver my inaugural lecture on elephants, which the audience must have thought deeply odd for a literary scholar. I suppose it is. Conveniently, Grahamstown hosts both the Cory Library for Historical Research and the National English Literary Museum, whose combined archives have provided innumerable sources and leads, and their wonderful staff have helped me out year after year. Anonymous readers helped me refine the manuscript, as did Monica Seeber, my editor, Victoria Hume, and the whole crew at Wits University Press.

Above all I pay tribute to my mother, Jill Wylie, whose devotion to saving animals remains paramount in my experience. I hope I am continuing her legacy in some fashion, though I doubt I will ever write as lucidly and deftly as she.

I have been to a number of conferences and colloquia to present nascent thoughts on elephants in literature; some of those eventuated in journal articles on which certain chapters of this book are based, albeit much modified, as follows:

'Elephants and Compassion: Ecological Criticism and South African Hunting Literature'. *English in Africa* 28, no. 2 (2001): 79–100.

'Elephants and the Ethics of Ecological Criticism: A Case Study in Recent South African Fiction'. In *Re-imagining Africa: New Critical Perspectives*, edited by Sue Kossew and Dianne Schwerdt, 175–193. New York: Nova Science, 2001.

'The Anthropomorphic Ethic: Fiction and the Animal Mind in Virginia Woolf's *Flush* and Barbara Gowdy's *The White Bone*'. *ISLE (Interdisciplinary Studies in Literature and Environment)* 9, no. 2 (2002): 115–132.

'Why Write a Poem about Elephants?' *Mosaic* 39, no. 4 (2006): 27–46.

'Feral Whispering: Conservation, Community and the Reach of the Literary'. *English in Africa* 41, no. 3 (2014): 119–140.

'Touching Trunks: Elephants, Ecology and Compassion in Three Southern African Teen Novels'. *Journal of Literary Studies* 30, no. 4 (2014): 25–45.

Introduction: Compassion for elephants?

'**A**re you an elefriend?' So asks a recent conservationist campaign for funds to help save elephants. What does the notion of 'friend' mean here? Is it true friendship to pop a few spare bucks in a distant organisation's account? What historical and natural processes have made this appeal necessary or attractive? What is the role of words themselves – the coinage 'elefriend', for one – in forming and disseminating ideas of compassion?

Elephants are in dire straits – again. They were virtually extirpated from much of Africa by European hunters in the eighteenth and nineteenth centuries, but resurged for a while in the twentieth, in the heyday of late colonial conservation efforts. Nevertheless, an estimated precolonial population of 26 million elephants now staggers at less than half a million – and is dropping at a terrifying pace. In one estimate, an elephant is being killed every 15 minutes. At that rate, in just a few short years they will be extinct north of the Zambezi – and the ivory merchants' attentions are already turning towards the still relatively abundant herds of southern Africa. On the one hand, a network of profiteers that has no compassion whatsoever for elephants; on the other, an embattled scattering of conservationists, local and international, who literally weep at the fate of our most charismatic mammal. All the literature, art, sentimentality, scientific research, legislation, fencing and even weaponry in the world seems next to powerless to resist the fatal snares, bullets and poisons deployed by Mammon, the God of Markets.

At the same time, reasons for being especially compassionate and protective towards elephants are now almost a cliché: their sheer size, high intelligence, rich emotional lives, capacity for mourning, caring matriarchal social structures, that enigmatic grace. In the twentieth century, a combination of conservation ethics and the aesthetics of the tourist gaze has profoundly affected the actual fate of elephants and their representation. Additionally, current ecological philosophies and sciences focus on the role of elephants within ecosystems, an angle gaining further importance from the gathering awareness of anthropogenic global warming and climate change.

It is one of the iconic conservation struggles of our time. Elephants have been with us for tens of centuries. They are integral to our history. It would be more than shameful to see them exterminated in the wild. It is vital that we understand how and why people develop compassion – or fail to – and what stories we tell ourselves in order to sustain those attitudes. In this book I hope to contribute to that understanding. I might have structured the book in a number of ways, but have chosen to explore how people have expressed attitudes towards elephants in several key genres of southern African literature over some two hundred years. Genre plays an important role in structuring feeling and even consequent action. A reader is likely to respond differently to factual than to fictional texts, and differently again to poetry. I do not wish to overstate the case here: there is no simple one-to-one consequence of reading this or that. Modern-day hunters, for example, read older accounts not only to gain support for their own attitudes towards killing animals; they may deliberately conform in behaviour to that depicted in admired predecessors' books and stories. In contrast, I am personally repelled by that very same hunting literature. Yet people write in certain ways in order to affect readers, sometimes just to entertain, often explicitly to persuade. I want to probe the primary features, and possible effects, of some major genres: indigenous forms, early European travelogues, hunting accounts, novels, game-ranger memoirs, scientists' accounts and poems. At numerous points, we will find these genres bleeding into one another at the edges, complicating the field further. While recognising that once oral performances – and, today, the visual arts including film, advertising and photography – have the greatest effect on the public imagination, I am confining myself to the written word – and that, mostly, in English.

Behind literary representations of elephants lies a tangle of deep and controversial philosophical debates – among them debates about animal mind and intelligence, animal legal rights, anthropocentric values as opposed to natural or intrinsic values, definitions and applications of community and aesthetic beauty, the ethics of killing. The literature on all these areas is vast. It is not my purpose to adjudicate in these debates as such, only to see how they appear in and inflect the tenor of selected literary works. For the interested reader, however, a good place to start would be Christen Wemmer and Catherine Christen's edited collection *Elephants and Ethics* which, though not specifically southern African in scope, contains several seminal essays. Unquestionably, elephants bring to a particular emotional head many current human-animal issues.

In short, I explore what southern Africa's literatures imply about who kills elephants and why; and who shows compassion towards them, in what ways and why. In particular, I follow a developing philosophical contestation between death and compassion, between those who kill and those who love and protect. It is a struggle that evolves in phases, has many dimensions and intersects with many other issues, but broadly it has intensified as modes of compassion have burgeoned and altered. And at certain unsettling points death and compassion become one and the same.

Death, though it may be inflicted for any number of reasons, has a certain simple finality about it. Compassion is more difficult to define. Take this passage from Edward Eastwood and Cathelijne Eastwood's fascinating book *Capturing the Spoor*, which surveys 'Bushman' rock art (including examples of elephants) and tries to divine the attitudes that inform it:

> The San have not only an intimate knowledge of animal behaviour but empathy with the animals themselves, sensing through their mythology and folktales and through experience that all creatures are kindred beings. Hunters, for example, might feel a strong bond of sympathy with the animals they hunt, experiencing sensations in their bodies that correspond with salient characteristics of the animal, such as the bearing of horns or bodily markings.

3

This attitude of respect and sympathy is best illustrated by the respectful way in which the San will talk about 'meat', meaning large prey animals. When a story demands that large prey animals are listed and mentioned, they are called by special respect names. The storyteller will say the names in a hushed tone, full of awe, and enumerates the animals as though entranced.[1]

This passage raises as many questions as it answers. It blurs the differences between 'empathy' and 'sympathy', between 'respect' and reverence, and perhaps between imaginative storytelling and reality. In any event, there is no sign, in either the rock art or the interpretation, that the reverence and awe that these paintings seem to express might be combined with anything resembling compassion.

The dictionaries tend to allow the terms 'sympathy', 'empathy' and 'compassion' to overlap or be vaguely equivalent, while philosophers and psychologists distinguish them in a bewildering number of ways, some of them contradictory. The writers studied here also use a range of related terms – pity, remorse, regret, guilt, sentimentality, love. Most dictionaries derive the word 'compassion' from the Latin *pati, passus*, to suffer (hence 'passive') and therefore align it with 'pity'. But 'pity' implies an inequality of conditions, a hierarchy of privilege over deprivation. 'Empathy' is different again. Martha Nussbaum, in *Compassion*, defines empathy as involving 'the ability to imagine the situation of the other'.[2] This is obviously a crucial element of the literary enterprise. An inability to behave empathetically or compassionately, in Nussbaum's view, results in part from a failure of the imagination. Imaginative failure may be societally induced or purely personal and even unstable from one moment or situation to another. Nussbaum outlines three thoughts or judgements she regards as essential to compassion. First is *seriousness*: one feels that the other's suffering is 'important and non-trivial'. Second is a judgement of *non-fault*: the sufferer is not deserving of that suffering or cruelty, or has not brought it down upon himself. The third judgement is of *similar possibilities*: the 'person who has compassion does often think that the suffering person is similar to him or herself and has possibilities in life that are similar'.[3] This of course is easiest with other humans; it gets more tricky across species, as with elephants, not only because they are so physiologically different, but also because the contexts in which they are approached can vary greatly. Empathy is not sufficient, nor automatically a ground for compassion, though it frequently does so serve. Action-orientated compassion is more firmly rationalised and contextualised, though there may be times, as Nancy Snow argues, when compassion can both be rational and independent of imagination – and even at times inappropriate.[4] In practice there are limits to compassion. Not only are some humans apparently immune to it, but even those who feel compassion can reach a certain boundary at which the feeling shuts down, or can be compartmentalised off. This kind of response is common to all of us, but is especially palpable in the writings of the elephant hunters. How we consider, couch, imagine and convey such feelings has a direct impact upon our concrete behaviour towards animals in the world.

We can, perhaps, over-refine our definitions. Many writers this book explores use the different terms loosely or interchangeably, and I will not attempt to parse the nuances in too rigorous a fashion. Still, it might be helpful for now to offer a working baseline. First, I link *pity* and *sympathy* as cousins of ineffectuality: they are kinds of an inner tut-tutting, which may recognise the other's suffering, but one neither identifies with the suffering nor is able or willing to do anything about it. Sometimes such a response is involuntary; it is also often predicated on some difference on a *scala natura*, a power differential in which the observer is seen as innately superior, or is buffered by being situationally better off.

Empathy, secondly, I take as a stronger imagining of the other's subjective feelings, especially suffering, an imaginative identification that might produce analogous physical responses in the observer. Empathetic feelings are founded on a greater sense of equality between sufferer and observer, or perhaps on a desire, *mutatis mutandis*, for fairness of treatment or life-possibility. This might involve what Nussbaum calls a 'capabilities approach' to animal rights: elephants, for example, should be permitted to fulfil their complete and essential elephant-ness.[5] Often, empathy will incorporate a belief in bodily or auditory *communication* of some kind – Bushman re-enactment or mimicry of animals for hunting or shamanistic purposes would count as empathetic. Empathy still retains an element of the involuntary and need not eventuate in action for the animal's benefit.

Compassion, finally, I regard as a more holistic term, a response that takes a more conscious place within an overarching schema of ethics (a considered animal rights philosophy, say, or a scientifically based conservation ethic). It may be provoked by instinctive responses of sympathy or imaginative empathy, but serves as a stronger call to action-in-the-world. Actions might take the rather distant form of, say, contributing funds to that 'elefriend' organisation or writing a supportive book; or a practical measure such as implementing animal rights laws, establishing and maintaining a sanctuary, or physically rescuing an individual elephant from a dire situation. Compassionate action, in practice, is probably seldom pure or unalloyed with human self-interest. It may even, as in the case of a mercy killing, mean the death of the animal. Nevertheless, compassion, crucially and by definition, is *intended to benefit the animal*.

In addition, I want to locate compassion in an echo chamber of communal meanings. I would like to relate it not only to the recognition of suffering, but also (admittedly with rather less etymological justification) to the Latin *passus* meaning 'step'. Hence, to be compassionate is also to be companionably *in step with*, alongside. It might thus be related to the words 'compass' and 'encompass', so that to be compassionate also means finding direction together *with* the other, and *within* some encompassing envelope, a community, or an ecosystem. Compassion says to the other, whether human or elephant: *We are on this journey together*.

Two related terms will keep resurfacing in this study: *sentimentality* and *anthropomorphism*. Sentimentality has a long and complex history, but in recent usage might be aligned with the ineffectuality of pity. Anthropomorphism – the attribution of 'human qualities' to animals – has been conventionally aligned with the imagination and so plays a major role in literary works. Philip Armstrong, in his essay '*Moby Dick* and Compassion', notes how both terms have routinely been disdained in the academic arena:

> The dismissal of human-animal studies relies on two strategies, often in combination. The first is the allegation of sentimentality, which presumes

the researchers of such topics are distracted from the real commerce of human life, presumably by an immature emotional investment in non-human animals . . . The second, perceived as both a cause and an effect of the first, is the allegation of anthropomorphism, which assumes – more often than it demonstrates – that any study not conducted according to rigid scientific principles inevitably misunderstands nonhumans by projecting onto them human characteristics.[6]

However, recent scholarship, in conjunction with the growth in animal rights activism, has been less resistant to admissions of feelings and of human-animal commonality.[7] In imaginative works, the question of anthropomorphism is not only unavoidable, but actually becomes a tool of attitude. Nevertheless, anthropomorphism's ostensible conflict with positivist science continues to niggle, even as it becomes more common for writers to imagine the elephant's point of view. The role of what Sara Ahmed calls the 'emotionality of texts' becomes crucial.[8] T.S. Eliot famously argued that the emotions involved in reading a literary work are quite distinct from those experienced in everyday life. Texts can even act as shield or distraction from the emotionality of the real. However, in some respects the literary emotion is arguably dependent on, or an extension of, our everyday ability to imagine ourselves, however tenuously or even falsely, *as* the suffering (or, for that matter, joyful) other, and so proves crucial to sociality itself.

Such imaginative identification, and therefore compassion, is relatively easy to extend to the domesticated and unthreatening pet, but much less so to a wild animal so physically different, ethically indifferent, free-ranging and potentially dangerous as an elephant. Indeed, one view suggests that the most compassionate thing one can do for wildlife is to leave it strictly alone – hence the idea of 'wilderness areas' or 'national parks' in which 'wild' animals can exist, apparently independent and unhindered. But, in effect, almost all situations involve the need to balance human self-interests with those of other creatures. The formal park, where only a small voyeuristic elite can arrange to visit or stay, is arguably itself a mode of exploitation. Animals benefit in certain ways, but the sector can succumb to untenable romantic notions of 'untamed' or 'pristine' wilderness, whereas scientists and managers often argue that the primary goal is 'ecosystem integrity', on which all ethical decisions should be based. Both stances are idealistic. At the same time, the 'animal rights' movement, advocating compassionate treatment on legal and philosophical grounds, has clashed with the managerial pragmatics into which the wildlife situation has been thrown, as well as with 'animal welfare' advocates less concerned with legal rights than with ameliorating the plight of individual animals. The texts studied here show the increasing presence of what Gregg Mitman has called 'pachyderm personalities' as being ethically significant.[9]

On the one hand, as Holmes Rolston III writes in his essay 'Ethical Responsibilities toward Wildlife', other animals have their own being, and any ethic applied needs to recognise their difference from us: 'Life in the wild is not . . . life in culture'. Or, to paraphrase one ecologist, whatever elephants deserve, they are not large, grey humans. Nevertheless, Rolston notes hopefully, 'Once we can discriminate the differences between wild nature and human culture, the *is* in nature and the *ought* in ethics are not so far apart.' Moreover, 'recent scientific activity has increasingly smeared the human/animal boundary line. Animal anatomy, biochemistry, perception, cognition, experience, behaviour, and evolutionary history are kin to our own . . . Ethical progress has also smeared the boundary. Sensory pleasures are a good thing, ethics should be egalitarian, nonarbitrary, nondiscriminatory.'[10] Much of the literature explored in this book evidences the tensions between these two poles of difference and egalitarianism.

Studying literary representations obliges us to consider words and emotions such as compassion (or, indeed, indifference or cruelty) as fundamental constituents in a network of ethical relationships. Emotional preconceptions, mediated through words, help to constitute the objects (elephants, say) *as meaningful* in ways that have directly physical and profoundly societal consequences. And those meanings shift and migrate over the historical phases covered in the ensuing chapters.

The presence of elephants pervades our cultures, in films and newspaper reports, common proverbs, tourist trinkets and advertising anything from cement to popcorn. Elephants appear regularly and iconically in the art world, as when the philosopher Adam Cruise symbolically erects and burns a pile of wire-and-plastic tusks, or when the sculptor Andries Botha sparks a political furore by arranging elephant figures, made of tyre rubber, on a highway island in KwaZulu-Natal.[11] All these forms deserve further study. My interest here, however, is more narrowly in *literature*, and that in just a few selected genres. I am therefore also obviously confined to the period of literacy in southern Africa that was introduced by Jan van Riebeeck's landing at the Cape in 1652. This should not be taken to mean that non-literary indigenous or 'precolonial' attitudes are less important, or do not continue to exert an influence today. Southern African humans must have harboured feelings about elephants, where they were encountered, for tens of thousands of years before literate Europeans invaded. Research into elephant-related oral productions in the subcontinent's many languages would be a valuable project, but it is not one for which I am methodologically trained or linguistically equipped. In some ways, this book is a study in the recent dominance of Western literacy, its translation of indigenous into written forms, and the ethical links of that literacy to domination over the natural world.

As I explore in chapter 1, our oldest access to precolonial attitudes towards animals is the subcontinent's widespread and bewitching rock art. However, this chapter centrally asks: is it even possible to divine 'authentic' emotional responses from such work? Other oral forms – notably folk tales, praise poems and proverbs – are also now inevitably mediated by layers of translation, censorship and public repackaging for literate audiences. This complex dissemination of ancient forms into modern media has both illuminating and troubling dimensions. In sum, it becomes difficult to say just whose cruelty, reverence or compassion we are finally seeing.

Indigenous attitudes towards wild animals were doubtless not always benign, but it is certain that they were never as comprehensively murderous as those introduced by European incursion. The difference, roughly, was religious respect and dependence versus commercial materialism and exploitation. In the seventeenth and eighteenth centuries this incursion was multinational, though ultimately dominated by the Dutch and English. The early travellers' accounts were German, Swedish, French and Scots as well as English. They were also largely of a class: highly literate and increasingly of a rationalistic bent. (We have to keep remembering that there were thousands of other invaders – farmers, traders, soldiers, hunters, sundry itinerants and escapees who never left a literary mark on history.) What was, and is, the role of science in structuring responses to elephant presences? These gentlemen-scientists' curiosity often came with a nationalistic zeal and an unthinkingly destructive approach to the African wilderness and its denizens.

Accounts of elephants are fairly rare in the seventeenth century. Chapter 2 focuses on a century of travel accounts bracketed by two key scientific events: the publication of Carl Linnaeus's *Systema Naturae* in 1735 and Charles Darwin's visit to the Cape in 1836. Many, if not all, of the eighteenth-century accounts draw on the systematising and curiosity-driven mentality of Linnaeus's Enlightenment Europe, while Darwin's brief but significant presence introduces the evolutionary perspectives that would subsequently dominate the zoological and ecological sciences. Understandings of and emotional attitudes towards elephants have been radically affected by the increasing dominance of the scientific stance (which is not to imply consensus among the many different branches of professionalising science), manifesting in palpable tensions between the emotional and the empirical in recent times.

Unlike the indigenous peoples, eighteenth-century European travellers and traders had sufficient firepower to obliterate literally millions of southern Africa's wild animals. They did so without much evident compunction. This nerveless slaughter accelerated throughout the nineteenth century. Why did men hunt elephants? Indeed, why do men hunt at all? The hunters' accounts of the period – the subject of chapter 3 – come to form as distinct a genre as their predecessors' travel accounts while echoing and extending them in many respects. Hunters and travellers both saw themselves as point men for imperial expansion. If the eighteenth-century travellers focused on information and specimen gathering, with wildlife slaughter as a concomitant, the bias was reversed in the nineteenth century. Now, commerce rather than discovery underpinned adventure. The opposite of compassion for elephants is ivory.

The killing was not wholly devoid of moral ambiguity, but compassionate feelings are, in these hunters' tales, from Roualeyn

Gordon-Cumming to F.C. Selous, observably and repeatedly shut down at the crucial moment, such that by the last quarter of the century there were scarcely any elephants left to hunt on the subcontinent. Loss modulated quite rapidly through 'preservation' philosophies into 'conservation' and restoration, for a mixture of motivations, not all of them especially honourable. The alliance of conservation ethics – exemplified by the establishment of the flagship Kruger National Park around the turn of the century – with rapid industrialisation, the spread of agriculture and ranching, and racially skewed land distribution, introduced a whole new raft of ethical dilemmas.

Can adult fiction, the focus of chapter 4, bring something specific to the compassion debate? Mayne Reid's *The Young Yagers*, originally published in 1850, sets many of the generic norms, but features elephants sparsely. Similarly, the wild Africa fantasies of H. Rider Haggard in the 1890s and early twentieth century represent the ubiquitous elephant hunt only tangentially. Between Haggard and Stuart Cloete nearly three-quarters of a century later, regionally produced fictional treatments of elephants seem especially scarce (barring various short stories, which I bypass in favour of novels). When elephant-orientated novels reappear halfway through the twentieth century, they first centralise a kind of David and Goliath duel, then begin to evince the appearance of the 'hands-off' or preservationist ethic appearing *within* the hunting manifold. The hunter grows sick of the slaughter as well as concerned for whole-species loss, so later novels begin to overlap with game-ranger memoirs in their location in or near formalised parks, with rangers themselves as more prominent characters. Hence, Wilbur Smith's *Elephant Song* can deal, if rather opportunistically, with the ethical dilemmas of culling elephants within a park; and in Dalene Mathee's *Circles in the Forest* – possibly the only southern African adult novel to portray the elephant's plight in a genuinely ecological way – a self-appointed elephant guardian is the central character.

If the adult fiction makes for reading as grim as the hunting accounts, fiction for children indulges the sentimental aspects of compassion. Anthropomorphism and empathetic emotions seem more permissible for the juvenile mind, to be grown out of eventually – or so the (adult) writers assume. Yet they raise a crucial question: how do we, and how should we, educate our children about the natural world? The teen fictions I examine in chapter 5 are appropriately grittier than those for younger children, and the shift in ethical stance is marked. Now the hunter is villainised, the game ranger is the moral hero, and there is no doubt that the elephant is the vector for compassion, even for companionship. The influence of all the developments in animal rights, consciousness studies, ecology and conservation ethics are made especially vivid in this range of work – and here, more than in any other genre, questions of didactic efficacy and of the roles played by literature in education are foregrounded. The links between the social construction of compassion and fictional affect are complex but crucial – to all genres, not just juvenile fiction.

Game-ranger memoirs, explored in chapter 6, come to constitute another quite distinct genre, but they owe much to the episodic structure and the laconic tones of the earlier hunting accounts. At the same time, they frequently make use of the techniques of narrative and description that one would readily associate with fiction. There is a good century of such works, starting with Harry Wolhuter and James Stevenson-Hamilton and the founding of Kruger. These two – though there were hardly any elephants to write of in their days – exemplify the shift from hunting to conservation ethics, from killing to photography and tourism. Such vicarious experiencing has become the dominant mode of our time. In the later twentieth century, game-ranger memoirs proliferate, usually popular and jocular, but also regularly grappling with the ethical issues of enclosing artificial ecosystems, and of elephant culling.

The game-ranger genre leaks into another, examined in chapter 7, which I term the 'field-research memoir' – popularised accounts of hard-science elephant research and/or reserve management. These books not only enhance perceptions of elephants as marvellous and complex animals deserving of protection, but also tackle the complex problems of artificially confined elephants' interface with neighbouring human settlements, encroachments, depredations and national politics. Lawrence Anthony's *The Elephant Whisperer* is probably the best known. These kinds of memoirs raise particularly sharply the question of whether our sense and definition of community – that grouping within which one might effectively exercise compassion – can really be extended to include megafauna as massive and awkward as the elephant. These works are predicated on the historical reduction of elephants to a shadow of their former populations and ranges, as well as on the forbidding fact that the threat is increasing, not diminishing. Protected areas, for all their problems, seem more necessary than ever.

Nowhere is this sense of the threatened remnant sharper than in the cases of the Knysna and Addo elephant populations, which have spawned a minor literature of their own. Departing from the structure of previous chapters, in chapter 8 I explore this 'cult of the remnant' across genres, pulling together a number of already latent themes. Oddly, even as science strives for ever-more refined knowledge of the elephant (the Addo herd is exceptionally well researched), in the Knysna case the very mysteriousness of the forest elephants becomes essential to their preservation, a symbolic mystique whose relation to compassion is intriguing.

Finally, one might expect that the genre best suited to expressing emotional attachment to elephants would be poetry – and to a large degree that expectation is fulfilled by the selection of poems I examine in chapter 9. These range from the precolonial to the present and are highly variable in thrust, but if one can risk a generalisation it is that in poetry the postulate of an elephantine inner life is imaginatively transmuted into, or reflected in, the human inner response in a highly refined fashion. Poems are, in their way, the verbal equivalent of gazing at close quarters into a lustrous elephant's eye; one cannot help but feel *considered*, weighed up, the lineaments of one's humanity gently exposed.

It is often said that what makes the elephant a suitable subject for compassion is its combination of near-human features: intelligence, memory, maternal tenderness, an evidently rich emotional life, and so on. So what makes some people from within the *same* culture feel so differently? I grieve with every elephant death and abuse I hear about; yet a school contemporary of mine who had a similar upbringing has no compunction in shooting them. And attitudes can change even within one person, in the course of a life. I know a state veterinarian who, for years, calmly justified culling elephants in the service of the 'bigger picture' – the economics of it, and ecological balance – but finally found it 'distasteful' (as he put it) and I could see that the thought of killing another elephant deeply pained him.

Lauren Berleant, in the introduction to her volume of essays *Compassion: The Culture and Politics of an Emotion* has this to say: 'When the response to suffering's scene is compassion – as opposed to, say, pleasure, fascination, hopelessness, or resentment – compassion measures one's values (or one's government's values) in terms of the demonstrated capacity not to turn one's head away but to embrace a sense of obligation to remember what one has seen and, in response to that haunting, to become involved in a story of rescue or amelioration: to take a sad song and make it better.'[12]

Chapter 1

No Simple Sort of Mirror:
Compassion and the precolonial

About five million years ago, when the West Coast region of South Africa was a lot more lush than it is today, a flash flood abruptly drowned an extraordinary number of animals. Entombed in mud until phosphate miners uncovered them in the 1950s, the bones of sabre-toothed cats, African bears and short-necked giraffes constitute one of the richest Pliocene-era fossil deposits on the planet.

Among the specimens are the remains of an early four-tusked elephantine species, a gomphothere whose descendants would evolve into the three main genera of modern-day elephants. Four million years ago *Mammuthus planifrons* roamed the region, twice migrating into Europe and Asia, founding the woolly-mammoth genealogies as well as the Asian elephant. Left behind was the line of *Loxodonta*, the African elephant. One of them shed a tusk, which fossilised around 130 000 years ago, eventually to be unearthed north of Durban.[1] These recent types thus virtually co-evolved with humans and some anthropologists have speculated that humans would not have been able to migrate out of Africa had the elephants not preceded them. Human and elephant histories are deeply entangled from the beginnings of memory itself.

The fossils of the West Coast deposit at Langebaanweg, solidified remnants of once living, eating, fighting, breeding and bleeding creatures, are today carefully preserved beneath a coating of yellowish resin.

Rather like these fossils, precolonial stories tend to be extracted from their original contexts, eviscerated of the vivacity of living performance and overlaid with a patina of modern attitudes. Once-oral meanings are simultaneously preserved and occluded, repackaged in literate forms, archived, retold, republished in lavishly illustrated books mostly aimed at children and in simplified tourist brochures and Internet sites. There are various problems, then: the infantilisation of stories that would once have been rich with adult meaning; their reduction to mere moralising; their increasing decontextualisation; and inevitable slippages in translation. Even as we moderns reach back into the past, in the very reaching we alter the nature of what we grasp.

Pre-modern depictions of human-elephant relations are so modified or fragmentary that it is hard to discern attitudes with any certainty. Did the earliest humans evince anything like compassion for the massive mammalians? Can we find traces of compassion for elephants in precolonial stories, folk tales, fables, legends, myths? Was there room for animal compassion in hunter-gatherer societies? What relationships pertain between compassion and reverence, between compassion and taboo? Precolonial societies are often praised for their ecological knowledge and attunement, but does that intimacy eventuate in compassion or just in more effective exploitation, defence or coexistence? Or is compassion effectively a modern invention? Is there, in modern times, a hidden link between compassion and taming, compassion dependent on control, on the reduction if not elimination of threat or necessary usage? How does this modern stance emerge in recent refashionings of the precolonial tales?

The oldest traces of elephant-human relations in southern Africa are those captured in rock art, either painted or chipped out of suitable surfaces. Elephants are depicted less often than many other species. It is hard to decipher these images, distributed across the subcontinent, from the Cederberg in the west to the Drakensberg in the east, from the petroglyphs of Twyfelfontein in Namibia to the life-sized paintings near Mtoko, Zimbabwe. Beliefs about elephants may vary, subtly or widely, from one region or era to another. The elephant, through its sheer size and its inherent danger to humans, probably provoked fearful awe or reverence among all peoples, but it seems unsatisfactory to collapse all

16

images into a single generalised realm of meaning, as Tim Forssman and Ken Gutteridge tend to do in their book *Bushman Rock Art*:

> The elephant is one of the Great Meat Animals and thus is one of the most powerful animals in the bush. Essentially, it contains more *n/om* [magico-spiritual force] than most other creatures. Bushmen view the elephants as powerful for a number of reasons. Firstly, it is an enormous animal and can be very dangerous. Secondly, Bushmen believe it maintained human qualities from the First Order of Existence, when all animals were human. For example, elephants are very affectionate. During typical herd or parent-offspring interaction they frequently appear to embrace, intertwining trunks, often touching, smelling or rubbing one another. Further, Bushmen perceive that elephant meat is similar to that of humans; they also believe elephants dance, something very important to Bushman society.[2]

The authors supply no specificity of sources, age or locations, and only a generalised explanation of what they take to be the informing dynamics. The notion that elephants continue to display quasi-human qualities once dominant in a mythical Early Age, when humans and animals were one, seems to be expressed in taboo rather than compassion. In support, Forssman and Gutteridge mention the story of the Elephant Girl, a tale that exists in more than one version, but seems derived in their version from Megan Biesele's research among the Ju/'hoansi of the Kalahari in *Women Like Meat* (more on this below). Forssman and Gutteridge credibly suggest that depictions of elephants being pierced by arrows are not hunts as much as they are metaphors for shamanistic acquisition of the elephants' intrinsic potency; their inclusion of an elephant petroglyph in which the animal is surrounded by obvious therianthropic figures – human-animal hybrids – supports this suggestion. (They do not say so, but this oft-reproduced image is from the Cederberg.)

But the trance-dance interpretation need not exclude the occasional hunt, such as a rare elephant depiction in the Drakensberg.[3] Bert Woodhouse's overview of elephant rock art in *When Animals Were People* argues for a number of elephant hunt depictions, including of hamstringing as a technique.[4] The elephant was obviously a formidable adversary, but not entirely beyond the capacity of arrow- and spear-wielding hunters to subdue, even if it took days of harassing the animal to exhaustion, as in an account from the 1860s.[5] Both Khoisan and Xhosa hunters used staked pits for elephants, probably for centuries, and certainly as early as the eighteenth century; somewhat comically, François le Vaillant fell into one in the Outeniqua area in 1782.[6] Such colonial-era accounts of indigenous hunting methods may be cautiously extrapolated back in time and across the continent. Killing an elephant would be a rare and therefore powerful event, worthy of rock art depiction.

Woodhouse has also argued that a number of elephant depictions – including examples as far-flung as Harrismith, Piketberg, Uitenhage and Zimbabwe – are associated with rainmaking; he points to trance-associated showers of lines in the vicinity, overarching 'rainbows' and preternaturally elongated trunks in some cases.[7] The latter features fascinatingly in a painting from the so-called Ebusingata panel, now in the KwaZulu-Natal Museum, Pietermaritzburg. A shamanic therianthropic figure bears ritual objects, including fly whisks, is apparently surrounded by a swarm of bees and sports an elephant's tusks, trunk and perhaps forefeet. One can only wonder if the living shaman felt that oft-encountered testimony of Bushmen hunters: they can detect or even attract animals through tremors and vibrations in their own bodies – a highly attuned form of somatic empathy, perhaps. Some are sceptical:

'In my imagination, I become the animal I am stalking', is linked to the supposed San cosmology that animals derived from humans. The zoologist Charles Handley who hunted with the Ju/'hoansi in 1952 while a member of the Marshall Family Expedition said that hunters 'could actually think like the animal enough so that they soon knew what its strategy was, where it was going. [It was] not some kind of mystical ability unknown to outsiders[:] the ability to track is learnt, not genetically encoded.[8]

The empathetic connection with rain and trance is persuasive in some cases, admittedly tentative in others, and certainly not always applicable. Some commentators eschew speculation altogether and settle for mere description, as in Peter Garlake's treatment of some Zimbabwean rock art:

> Through the sheer size of the images, elephants dominate the paintings in many caves. Many are shown in outline only and some are huge – up to 4 m across. The tusks and ears of elephants caused particular problems of representation in profile, the eartips because they lie against the body, the tusks because only one is visible from the side. The ears were therefore represented either by showing the tip breaking and extending beyond the outline of back and head or by adding two quite unrealistic curved mop-like shapes to the top of the head. Mop-eared elephants were almost never drawn in outline only. There is probably some genuinely stylistic and chronological significance to these two sorts of representation. Elephants with 'mop' ears in solid paint seem to be altogether cruder, more lifeless and less realistic . . . To judge by superpositions, the solid images are later paintings than the others.[9]

Garlake believes that each painting 'was conceived as representing a generalised archetype, not a particular individual', but some paintings evince a creditable closeness of observation, as in the raised tail of alarm in one Zimbabwean example, the searching, scenting raised trunk in a depiction from the Dordrecht area of the Eastern Cape, or one elephant holding another's tail in a Cederberg image. Such close observation presumably embodies some form of familiar coexistence; hunting scenes might evince the associated frissons of fear, challenge, excitement or triumph; shamanic scenes might well express bodily felt empathetic resonances or reverential taboo. But these are generalisations and the degree to which any of these ideas entail *compassionate* action designed to benefit the animals must remain somewhat open.

Edward Eastwood and Cathelijne Eastwood's *Capturing the Spoor*, quoted in the introduction to this volume, and Forssman and Gutteridge above, are examples of a commonly used attempt to explicate rock art by reference to recorded oral tales and similar testimonies. These writers make an assumption that 'sensing through the myths' and through bodily sensations, an empathy with the animals is established analogous to that interpreted in the rock art.[10] But do the myths and tales 'say' the same thing as the rock art? As the researcher Janette Deacon writes, 'neither one is derived from the other'.[11] Matthias Guenther similarly argues that the naturalistic rock art cannot be said to be 'illustrations' of particular myths and legends, like illustrations accompanying text in modern coffee-table books.[12] Biesele convincingly shows, moreover, that the folk tales and legends themselves are 'no simple sort of mirror' of their society.[13] Hunter-gatherer social organisation is highly variable. Far from being static or unified in their 'traditions', those societies were characterised, Guenther writes, by 'flexibility, fluidity, adaptability, individual autonomy, organisational ability and ambiguity and lack of standardisation of belief'.[14] Similarly, Bushman stories or *kukummi* are impelled by a wide variety of motives; the very term *kukummi* encompasses all kinds of myth, tale and anecdotal account, rendering Western generic terms such as legend, poem or folk tale of shaky analytical value. Guenther calls the myths 'hauntingly asocial and pre-cultural'. This may be overstated: products of the imagination, however 'liminal and surreal' they may appear, must still somehow be connected to and illuminative of the way a people thinks of itself (its culture). In any event, notably missing from the analyses of Guenther and others is any thorough consideration of the *emotional* import of stories and representations. It is impossible to divine what the artists *felt* towards the animals, including elephants, that they were depicting.

Southern African literature is replete with collections of so-called folk tales, stories undying in their appeal, retold and recycled in various formats, sometimes over many decades, tapping the deepest layers of the psyche. Animal tales have always been particularly powerful and vivacious. Ruth Finnegan, the doyenne of oral literature studies, neatly calls this modern-era recycling of tales a 'snaring into writing' – new in form, but also 'the kind of human processing and negotiating that has always been going on everywhere . . . founded in the interaction of many participants, using and negotiating and adapting them in multifarious transformations to a whole variety of purposes'.[15] One may be inclined to take the tales for what they are: innovative and vivid collaborations across eras and cultures but, still, some cautionary notes are necessary.

Firstly, the ethnicities these collections purport to illustrate or identify are seldom as stable as they seem, nor are their folk tales as timeless as they are said to be. The 'Zulu', for example, came into being as a self-identifying unit only in the eighteenth century, and the name has proved a highly mobile signifier, flexing and narrowing through successive stages of colonial boundary-making and civil wars. This applies even more to larger ostensible groupings such as 'Bantu', whose provenance and coherence are matters of intense debate, but whose commonality has often been taken for granted. An example is the volume *Bantu Folk Tales from Southern Africa*, rewritings by a tireless compiler, Phyllis Savory. Her introductory outline of Bantu migration, her implication that all 'Bantu' people somehow think alike and her view that these stories are 'age-old' unalloyed transmissions from 'the deep, dark ages of man' are all at best doubtful, demonstrably false in some cases and in most others impossible to verify.[16]

A second caution, though, is that many of these tales have indeed migrated over time and space from one community and group to another, so that similar but variant versions of the same tale can be found across vast swathes of Africa. This means that we need to pay attention to who exactly is involved in the collection or transcription of any particular version.

Thirdly, then, suggestions that there was ever an *original* story, which might somehow be reproduced, or even referred back to, are usually delusory. Layers and networks of long-transmitted memorised elements are shot through and transmogrified by modern poetics, narrative techniques and print-publication technologies. With both positive and negative effects, this 'snaring into writing' has resulted in widespread infantilisation of the tales. What is now often advertised as learning about 'other' cultures, began as a cultural prejudice. Wilhelm Bleek, the German philologist or linguist, was voicing a common attitude in the preface to *Reynard the Fox in Africa*, his 1864 collection of 'Hottentot' and 'Bushman' tales, when he asserted that they would appeal to 'children, and also simple-minded people, whose taste has not been spoiled by the poison of over-excited reading'.[17] In 1924, his daughter, Dorothea Bleek, publishing further Bushman tales from her father's archive in a seminal text, *The Mantis and His Friends*, added that the Bushman 'remains all his life a child, averse to work, fond of play, of painting, singing, dancing, dressing up and acting, above all fond of hearing and telling stories'.[18] This default attitude affected even academic circles. Until the 1970s, as Thomas Dowson and David Lewis-Williams state, 'the stereotype of the Bushmen as "children" living close to nature had obscured [their real] complexity and had discouraged researchers from giving anything but the most cursory attention to what appeared to them to be superstitious, naive and trivial beliefs, rituals and myths'.[19]

We can exemplify these issues, as well as track certain changes in attitudes towards elephants, by unpacking versions of just two Bushman stories over time. Both begin in the Bleek-Lloyd archive, which may be as close to the precolonial as we are now likely to get.

In the 1870s, Wilhelm Bleek, his sister-in-law Lucy Lloyd and, later, Dorothea, interviewed ex-convicts from Cape Town's Breakwater Prison, most of them /Xam men from the Kenhardt area of the Northern Cape. The archive's 12 000 handwritten notebook pages are fascinatingly rich, but come with a number of caveats. Firstly, the material is fragmentary, translated and decontextualised, and can only be interpreted with great caution. Secondly, it pertains to only one small and (even then) already dying-out segment of those peoples popularly lumped together as Bushman or San, but in fact consisting of some 200 mutually unintelligible dialects, many demonstrably different in beliefs and practices. Thirdly, the semi-desert Kenhardt region was never more than sparsely populated by elephants, which had probably been shot out by 1800 – though there are some rock art depictions there, the /Xam informants have relatively little to say about them. Nevertheless, what they do offer is interesting enough.

Two stories begin with the Bleeks, and subsequently appear in several versions. Here, firstly, is a testimony given by Bleek's informant Rachel, told to her by her mother:

> While he [the springbok man] lay sleeping, the elephant and the young elephant came above him; while he lay [on the earth which he had thrown out of the hole] sleeping; and he lay asleep; and she (an elephant) took up the young springbok, and she put down the young elephant; and she took up the young springbok; she took it away. And he [the springbok] lay there, and he awoke. He arose again, he dug,

while the young elephant sat above him. He awoke, he again dug, he saw the hole's shadow, and he saw that the young springbok did not sit above him. Therefore it was that he came out of the hole and he espied the young elephant's ear's shadow on the hole's earth, when he thought he would arise. He again, he dug, he dug, he beheld that young elephant's ear's shadow was great. And he came out of the hole, he looked, looking about, and he espied the elephant's foot's spoor. And he went to the young elephant, and he looked about at the young elephant, at the young elephant, that then people's child (it) was, they had taken away his child. And he took up a knobkerry, and he beating knocked down the young elephant; and he returned, he [reflected] thought that he had killed the young elephant. And when he returned, he went to tell his younger sister that the elephant had taken away his child.[20]

And there it ends, apparently a tantalising fragment of a larger story that might or might not have an ending – or what Westerners habitually regard as a suitable ending. What do we make of this unpolished account, with its hesitations and repetitions, its tentative syntax and awkward expressions, all redolent of the jerky progression of a difficult translation process? Is this a fantasial transposition of some actual event, or the refraction of a shamanistic transformation of springbok and human? Is the hole a game pit (similar to that in another elephant story – see below) or something more spiritual in significance? At the very least, the story seems to express a kind of family loyalty, of necessary vengeance in the face of theft – it would not be uncommon for either other human groups (including Boer commandos) or wild animals such as hyenas to snatch a child while the parent was dozing or distracted. But this does not explain why it should be the springbok and the elephant; there are evidently invisible connotations that elude analysis here. As in many *kukummi*, human and animal behaviours and relations often seem to be much the same, with the vocabulary of personification (or anthropomorphism) applied equally to either. At any rate, there is no obvious compassion *for* the elephant expressed here.

Rachel's fragment seems to be a watered-down or ill-remembered version of the story as told by the more accomplished informant Dia!kwain. Dia!kwain's tale is richer with mythological detail and purport, with the springbok-man figured explicitly as /Kaggen, the mantis-like trickster-god who features so strongly in Bushman myth. Bleek summarised Lucy Lloyd's laborious transcription:

> An Elephant carries away the little Springbok on her back while /kaggen (the Mantis) is inside a hole digging for food. /kaggen calls to the little Springbok from inside the hole but it does not answer him. The Elephant-calf answers him instead, but not with a nice sound. /kaggen thinks that the soil he has thrown out of the hole has stuck in the little Springbok's throat. /kaggen emerges from the hole to see why the child's throat sounds as it does. He finds the Elephant-calf lying there covered with soil from the hole, strikes the calf and knocks it down, killing it. /kaggen tracks the departed Elephant by its spoor but decides to return home to tell his sister (who is the Blue Crane) about the theft of the child. The sister scolds him for sleeping in the hole and not hearing what occurred. /kaggen asks for food so that he may follow the Elephant to its place. He tells his sister she must watch for when the grass blows from another direction, for that is when he will return with the child. He finds the Elephant's house and sees the little Springbok playing with the Elephant children, and calls out to it. The Elephant sees /kaggen coming and swallows the Springbok child. /kaggen demands that the Elephant give the child back and enters her navel to fetch the child, whom he fastens onto his back. The other people try to stab /kaggen to death, so he exits through the Elephant's trunk and flies away to return the child to his sister.[21]

More 'ecological' relations between animals and environment (tracking spoor, grass, wind, food) are evident, but the imaginative elements are much stronger – not to say more bizarre from the outsider's perspective. A /Xam person would be connecting almost unthinkingly with a network of related *kukummi* and culturally sanctioned images. Some aspects appear to be based on nothing more substantial than a pun: Bleek noted, for example, that the term *urina* or 'little hole' is a /Xam name for the springbok kid and that this was playfully and imagistically connected to the common use of a springbok hide, tied up by its feet as a deep sling for a baby on the back. So much of this kind of resonance inevitably escapes anyone not thoroughly versed in the /Xam language, its physical and artefactual environment, and its immemorial narrative resources.

A third version, quite close to the original transcription, but in a quite new conversational style, would be included by Dorothea Bleek in *The Mantis and His Friends*:

> The Mantis was digging out wild bees' honey and throwing it to the little Springbok. He said: 'Are you eating, as I am eating?' The little Springbok was silent and did not answer the Mantis. The Mantis said: 'What is the matter that the child does not speak to me, when I ask it whether it is eating as I am eating?' And he took out more honey; he said: 'Are you eating as I am eating?' Then the Elephant calf said: 'Kurru!' And the Mantis said: 'Listen! What is the matter? My child does not usually speak so that I cannot understand it. Let me take out some more honey and throw it out again, so that I may hear whether it is my child speaking; for I do not understand what this child answers; I do not hear plainly. What can have happened to the child's throat to make it answer me like this; that is what I must find out. Therefore I will throw up more honey.'[22]

Although Bleek deliberately excised what she regarded as tedious repetitions, and replaced such exoticisms as '/Kaggen' with 'Mantis', this retains at least some features of a clear, carefully incremental oral performance. What is interesting is which aspects are retained or modified in order to suit non-Bushman target audiences – and how this might affect emotional responses.

A fourth retelling, derived from Bleek, was by Laurens van der Post, whose books *The Lost World of the Kalahari* (1958) and *The Heart of the Hunter* (1961) did much to popularise an emergent if romanticised image of 'the Bushman' as complex, ecologically valuable and tragically diminished – a possible philosophical antidote for what Van der Post deplored as the ills of the industrialised West. Van der Post tended grandiloquently to assimilate Bushman belief to his own quasi-Jungian cosmology, even as he insisted on Bushman uniqueness. This shows in his version of Bleek's transcription:

> Mantis killed an elephant because it swallowed a small first thing of life, his beloved pet, a little springbuck lamb. He was feeding it with honey which he was digging out of a hole, devoting the sweetness of his nature to nourishing the tender and the small, when an elephant came

along and swallowed the lamb. When Mantis discovered this he went after the elephant, entered it by the navel, going as it were to the origin of the monstrous, killed it from within and emerged with the lamb, to carry it to his home – that is, to give the small a permanent place in his spirit. Way back there at his home, his sister looked at the grass on the veld and saw the wind blowing over it: the wind was coming out of the East. 'Oh! people, look!' she cried; 'why is the grass blowing this way? The wind is where the Master told me it would be when he turned back, when he was coming home . . .' The wind, the spirit, was coming out of the East where the day is renewed after the night, to bear witness to the fear that Mantis, in rescuing the small from the tyranny of the great, had renewed life on earth.[23]

'Beloved', 'honey', 'lamb', 'spirit', 'the East': the Christian echoes in Van der Post's diction show how this has become a redemption tale, a narrative of movement from the 'origin of the monstrous' to 'renewed life'. The succour of the small against the 'tyranny of the great' is both Christlike and in tune with his grander project of spiritualising the 'vanishing people', as he termed the Bushmen, in the face of juggernaut imperialism.

We might rightly feel uncomfortable about this treatment, but it is only a particularly vivid example of what inevitably happens to such indigenous material. As for elephants themselves, Van der Post considers that in the Bushman world the elephant was 'the great image of exaggeration and brute power', of 'the exaggeration and excess from which his spirit had to free itself if ever it were to become symmetrical and whole'.[24] This sounds more Jung than Bushman, but it seems right to see antagonism between human and elephant as fundamental. Compassion for the elephant *as elephant* is no more evident here than before; ecological knowledge, cross-hatched with relations of respect or fear, does not automatically result in compassion as I have defined it. Nor does respect preclude hunting and consuming the elephant – though in another fragment from the Bleek-Lloyd archive it appears that eating the elephant's heart is forbidden, as it could result in an elephant coming back to kill the hunter. Contrarily, the taking on of elephant 'power' in magical fashion might actually preclude compassion. In this world view, respect and compassion are, surprisingly, in opposition.

The second series of versions begins with Bleek's collection of independent Bushman narratives, already refracted through transcriptions by various frontier missionaries, refurbished in 1864 in *Reynard the Fox in South Africa*. Two of these narratives involve elephants. 'How a Nama Woman Outwitted the Elephants' is a particularly (to us now) puzzling story.[25] A Nama woman is married to an elephant; as with bears in certain North American myths, the possibility of this union is taken as a given. Things somehow go wrong, however; the woman and her cattle flee, and implore a certain rock to split open and allow them in, which the rock does. The elephant, in pursuit, makes an identical request; the rock opens, but then crushes the elephant. Precisely because its motives, its turn of plot, some of its conversational details and its denouement elude explanation within Western narrative logics, this story is never (as far as I know) retold by later compilers. If anything, though, it speaks to that original, mythic communion of human and animal, which is then broken, leaving them in a state of antagonism.

The second story has proved more accessible. This is 'The Elephant and the Tortoise', which Bleek identifies as Damara, originally recorded by the missionary J. Rath:

Two powers, Elephant and Rain, had a dispute. Elephant said, 'If you say that you nourish me, in what way is it that you do so?' Rain answered, 'If you say that I do not nourish you, when I go away, will you not die?' And Rain then departed.

Elephant said, 'Vulture! cast lots to make rain for me.'

Vulture said, 'I will not cast lots.'

Then Elephant said to Crow, 'Cast lots!' who answered, 'Give the things with which I may cast lots.' Crow cast lots and rain fell. It rained at the lagoons, but they dried up, and only one lagoon remained.

Elephant went a-hunting. There was, however, Tortoise, to whom Elephant said, 'Tortoise, remain at the water!' Thus Tortoise was left behind when Elephant went a-hunting.

There came Giraffe, and said to Tortoise, 'Give me water!' Tortoise answered, 'The water belongs to Elephant.'

There came Zebra, who said to Tortoise, 'Give me water!' Tortoise answered, 'The water belongs to Elephant.'

There came Gemsbok, and said to Tortoise, 'Give me water!' Tortoise answered, 'The water belongs to Elephant.'

There came Wildebeest, and said, 'Give me water!' Tortoise said, 'The water belongs to Elephant.'

There came Roodebok, and said to Tortoise, 'Give me water!' Tortoise answered, 'The water belongs to Elephant.'

There came Springbok, and said to Tortoise, 'Give me water!' Tortoise said, 'The water belongs to Elephant.'

There came Jackal, and said to Tortoise, 'Give me water!' Tortoise said, 'The water belongs to Elephant.'

There came Lion, and said, 'Little Tortoise, give me water!' When little Tortoise was about to say something, Lion got hold of him and beat him; Lion drank of the water, and since then the animals drink water.

When Elephant came back from the hunting, he said, 'Little Tortoise, is there water?' Tortoise answered, 'The animals have drunk the water.' Elephant asked, 'Little Tortoise, shall I chew you or swallow you down?' Little Tortoise said, 'Swallow me, if you please!' and Elephant swallowed him whole.

After Elephant had swallowed Little Tortoise, and he had entered his body, he tore off his liver, heart, and kidneys. Elephant said, 'Little Tortoise, you kill me.'

So Elephant died; but little Tortoise came out of his dead body, and went wherever he liked.[26]

This is clear, even to a child, and obviously amenable to a moralistic interpretation – a warning about greed and possessiveness, say, and James Honey, in 1910, had no qualms about reproducing it verbatim in his influential collection *South-African Folk-Tales*.[27] If Bleek had been somewhat condescending towards his indigenous subjects, implicated as he was in the nascent 'science' of European ethnology, Honey descends into outright racism. He cites with approval the opinion that South African folklore is 'in its very nature plain, and primitive in its simplicity . . . descriptive in great measure of the events of everyday life, among those in a low state of civilization . . . very little that is grand or magnificent must be looked for in it'.[28] Demeaning, distortive and downright ignorant, this establishes the ground for further infantilisation. Honey (following Bleek) at least does not eschew the repetitiveness that might have accompanied an oral performance of the story – though there is no original performance to gauge it by. The slight archaism of the language expresses the underpinning assumption that this is a kind of relic of a less developed, quasi-biblical age. Honey resists tacking on an explicit moral, though it is not hard to see a certain valorisation of the small against the large here. This is emphasised by a parallel tale, also derived by Honey from Bleek, involving the giraffe rather than the elephant. The elephant as such is not the villain, then, so much as symbolic of an attitude of oversized bullying countered by a certain cunning in the underdog – or under-tortoise.[29] In the end, if there is compassion underlying this in any way, it is clearly not for the domineering elephant.

A version of the same story is retold by the assiduous compiler Jan Knappert in a 1981 booklet, *Namibia: Land and Peoples, Myths and Fables*. Knappert includes it under Herero tales, but because he gives no indication of its provenance it is impossible to say whether this is one of those stories that has migrated across peoples, taking on local colour, or whether it has somehow found its way through publications into Herero circles, to become a kind of pseudo-tradition. Knappert's version is similar to Bleek's, but it omits the zebra and the slightly puzzling casting of lots, inserts some Herero names for the characters and some more colloquial narrative detail, and appends a coda, which bluntly lays out the moral:

> This fable teaches us not to be proud, for even an elephant cannot make rain. Nor is it useful to try and engage the services of such a weird character as the vulture. As for the tortoise, he should have been more careful in his choice of employer and not get involved with the ruthless elephant. The most stupid thing he did, though, was to try and stop the lion from drinking the water. The Herero proverb says: 'An elephant can swallow many big lumps, but he should know that *even* an elephant cannot swallow a tortoise.'[30]

In its modern phraseology – 'engage the services', 'weird', 'choice of employer' – this is palpably more Knappert than Herero. There are subtle judgements – of what counts as weird or stupid, for example – that take us ever further away from what might have been the feelings of the Herero informant – if indeed there ever was one.

Yet another version appeared in 1950 in *Bushman Stories*, which E.W. Thomas claimed to have collected in the Kalahari from a 'little old man' named Gaira in the Nama dialect. The general structure is the same, but the details and language are rather different. The narration feels distinctly more Westernised, with a deliberately archaic cadence and phrasing. An extract:

> The Elephant spoke to Rain. The Elephant said, 'If I should tear out all the trees and destroy the greenness of the earth, what would you do?'
>
> Rain said to the Elephant, 'If I should withhold my refreshment, so that the earth should wither and die, what would you do?'
>
> And they parted.
>
> The Elephant, trumpeting loudly, tore out the trees, to destroy the greenness of the earth. Rain quietly withheld his refreshment, so that the earth withered and died.
>
> Water vanished from the face of the earth. Then the Elephant, panting, made a big hole in the dried-up pan, and lay down on his side for the coolness of the deep fresh soil. And that side of him next the earth perished, and the Elephant was in sore distress.[31]

The behavioural details are a little unusual for such fables – this sounds almost like a prescient foreshadowing of later arguments about elephant damage to vegetal ecosystems. Unlike the series of animals seeking water in the Bleek version, here Elephant asks the korhaan to beg for water on his behalf; the bird gains its characteristic white collar as a sign that the prayer is answered. Elephant then sets Tortoise to guard the water; having failed to deter the lion and others from drinking, Tortoise actually chooses as his punishment of being swallowed by the elephant. Having plucked out Elephant's heart from the inside and emerged, Tortoise boasts: 'Today I will hold converse with no man, for today I am exalted above all men. Today I have laid low the trumpeting tyrant that vexed the land!'

Again, the elephant is a vector of antagonism, an icon of fearful dominance. A tale of its being felled by the little creature is, perhaps, a kind of wish fulfilment and a defusing of understandable fears, especially in conditions of drought. Common environmental conditions are psychologically addressed through the medium of imaginary triumph. Yet it is not the fable's purpose to teach us much about elephants per se. While it may in some indirect ways derive from real-life human-animal relations, it is not designed to describe them. Rather, these tales anthropomorphise in order to affect humans' view of themselves.

It would appear that Dianne Stewart, another prolific reteller of folk tales, bases her version in *The Zebra's Stripes* on Thomas's edition. Aimed at children, its naturalistic style includes more sensory texture, interiority and authorial intrusion, in the manner of conventional Western realism. For example:

> To prove his strength, Elephant twisted his long muscular trunk around a large, sturdy mopani tree, uprooting it and trumpeting so loudly that it drowned the thud of the tree as it slumped to the ground.
>
> Rain who wore the rainbow draped around her waist, observed him angrily and wondered whether she should strike him with her lightning tongue.[32]

Stewart sanitises the ending, merely shaming the elephant rather than killing it off. She also appends, as with all her stories, a box of 'interesting facts' about the elephant, a kind of scientific or conservation-inspired sidebar, as well as realistic, sometimes slightly comical, often exquisite illustrations, which are worlds away from the rock art of the ancient Bushmen. In several ways, then, Stewart injects a very different attitude towards elephants, a different realm of understanding and empathy wholly absent from the earliest versions, but deemed more appropriate to modern conditions. The antagonism evident in the early versions is obscured, even as a more complex, respectful and better-researched attitude towards the Bushmen has developed.

Published texts constitute one strand, but Bushmen themselves continue to tell stories into the present – a different genealogy of versions, no less complex. Biesele's study of the Kalahari Ju/'hoansi, *Women Like Meat*, includes a series of episodes involving G!kon//'amdima, daughter-in-law of the trickster figure Kaoxa, for example. As Biesele notes, these tales only somewhat indirectly reflect aesthetic and psychological states. Fossilised memorisations are overlaid with spontaneous

31

imaginative transformations, and may involve a number of interlocking themes: 'marriage and marriage-service, murder and blood-vengeance, the origin of meat animals, sex, birth, and the balance of power between men and women'.[33] Though G!kon//'amdima is primarily connected with the antbear, alternatively with the python, she is also in some versions known as !Xodi, the elephant-girl.

The version of 'The Elephant-Girl' transmitted in *Women Like Meat*, recorded in 1972, covers some eight pages. In summary: the elephant-girl seems simply to exist, and marries into another family. The narrative is complex; in its course the elephant-girl is killed and butchered by her husband's brother. As family members are offered the meat, some suspect it is in fact their relative, the elephant-girl, and they object. Meanwhile, drops of blood that had come to the grandmother on the wind and been stored in a bottle, begin to grow and grow until the elephant-girl herself is reconstituted. After more complicated machinations, she takes her revenge, fatally flattening her brother's people by blowing on a magic horn.

One thing this tale is *not* about is real elephants. Biesele supplies another structurally and thematically similar story involving a duiker, with no elephant-girl at all. These mythic animals are frequently fluid in their identities: their qualities – power, capaciousness or greed – are not necessarily unique to them. A visual homology, such as between a python and the elephant's trunk, for instance, means they can become symbolically interchangeable. That said, Biesele does supply some fascinating commentary on this story's motif of meat-eating prohibitions. Importantly, she records 'a range of attitudes' even within Ju/'hoansi society towards eating elephant meat: 'Some people eat it gladly, while others regard it with distaste.' One informant said: 'There's human meat there, and gemsbok meat, carnivores' meat, eland meat, every kind of meat, red, black, and white. It's very fat. When it's dead, an elephant smells bad like a dead person.' And another: 'You don't eat it because it's like a person. The female has two breasts and they are on her chest like a woman's. When she's young they stick out and when she gets old they fall. Also, her crotch is like a woman's with long labia.'[34] These observably human-like qualities of the elephant might conceivably provide some basis for empathetic kinds of coexistence. The recognition of commonality also involves respectful taboos in some places, even reverence in others – but 'compassion' would be overstating it.

What of other indigenous peoples, those who invaded, overwhelmed, displaced, or in some ways assimilated with the Bushman autochthons? Elephant tales are scattered throughout these cultures – though not, perhaps surprisingly, in large number.

As in the case of the Bushmen, assiduous collection of southern Africa's other indigenous peoples' traditions by literate research-ers began only in the mid-nineteenth century, with Henry Callaway's *Nursery Tales, Traditions, and Histories of the Zulus* in 1868. By then, though many local societies held fast to established beliefs, their social structures and cultural expressions were already fraying under the impact of European invasion and the technologies of modernity. Callaway, despite his location in mid-imperial thrust, remains in many ways exemplary. He provided parallel Zulu-English texts, acknow-ledged individual informants and discussed linguistic issues in detail. Unlike many of his contemporaries, he believed that a careful study of their stories would 'bring out unexpected relationships, which will more and more force upon us the great truth, that man has everywhere thought alike [behind] mere external differences'.[35] He was also pres-cient about future treatment of these testimonies: a popular edition, he thought, 'with a few alterations in the tales, and a condensation and modification of the phraseology, might become an interesting and not uninstructive book for the people generally and especially for the young'. He stressed, however, that they were 'not the invention of a child's intellect; nor all invented for a child's fancy' – and he worried about what such children's editions might lead to.

Callaway's Volume 1 contains two snippets of relevance to ele-phants. The first echoes Biesele's Ju/'hoansi testimony, this from one Umpengula Mbanda:

> There are many things that are abstained from among black people through fear of bad resemblance; for it is said there was a person who once gave birth to an elephant, and a horse; but we do not know if that is true; but they are now abstained from on that account, through think-ing that they will produce an evil resemblance if eaten; and the elephant

is said to produce an evil resemblance, for when it is killed many parts
of its body resemble those of a female; its breasts, for instance, are just
like those of a woman. Young people, therefore, fear to eat it; it is only
eaten on account of famine, when there is no food.[36]

Where human resemblance might in some views provide grounds for
fellow feeling and some kind of empathy, here likeness is seen as evil.
In animist world views such as the Zulus', visual or textural homologies
can as easily be used for nefarious magical practices (witchcraft) as for
good.

Callaway's second example probably *was* directed towards children.
It is structurally a fairly straightforward tale, made long and suspense-
ful only by dint of much repetition (the kind of repetitiveness that
would be cut from most later versions). Again, the elephant here is
not a beneficent figure, but rather a rapacious and deceitful one whose
capaciousness proves his downfall. The story – 'Unanana Bosele', attrib-
uted to 'Lydia' – involves a self-confident woman who builds her hut in
the middle of a road. Two of her children are swallowed by an elephant;
she searches for them, finds the elephant, and is swallowed herself. Inside
the elephant, she discovers an entire country, full of people, including
her children. But the children are hungry. The woman asks: '"Why did
you not roast this flesh?" They said, "If we eat this beast, will it not kill
us?" She said, "No, it will itself die; you will not die." She kindled a great
fire. She cut the liver, and roasted it and ate with her children. They cut
also the flesh, and roasted and ate.'[37] Eventually the elephant, now in
great pain, dies; the woman cuts through a rib with an axe; the people
and animals emerge, and the woman departs, enriched by many gifts.

While many aspects of everyday life appear in the tale, it is neither
a 'simple sort of mirror' of that life nor a straightforward expression of
a coherent culture's beliefs. While it may draw on the aforementioned
notions of taboos on eating elephants, this magically roomy beast is no
more a direct reflection of reality than is an invented super-beast from
a computer game. The tale is entertainment, perhaps not even carrying
an obvious moral.

The phenomenon of white writers recirculating indigenous stories
is a fraught one in the tangled, uneven, racialised politics of South

African letters. Such writing, to be sure, has migrated from patronising, through anthropological curiosity, to a post-apartheid effort at restitution and recharged nation building. Now, black African writers are taking advantage of the technologies of publication to promote both broadly African and more narrowly ethnic values and identities through the refurbishment of folk tales. An interesting example is the recent repackaging of a traditional Yei tale from Botswana about how the elephant came to be: *Tlou: The Elephant Story*, written by Bontekanye Botumile. The essential tale is not unlike that underpinning Bushman animal stories – the original union of human and animal. The difference is that this story works in reverse: a human, visited by the ancestors, turns into an elephant and returns to the wild. The human is a young, hungry mother; the transformation is an act of rescue from her impoverished life. The style is Westernised to the extent of italicising (and translating) Tswana words, and giving the woman/ elephant protagonist, Tlou (elephant), fairly complex interiority:

> Out of the corner of her eye she saw something move. It was the *leselo*. The flat winnowing basket rolled like a wheel. It was as if someone was moving it. It spun gently towards her and landed at her feet. Tlou slowly approached the basket. Puzzled, she picked it up and turned it over. Her eyes flashed back to where it had rolled. There was still no one there. She felt the eyes still watching her. She looked at the *leselo* one more time. What was the basket trying to tell her? Who was in the *lapa* with her? What did they want?
>
> She shuddered in fear. She closed her eyes to try and calm herself down. She mouthed a silent prayer for the ancestors to protect her and her baby.[38]

Magicality and the presence of the ancestors are taken for granted, even as the story is inserted into a modern context. The illustrations by Moira Borland are, unlike rock art, highly naturalistic, almost photographic, and the story itself, as was the case in Stewart's *The Zebra's Stripes*, is amplified by ancillary 'natural facts' about elephants. There is also a kind of anthropological page of 'common Yei beliefs about elephants'. Among these are a number stressing the commonality of humans and elephants, such as: 'The back of an elephant is shaped like that of a woman', an elephant will bury the body of a human it has killed, has to undergo a period of penance for that act and will also protect the human body from scavengers. The story itself stresses this commonality. While the men of Tlou's village are afraid and want to kill her, her friend MmaPelo recognises her and leads her to the forest, where the birds welcome her. MmaPelo says:

'You will be the queen of your kind. Through you, all the knowledge and wisdom about human and animal life will be passed on. Tell this to all that will come after you. Let them know that you and your kin are first cousins of human beings. Treat all the humans you will encounter with the same quiet dignity you have always carried. Remember always, that we were, and are, one thing. Finally, respect the wild and everything in it. Look after it, and it will look after you.'[39]

MmaPelo's act of empathy and compassion – feeling *with* Tlou, and then literally walking with her into the wild – is a call to all humans to recognise similarity, and to preserve the wild for their own good. It is an effective marriage of the traditional and the ecological.

Credo Mutwa is the self-styled guru of all sangomas – not uncontroversially. Outside South Africa, Mutwa is 'introduced to the public as an authentic Zulu prophet, who is willing to share his pure and uncontaminated indigenous wisdom with the world, while within South Africa [he] is mostly seen as a fake, an opportunist and a charlatan'.[40] The introduction to his book *Isilwane: The Animal* includes an impassioned denunciation of Western destructiveness, and an attempt to resurrect ancient African values that he labels 'green' – a term now pervasively but often too loosely used:

Western man is taught that he is the master of all living things . . . A very dangerous attitude that ought to be erased from our minds and from those of our children is that human beings can build a glittering technological future without animals, and without trees . . . Expelling God from everyday life leaves the field clear for super-capitalists, colonialists and other plunderers to rape the Earth . . . In old Africa we did not regard ourselves as superior to the animals . . . We believed that we had nature within and beyond ourselves.[41]

In the course of some woolly philosophising, Mutwa rattles off frag-
ments of information about widely scattered parts of Africa and
African peoples, occluding possible differences between them. In a section devoted to the elephant, he makes some comments on Botswanan
beliefs, generally supportive of Botumile's children's story:

> The Batswana Batloung tribe, whose name means 'people of the ele-
> phant', were sworn to protect the elephant . . . It was believed that
> an elephant would not injure a person who carried the Batloung
> name.
>   But what if an elephant became a rogue and started devastating vil-
> lages . . . and started terrorizing the people? If this occurred, the tribe's
> king would call a gathering of his wisest people, among whom would
> be the traditional healers. They would throw the bones of divination
> and seek the answers from spirits so as to [discover] exactly why the
> elephant had become an enemy.
>   If the diviners found that the elephant was sick or had been har-
> assed by human beings in any way, strenuous efforts – some of them
> quite dangerous and bizarre – were made to entice the rogue elephant
> away from Batloung territory without it being killed. However, should
> it prove absolutely necessary to kill the elephant, a group of elephant
> hunters who were not of the Batloung nation had to be brought in from
> far away.[42]

Though subtitled *Tales and Fables of Africa*, Mutwa's book in effect
incorporates several different genres. His section on the elephant consists of three subsections. The first is a praise poem (evidently of his
own composition), which reinforces his earlier comments – a vivid,
canny, slightly argumentative mix of ostensibly 'traditional' belief and
New-Age-style 'green' environmentalism:

> You are the elephant!
> You, whose loud trumpeting heralded the birth of the world
> You, whose last trumpeting will herald the end of the world we know
> Be angry, great elephant
> . . .
> *Shwele*, forgive the people who kill you, not knowing whom they kill

37

Who destroy you, not knowing whom they destroy
Who disrespect you, not knowing to whom they are speaking
Indhlovu, elephant, servant of the great Earth Mother![43]

A rather contradictory appeal to anger, biblical forgiveness ('they know not what they do') and a milky admixture of earth-mother mythology, transmigration of souls and second-hand Gaia-think is continued in the second, discursive section. It is resonantly titled 'Reincarnation of Murdered Gods' and drifts somewhat incoherently through a slew of summarised beliefs. He notes, interestingly, that the Zulu *ndhlovu*, elephant, is derived from *dlovu*, meaning 'to crash through', 'to pierce savagely', 'to act with extreme brute force'. Power, logically, can produce a sense of reverence, which Mutwa claims seamlessly for all African peoples. As already noted, it is rather more complicated than this.

The third subsection – 'The Elephant Who Did Not Forget or Forgive' – is not so much a traditional tale as a modernised parable. It features a 16-year-old Zulu lad, Shungu, in Natal in the early 1900s, who joins an elephant hunting expedition, seeking meat for a starving village. A pit-trap is dug and an elephant caught, but an overexcited Shungu impetuously wounds another elephant with his assegai. Many, many years later, Shungu, now a Christian missionary, happens to be passing by the fence of a game reserve in that very area. And an elephant – obviously the once-wounded one – charges through, picks Shungu up, and wedges him in the high fork of a tree, from where he is rescued by passers-by a few days later. The moral of the story, perhaps, is 'respect, if not be nice, to the elephant'; or, 'cruelty against nature will return to haunt you'. Moreover, Mutwa credits the elephant with a certain compassion of its own: rather than killing Shungu, it merely gives him a good hard look and punishes him.

The contemporary influence of conservation ethics, with a spiritual leaning, is reinforced by a foreword to *Isilwane* by the late Ian Player, conservationist extraordinaire and saviour of the white rhino. Player ignores Mutwa's more controversial aspects, and aligns him with

James Lovelock's 'Gaia hypothesis' and with the bush-philosophy of Player's own mentor, Magqubu. Such syncretism can be at once seductive and vacuous, scientifically dubious, but emotionally appealing. The interracial element to these late productions is also a pointed element; Mutwa is participating in a trend deliberately to refract folk tales through print and even electronic media to support the post-1994 notion of the rainbow nation. Conservation strategies that ignore our racialised histories are ultimately bound to fail. Elephants are at the very core of those strategies.

I end this chapter with a glance at a few examples of two genres of traditional lore other than folk tales: the praise poem and the proverb.

The praise poem or panegyric is as distinctively 'African' a genre as one is likely to find. Praise poems are sung or performed at every level, from the ordinary person praising a cow or a wife to a designated praise singer – the griot in West Africa, the *imbongi* among the Xhosa and Zulu – reciting more formalised eulogies to the chieftain or king. A Zulu example, the praises of Dingane, will illustrate some essential features.

Dingane, who ruled the emergent Zulu polity between 1828 and 1840, inherited some praise lines and epithets from his predecessor and half-brother, Shaka – despite having murdered him. Among the praises are a number aligning kingly power with aspects of the elephant, primarily strength and destructive power. The first whites to leave records of Shaka's reign noted the elephant praise line – which did not stop Shaka helping them hunt for ivory now and then. There is no telling how far back the epithet might have been used; we know only that from the 1820s onwards it was used continuously for the succession of Zulu leaders. The praises of Dingane were recorded several times, as more white missionaries and administrators arrived in Zululand. James Stuart, a magistrate and assiduous collector of Zulu oral history, eventually put together a composite of the various versions available to him – a problematic venture, since each praise event would have been tailored to the demands of a particular situation, and each performance inflected by the particular mix of memorisations and inventiveness of the *imbongi* concerned. But these are some of the lines concerning elephants recorded by Stuart, and exhaustively annotated by D.K. Rycroft and A.B. Ngcobo:

Crimson one who is an elephant with wounds.

. . .

Elephant whose sleep is fitful,
While others sleep happily.

. . .

Tusk-of-the-elephant, Penetrator,
He pierced Madlanga near the Fasimba.

. . .

Turner-away, like elephants,
being slaughtered even by the owners of the fields.
Whichever way he took, they ran away from him.

. . .

The elephant smashed everything; there was nothing left!
The branches of the trees were broken; there was nothing left.
There were only the uprooted stumps to be seen,
They were turned upside down![44]

As these epithets show, the primary associations are with power, size, ferocity and lordliness – qualities as easily derived from lions and leopards as from elephants. The elephant content is largely symbolic, even when it is evidently derived from observation of actual elephant behaviour: the smashing of vegetation, the flapping of ears. But as Rycroft and Ngcobo's extensive notes attest, there is not much more than this to be said, though nuances emerge from close examination of the Zulu originals. For example, the Zulu word here translated as 'Penetrator', *uMashiqela*, has 'the meaning of "autocrat, dictator, one who uses force in government". However, it is derived from the verb *shiqela*, meaning "ram in, push down, squeeze in", which is related to the ideophone *shiqe*, "of sinking in or sinking down". Other associated nouns are *isishiqe*, "rough abusive words or unkind words" and *isishiqeli*, "a bitter-tongued person".'[45]

Given that the murderous usurper Dingane had a rather mixed reputation among his own people, it is possible that in its performative context, what might be read by the vain as overweening praise, might to the cynical listener carry undertones of criticism. In any event, fellow feeling or empathy *for* elephants, let alone active compassion, plays no part in such praises.

The other 'traditional' form frequently said to express the root values of a people are proverbs, compact wisdoms likely to have survived unchanged down the generations, perhaps better than any other. Here I will air just a few from one collection of Zimbabwean Shona proverbs, or *shumo*, with explanations as provided by Mordikai Hamutinyei and Albert Plangger:

> An elephant with calves does not cough up phlegm.
> One who is holding a treasure does not expose it to danger. He is afraid of losing it one way or another.
>
> An elephant is taboo in public but in private is delicious.
> Usually people pretend in public to be of good character but under cover of privacy they show their loose morals.
>
> An elephant is not burdened by its own tusks.
> Nobody will resent the burden of something he knows to be part and parcel of himself. Also, one should be equal to one's responsibilities.
>
> The elephant died on account of the ant.
> A small habit left uncontrolled may develop into a serious defect which disqualifies a man and does harm to the whole community.[46]

In all societies, proverbs can be slightly riddling, interpretable in different ways for different situations; seeing them as reflective of their society needs to be hedged about with as many qualifications as rock art and folk tales. They are almost exclusively directed to human behaviour, not to human-animal relations as such. We learn little or nothing about elephant behaviour, or real-life attitudes of the humans towards elephants, even as the proverbs might keep the mere existence of elephants in people's minds. But proverbs on their own have no power to keep the animals themselves alive or safe; despite them, even elephants might soon be – to put it proverbially – as dead as the dodo.

Chapter 2

Experiments and Devastation:
Early travelogues and the advent of zoology

François le Vaillant, reminiscing on his attitude prior to his travels into South Africa in the early 1780s, reveals that

> above all, I continually dreamed of portions of the globe which, having not yet been searched, could, by giving new knowledge, rectify the old. I regarded as supremely happy the mortal who would have to be brave enough to go and find it at its source. The interior of Africa . . . was still virgin earth. With my spirit full of these ideas, I persuaded myself that the ardour of zeal could supplement genius and that as long as one were a scrupulous observer, one would always be a great enough writer.[1]

In many ways, Le Vaillant represents a culmination of trends that had been developing in the conjunction of Europeans' philosophical and scientific thought with their 'discovery' and thereafter conquest of other parts of the globe. The early European travel accounts and related journals – starting with Jan van Riebeeck's Cape diaries of the 1650s, to Carl Peter Thunberg and Anders Sparrman in the eighteenth century and William Burchell and John Barrow in the early nineteenth century – coincided with the growth of the scientific paradigms of the Enlightenment. Many of these travellers were 'naturalists' of one or another stripe, and even those who were not drew heavily on them, interpolating greater or lesser 'scientific' observational detail about the flora, fauna, geology and native customs. Increasingly, this positivist strain of European thought, utterly alien to indigenous thought patterns, would come to dominate the treatment of animals in the wild. But has zoological science, modulating into 'ecology' in the twentieth century, really done much to save the animals from human destruction, or does it remain marginalised by economic forces? Or might the animals have been even worse off without scientific revelations?

A deep rift is often asserted between professional scientists, who insist that empirical objectivity is the only valid method for assessing the value of the animal presence, and the (put broadly) animal rights lobby, who are accused by the first of distorting the picture with inappropriate emotionality. Yet it seems clear enough that an emotional investment – often on the part of a scientist, indeed – is most often what drives a rescue operation or efforts to preserve a species. So the fundamental question underpinning this chapter is a simple but crucial one: what is the relationship between science and compassion, particularly with reference to elephants? Along with most other wild animals, southern Africa's elephants were caught up in a contradictory whirlwind of quasi-military invasion and killing, commercial networks and the West's thirst for scientific knowledge.

Enlightenment science projected itself as perfectly objective, the production of supra-cultural knowledge by 'scrupulous observers'. But it was also – as Patricia Beer, among many other commentators, has noted – in itself a cultural movement. Moreover, during the period examined in this chapter, the humanities dominated and scientific observations were habitually embedded in poetics and narrative, not least of all the travelogue.[2] Le Vaillant's own ambition to rectify faults in received knowledge implicitly recognises the effect of cultural preconceptions; so too does his ambition to be a writer, which implies compiling a work for a particular audience within a particular cultural matrix. The cultural historian Mary Louise Pratt has explained how 'one of Europe's proudest and most conspicuous instruments of expansion, the international scientific expedition . . . was to become a magnet for the energies and resources of intricate alliances of intellectual and commercial elites all over Europe'. Other parts of the world, even as they were being aggressively colonised, served as 'testing grounds for modes of self-discipline which, imported back into Europe in the eighteenth century, were adapted to construct the bourgeois order'.[3]

One avowedly disinterested project, to collect knowledge for its own sake, finds itself somewhat at odds with a more narcissistic one, to present the adventurous individual 'penetrating the virgin interior'. Both projects would find themselves in awkward entanglements with the more rapacious and militaristic strands of imperial conquest. Even more than upon indigenous peoples in southern Africa, that rapacity was unleashed upon animals. John Miller's summation refers to the nineteenth century, but it applies just as well to the eighteenth:

> Natural history provided romancers with an alluring context for adventures in the earth's wilder reaches and one which raises key questions concerning racial, gender and species identity. In promulgating an ostensibly ideologically neutral objective order of creation, natural history often served to naturalise colonial structures of domination . . . The march of 'truth', then, went hand-in-hand with death, illustrating natural history as an aspect of imperial violence and a deeply problematic enterprise from the point of view of animal ethics.[4]

The collection of 'specimens' for the cabinets of curiosity, early museums, menageries and zoological societies that began to proliferate in the eighteenth century could be combined with what these writers called the 'romance' of the travelogue, denoting a congeries of features – manly travel into exotic landscapes among strange people, the paradoxical pleasure of daring and ordeal, and the assertion of imperial ideals. In practice, the emergent genre of the travelogue was characterised by, as Le Vaillant himself put it, 'experiments and devastation'.[5]

The impact on the elephant would be catastrophic, the holocaust beginning almost the instant white men set foot at the Cape in 1652. However, this chapter concentrates on the century between 1735 and 1836. The first date is when the Swedish naturalist Carl Linnaeus, published the first edition of his *Systema Naturae*. His binomial nomenclature, though not the only one in circulation, largely prevailed, and exemplified the thrust towards precision, order and hierarchy that came to dominate the European natural sciences. Several travellers in South

Africa were acquainted with his work or were, like Sparrman, actual
students of his. The second date, 1836, is marked by Charles Darwin's
visit to the Cape on the *Beagle* voyage. Though in itself brief, his visit
symbolises the imminent rise of evolutionary theories which, combined
with Linnaean mapping of species, would prove the foundation of the
conservation-orientated and ecological sciences to follow. The impact
of these sciences on the fate of the elephant can hardly be exaggerated.
This chapter, then, probes the initial stage of that scientific incursion
on the world of the southern African elephant, and on the ethics of its
literary treatment within the ambit of colonial power.

When Van Riebeeck, first Dutch commander of the Cape of Good
Hope way station, occasionally mentions elephants in his daybook, it
is only in relation to tusks and his hope for some trade in ivory. The
local people, the Khoikhoi or 'Hottentots', as the Europeans habitually called them, found elephants formidable to hunt, so what ivory
they had – sometimes fashioned into arm-rings – was mostly obtained
from natural or accidental deaths. They did take on elephants at times,
though, as described by O.F. Mentzel in 1787:

> When the Hottentots observe a lone elephant with good tusks in their
> vicinity, they collect a large crowd of their people, and when they con-
> sider themselves strong enough to surround the elephant, they spare
> no pains and trouble to make him *malkop* . . . mad, foolish and queer.
> Unless the elephant evades the snare before it is surrounded, the animal
> is as good as lost, for then it can definitely not escape them. This is the
> procedure: The Hottentots, each armed with an assegai, unfasten their
> karosses and put them over their shoulders or arms. They then form a
> wide circle around the elephant and approach it with slow steps. In this
> way the circle shrinks gradually and is tightened by the men. When they
> come closer to the animal, it tries to run aside, since it has not in any way
> been angered; whether it be to escape from such a crowd or to knock a
> few of them down and trample them out of spite. But to whichever side
> the elephant moves, the Hottentots immediately close their ranks and
> hasten to approach it on that side. As soon as the animal comes close
> enough for some of the Hottentots to reach it, ten or twelve of those
> nearest throw their karosses over its head. The elephant, unaccustomed
> to such coverings on its head and blinded by them, remains standing

on one spot and, since its eyes are covered and even its trunk entangled in the karosses, has its work cut out in attempting to shake them off and free itself; but this avails it nothing. For while it is shaking off the first karosses, twice as many Hottentots come forward, to throw their karosses over its head. As more and more Hottentots approach and the first ones recover their karosses and keep bombarding it with them incessantly, it becomes confused and undecided where to turn. The one of the most courageous Hottentots leaps up behind the elephant, seizes its short tail with his left and clinging to it thrusts his poisoned assegai with his right hand repeatedly into its body through the rectum as far as it can go. The elephant, which necessarily must suffer great pain from such a wound in its intestines is made quite frantic . . . But as this person cannot hold on to the elephant's tail for long with one hand, he leaves his assegai sticking in the elephant's anus and runs off. Should another Hottentot grasp the tail and twist the assegai already driven in by the first still deeper in its intestines, the animal would be felled all the sooner and the hunt more quickly finished; if not, it does not matter; for the elephant, blinded by the karosses, can do nothing than keep on turning in a circle, and the Hottentots who come closest to it, meanwhile thrust their poisoned assegais into its body in such number and so mercilessly that it soon collapses and bleeds to death.[6]

Mentzel's recognition of the elephant's confusion and pain and the 'merciless' nature of the hunt, evinces perhaps a glimmer of *his* empathy. However, this cannot be extended to whatever the Hottentots might have felt, beyond evident fear mingled with excitement.

There is no sign in Van Riebeeck's daybook that many elephants inhabited the immediate vicinity of the Cape station. Only when he and his successor, Simon van der Stel, began despatching expeditions further into the interior, did significant encounters begin to occur, and over the next century a holocaust of firepower was steadily unleashed. Even C.J. 'Jack' Skead's thorough survey of mammal incidences reveals only fragmentary information about elephant numbers, distribution and behaviour, let alone subtleties of attitude.

Here I highlight a few of the fuller accounts. To begin, in October 1653, one Corporal Verburgh, heading north for Saldanha Bay, reported 'a herd of seven and another time a herd of eight elephants of which our men were rather afraid as they, like the rhinoceros, remained standing firm so that our men had to get out of their way'.[7] Those elephants, it would seem, had never had anything to fear from humans. How quickly that would change. In 1705 Johannes Starrenberg, sent into the Piketberg region, found that elephants were being hunted more frequently by Hottentots, mostly because so-called white freemen had attacked them, run off their stock, and reduced them to poverty. Hence, when they did come across an elephant, they would run it to exhaustion, then trade its tusks for trinkets – the only livelihood left available to them.[8] Peter Kolb (or Kolbe) wrote in 1731 that elephants in the Groene Kloof in the Malmesbury district, which happened to be young and tuskless, were apparently neither bothered nor a threat. Nevertheless, as related by Mentzel, resident in the Cape between 1732 and 1741, the tipping point was already being reached:

> But after the arrangement whereby Groene Kloof was consigned to the meat contractors for fattening the cattle, an attempt was made to drive them away little by little as the elephants ate up much of the fodder to the detriment of the pasture. On the arrival of increasing numbers of farm labourers and cattle herds, they were sensible enough to withdraw to the further side of the Berg River. This they still occasionally visit in years of drought for drinking purposes, and stay there for a short while. But they never cross the river any more, and would have an unpleasant reception if they did.[9]

So it began.

These literate travellers generally followed established (if at times fearfully rough) paths already opened up by the settlers, itinerant traders and the ever-present and indispensible locals – most of them 'unlettered, unnumbered and sparsely recorded'.[10] Most elephant slaughter went entirely unremarked. As early as 1752, when August Frederik Beutler crossed the Great Fish River, deep into Xhosa country, he was following trails known to hunters and ivory traders. The later travellers therefore had a tendency to pump up their own hardships – the romantic adventurer's narrative, precursor to the romantic novel, demanded it. Kolb was one of the earliest, and would begin to delineate the genre – and be regularly critiqued by his successors for his inaccuracies. Most published accounts recorded journeys made in the second half of the eighteenth and early nineteenth centuries. The most important of these were Kolb (visiting the Cape in 1706, published in English in 1731), Thunberg (1772–1774), Sparrman (1775–1777), Robert Gordon (1777–1780), Le Vaillant (1781–1783), Barrow (1797–1801), Henry Lichtenstein (1805–1806) and Burchell (1821–1824). Though the Enlightenment sciences are varyingly evident in these multinational travellers' approaches to astronomy and geology, navigation and cartography, entomology and above all botany, the attention paid to larger mammals seems slight. The thrust was towards the collection of skins and specimens for the emergent technique of taxidermy – for which purpose the specimens obviously had to be dead – rather than towards close observation of living behaviour within functioning ecologies.

Such zoological commentary was not wholly absent. Kolb differed from those who came after him in *not* narrativising his observations, being more impersonally observational, but he 'seems to have had no special interest in, or training for, zoology'.[11] Mentzel drew explicitly on the zoological work of Georges-Louis Leclerc, Comte de Buffon, and belatedly on Sparrman. He thus includes a chapter on 'game and other wild animals', discussed in alphabetical order, a separation of zoological description from personal narrative that would feature strongly in later texts. On elephants he notes: 'This, the largest of all animals on earth, is so well known, and has so often been seen alive, that it would be superfluous to give another description of it. I shall therefore touch merely on the remarkable facts about it, and on points which have not yet been properly explained.' He discusses the position of the sexual organs and the mystery of the sex act, drawing on Sparrman and disparaging Abbé Nicolas-Louis de la Caille, who had merely repeated the invented myths of his predecessors. He reserves his most trenchant criticism for Kolb, especially his inflated and pompous style. According to Mentzel, some inland elephants may have appeared tractable: 'At the Cape of Good Hope, however, they are shot by the colonists at point blank range.'[12] He gives a detailed account of shooting elephants, with most of his focus on the proper weight and composition of shot, and how best to preserve the safety of one's horse. In this, he foreshadows the detachment of the hunters of the later nineteenth century.

The Swede Sparrman, visiting the Cape after voyaging to the Far East, was a student of Linnaeus's and, especially in his botanical studies, employed Linnaeus's binomial nomenclature. Like many of his predecessors, he referred also to the great Comte de Buffon – not without the courage to make corrections, such as on the ear shape of Buffon's drawing of an African elephant, and the number of toes on an elephant's foot.[13] He similarly demurred from accounts by previous visitors to the Cape including a story, related by Abbé de la Caille, about colonists hunting elephants 'with lances':

> Once upon a time three brothers, natives of Europe, who had already made a handsome fortune by following this profession, had, each of them being on horseback and armed with a lance, attacked an elephant by turns; which, however, at length, laid hold on one of the horses that had stumbled, and threw him, together with his rider, up into the air, a hundred paces from him; then taking up the latter, ran him through the body with one of his large tusks; upon which the animal held him up with exultation, as it were, thus impaled and shrieking in a horrible manner, to the two other horsemen, his unhappy brothers.[14]

Sparrman wryly comments, 'It is not extremely probable.'

Sparrman conducted one of the longer journeys eastwards from Cape Town, starting out in 1772. His main contacts with elephants first occurred in the Outeniqua region, 500 kilometres from the Cape. Just over a century since white men first set permanent foot at the Cape, he noted: 'The *elephants* are now, by being shot at continually, in a great measure expelled from the *Houteniquas*, and have taken refuge on the other side of the *Keurebooms-river*, in the woody, and almost entirely unexplored country of *Sitsikamma*.'[15] So it would remain for another two centuries. He devoted a lengthy section to a local 'Bushman' scene of drying elephant meat in the Humansdorp area. Contrastingly, he found that the colonists there 'look upon it as almost as horrible an action to eat the flesh of an elephant as that of a man; as the elephant, according to them, is a very intelligent animal, which,

49

when it is wounded and finds that it cannot escape from its enemies, in a manner weeps; so that the tears run down its cheeks, just as with the human species when in sorrow and affliction.' This would appear to be based on local experience rather than sourced from books, perhaps even derived from indigenous mythology, and a rare glimmer in the early literature of compassion for elephants. Sparrman was able to salvage some anatomical information from the remnants of the feast, and compared observations of the dead animal's teeth with those he would later inspect in 'the cabinet of the Royal Academy of Sciences'.[16] He also comments briefly on elephants' dependence on water and their capacity to swim.

But there the zoology ends: Sparrman's subsequent discussions of elephants are all about hunting them. A little further inland, he noted that in 'the *Lange Kloof*, and other places which the Christians had begun to inhabit, these animals were obliged immediately to retire from them'. He gave chase himself, detailing an elephant hunt on horseback. The process was grotesquely inefficient: 'The elephant, even after the third ball, still threatened vengeance; but the fourth entirely cooled his courage: however, he did not absolutely drop till he had received the eighth. Several experienced hunters of elephants have nevertheless assured me, that one single ball is sufficient to bring an elephant to the ground.' He then embarks on a long discussion of the firearms necessary: musket balls needed to be one part of tin and two parts of lead, and so on.[17] In this he anticipates much subsequent hunting literature, as he does in recording the often underreported role of indigenous hunters drawn into the modern technology of slaughter:

> Some Hottentots, who are trained up to shooting, and often taken out by the farmers for this purpose, are particularly daring in this point; as they are swifter in running, and at the same time, not without reason, suppose that they have a less suspicious appearance than the white people in the eyes of the elephants and other animals; and, on account of the rank odour they have, (somewhat like that of game) which proceeds from their skin-cloaks, their grease, and their bucku powder, are less liable to be discovered by the scent.[18]

50

The ivory trade, unsurprisingly, is at the heart of it. Sparrman wrote: 'It is merely for the sake of the teeth that the elephants are hunted by the colonists, though at the same time they contrive to preserve the flesh for their servants . . . [Since] a man may sometimes earn three hundred gilders or a hundred rix-dollars at one shot, it is no wonder that the hunters of elephants are often extremely venturesome.' He revelled in the thrilling account of one Dirk Marcus, who was nearly killed by a wounded elephant, anticipating many a subsequent anecdote of narrow escape, as well as another story of a colonist beaten to death by an enraged elephant. These illiterate and small-scale farmer-hunters are elevated to the status of 'bush-fighting gentry' – not so much by Sparrman himself as by his successive editors: a footnote in the Van Riebeeck Society edition acknowledges that 'Stalkers is the correct translation [of the Swedish] here, but the free translation of the London editions, "bush-fighting gentry" is too picturesque for rejection.'[19] None too picturesque for the elephants. So an enduring mythology begins – an ideal to mask the grim reality.

Le Vaillant is worth lingering on, not only for his relatively extensive accounts of elephants, but also for his ruminations on both science and ethics, and for the laconic, self-deprecating style that would become a feature of later hunter and game-ranger narratives. In the opening chapter of his *Travels into the Interior* Le Vaillant relates his childhood in Surinam where he built up an extensive collection of dead insects and experimented with methods of preserving the skins of the many birds he killed. He became a patient observer of the natural world, but largely in the service of becoming a 'determined hunter', a passion he confesses never left him: 'Some friends have accused me of coldness and insensibility. More have found the strange voyages I undertook later reckless. I gladly forgive the former and have nothing to say to the latter. Nonetheless, if they deigned to stop and look at the first steps of my childhood, the appearance of originality would be less surprising and they would see that my education is at once the cause and the excuse for it.'[20] The first sentence here implies a pre-existing ethical debate. By taking on himself the task of forgiveness, rather than asking for it, Le Vaillant sidesteps taking responsibility for his actions, shifting the blame to his education. Yet he is not entirely insensible of a moral troubling. He confesses that during his time in Europe, between Surinam and South Africa, he caused 'incredible havoc among the birds', even as he was trying to advance the cause of science – 'experiments' were inseparable from 'devastation'. Yet there was a side to Le Vaillant that leaned towards life and beauty, as he expresses when reviewing various European natural history collections: 'These superb displays soon made me uneasy; they left in my spirit a void that nothing could fill. In this pile of foreign trophies, I saw only a general deposit where different beings, stored without taste and without choice, slept profoundly for science. Their manners, their affections, their habits – did nothing give me any precise indications about these essentials?'[21] Though he was 'dazzled, enchanted by the beauty and the variety of forms, the richness of colours and the prodigious quantity of the individuals of every species', these collections did not satisfy a hunger for experience itself. Hence, he headed for the Cape, to continue in most respects the very collecting mania he disparaged. He is famous for his contributions to the science of ornithology, but how far did this mentality extend to mammals such as elephants?

The short answer is: not much. Elephants' manners, affections or habits are described only insofar as they impinge on his ability to shoot them. The following account helps set the narrative pattern for at least a century to come:

One of my Hottentots had climbed up a tree to survey the surroundings. He looked in all directions and, putting a finger in front of his mouth, he signals us to keep still. By opening and closing his hand several times, he indicates to us the number of elephants he sees. He climbs down, we consult and go downwind to approach without being noticed. He leads me so close, through the bushes, that he brings me into the presence of one of these enormous animals. We were almost touching and I could not see him. Not that fear had fascinated my eyes. I realized that in such a situation one must take a risk and be ready to face danger. I was on a little hillock just above the elephant. In vain did my good Hottentot point it out to me and in vain did he repeat twenty times in an urging and impatient voice, 'HERE IT IS . . . BUT HERE IT IS!' I still could not see it. I was looking much further into the distance, as I could not imagine that what I had twenty paces below me could be anything else than part of a rock, as this big mass was utterly motionless. At last, however, a small motion caught my eye. The head and the tusks which had been hidden by its enormous body turned toward me in alarm. Without losing time or my advantage in vain contemplation, I rested my largest gun on its pivot and shot him right in the middle of his forehead. The noise sent another thirty or so running as fast as they could. It was funny to see their big ears flapping in proportion to their speed. But this was only prelude to a livelier scene.

I was enjoying watching them when one of them went past us and was fired at by one of my men. From its bloody excrement, I judged it was severely wounded. We began to chase him. It kept lying down, getting on its legs, falling again. But as we were hard on its heels we made it get up by shooting at it. The animal had led us among high bush strewn with dead tree trunks which had fallen over. At the fourteenth shot, it turned in fury against the Hottentot who had fired it. Another man hit it with a fifteenth shot which only increased its rage. The man jumped out of the way shouting at us to watch out. I was only twenty-five paces away and was carrying my gun which weighed thirty pounds as well as my ammunition. I could not be as nimble as my men who had not gone as far forward as I had and who found themselves that much more ahead and better placed to escape the vengeful trunk and run to safety. I was running but the elephant was catching up every second. I was more dead than alive, I was abandoned by all of my men (at that point only one was running to my rescue) and there was nothing left for me to do but lie down and huddle against a big tree trunk which had fallen over. I was hardly there when the animal comes and goes over the barrier. But he stops to listen, quite frightened himself by the noise my men were making ahead of him. From my hiding place, I could easily have shot him, as luckily my gun was loaded, but the animal had already been shot at ineffectually so many times, and he was at such an unfavourable angle, that I had no hope of killing him with a single shot and therefore I lay still and waited for the worst. I never took my eyes off him, however, and was determined to sell my life dearly if I saw him coming back towards me.

My men were worried about their master and were calling out to me on all sides. I was careful not to reply. My silence persuaded them that they had lost their leader, and they called even louder and in despair they came in my direction. At this the frightened elephant turns about again and again jumps over the tree trunk about six paces off from me,

53

without noticing me. I then stand up, in my turn annoyed with him and wanting to give my Hottentots some sign of life, and let him have a shot in the rear. He totally disappeared, leaving behind him a trail which was clear evidence of the cruel state into which we had put him.[22]

Apart from that word 'cruel', and a subsequent comment that they had 'savagely mistreated' the animal, little remorse is expressed at this excruciating scene. Its essentials – the blithe ignorance, the self-promotion as white leader, alongside wry self-deprecation, the scene of the enraged elephant confronting the isolated hunter, the hair's breadth escape – would be mimicked and repeated ad nauseam in later accounts. Rather than evoking misgivings in the hunter, the wounded animal is abandoned. The dead one is devoured – 'I had never eaten anything so delicate' – and the tusks removed (disappointingly light at only 20 pounds). And if there *is* a quiver of guilt, in the recognition that the elephant was 'frightened', this appears only to set the scene for a repeat performance. The fear is actually found amusing. This is the case even when nestled within some naturalistic observation, which might at a pinch be passed off as zoological study:

Early the next morning I went on the trail [of the elephants]. From the top of a hill, on the edge of a wood, I spotted four of them in thick bush. I made sure I kept downwind of them and carefully came close to them. I treated myself to the pleasure of watching them at my leisure for half-an-hour. They were eating the leafy tips of trees. Before breaking them off, they thrashed them three or four times with their trunks. I believe this was meant to shake off ants and other insects.

After this preliminary operation, they always gathered as many branches as they could bundle with their trunks. Then they took this to their mouths, always from left to right. They did not chew much before swallowing. I noticed they chose the branches with the most leaves and they seemed to be very fond of a kind of fruit, which is yellow when ripe and which people in this country call the *Cherry*. When I had sufficiently observed their feeding method, I shot the one nearest to me in the head and in less than ten minutes did the same with the other three.[23]

Half an hour of proto-tourism is sufficient, before the indiscriminate slaughter begins. One elephant turns out to be a lactating mother; a

Hottentot shoots the orphaned calf: 'I scolded him severely . . . I could easily have tamed it.' Compassion for the young, something that would become more intense in time, does not appear here. Instead, Le Vaillant turns to the mother's corpse, to discover an anatomical anomaly:

> Naturalists, following the admirable custom of approving as undeviating and certain truths only the routine stuff of books and hunters confined to their studies, will probably contest what I saw: the female . . . had only one teat, placed in the middle of the breast. It was full of milk and I squeezed some into my hand. I found it quite sweet but the taste was not pleasant . . . The other females had the two nipples in the normal place on the breast and of the same form as that of women. They were in such good proportion that more than one highly fashionable young lady worried that she is over-endowed might have envied my female elephant this charm.[24]

The gendering of the gaze is indivisible from the spectacle of death, and also from the position Le Vaillant claims as the veracious participant-observer. He is poised in between the book-bound naturalist and the single-minded hunter, partaking of both views.

In yet another case, an elephant shot by Le Vaillant resists the bullet, gets angry and runs off, losing 'lots of blood': 'I regretted this a lot as he was the best one I had seen to that time. He was at least twelve to thirteen foot tall and his tusks looked to us as though they weighed more than twenty-five pounds each.'[25] Even in the avowedly disinterested naturalist, desire for ivory is ultimately paramount. So, in another instance, he would observe differences between left and right tusks in (dead) elephants, occasioned, he surmised, by the invariable left-to-right motion of carrying food to the mouth – and then deliver himself of another meditation on the meaning of hunting them. It is almost the last word on the subject, the next two centuries of disquisition a footnote:

> I was beginning to enjoy this hunting: with practice I came to find it more interesting than dangerous. I could never understand, and have understood even less subsequently, why authors and travellers have stuffed the stories they have told us with so many lies about the powers and tricks of this animal. Why have they excited the reader's imagination

about the dangers to which hunters who pursue the elephant expose themselves? In truth, if anyone were stupid and rash enough to attack an elephant in open countryside, he would be dead if he were to miss his shot. The greatest speed of his horse would never equal the trot of the furious enemy pursuing him. But if the hunter knows how to use his advantage, all the powers of the animal must give way to his ingenuity and his cool-headedness. I admit that the first view of it causes an astonishment that is close to stupor as it overwhelms and frightens one, but, with a little courage, and calm, a prudent man should strive to discover the character, the pace, and the resources of this animal. He should, above all, depending on the circumstances, make sure that he can retreat and take shelter from all danger if he should miss the animal and be pursued. With such precautions, this kind of hunting is no more than an entertaining exercise, a game in which the odds are fifty to one on the player.[26]

In this 'prudent' perspective – 'more interesting than dangerous' – almost all subsequent elephant-hunting accounts read as the self-centred exaggerations of the rapacious and the rash. Which is precisely what some readers' imaginations would seem to adore. Not all writing about elephants at the time was so brutal, however:

Beneath a form vast and uncouth
    Such excellence is found:
Sagacious Elephant! thy truth,
    Thy kindness is renown'd.
More mild than sanguinary man.[27]

William Hayley's long ballad on the elephant, published in London in 1802, evinces a sentimental admiration of the elephant – sage, 'resolutely kind' and morally superior to humans. By way of example, the ballad relates how a 'menial' or captive elephant rescues its handler or 'gard'ner' from a tiger attack. The portrayal is derived from a mingling of inherited mythologies and captive Indian elephant presences in England's embryonic 'zoological gardens' – a situation very different from that encountered by southern African travellers.

Almost simultaneously, Barrow was approaching the eastern reach of colonisation in what was then known as Kaffraria. In his *Travels into the Interior of Southern Africa* (1806), he wrote of the area between the 'Bosjesman and Kareeka rivers':

> The ground here has been rent and torn into vast chasms, separated by high ridges of rude and massy rock. The glens were choked up with thick, tall shrubbery, and the smaller kinds of the trees of the country. These wild and dismal dens, of many miles in extent, were considered by Rensburg, the [local] person before mentioned, as the nursery of elephants, where, he asserted, he had once seen in one troop between four and five hundred of these enormous brutes, scouring the plains, and making for the forests.[28]

Barrow was concerned to disperse poetic mythologies by gathering direct observations, even second-hand ones:

> Several of the persons with me pretended to have been eye-witnesses to the manner in which elephant performed the connubial rites; and they invariably asserted that, agreeably to the old accredited story, the female went down on her knees to receive the male, which, however, is not the fact. The manner in which this huge animal contrived to propagate the species is a subject that has long engaged the closet-naturalists of Europe, and which has produced many strange opinions and hypotheses. Some imagined that, notwithstanding the grossness of the body, the feelings of this animal were so delicate, and others, that its sense of slavery was so powerful, that shame in the one instance, and indignation in the other, were impediments to their indulging, in a domesticated state, in the gratifications of love. Such-like hypotheses, founded on false suggestions of travellers, have of late been most completely set aside by facts performed in the presence of many hundred spectators. In a letter from one of these gentlemen to his friend, dated Tipperah, July 11, 1793, and now published, the whole process of courtship, consummation, and time of gestation, are minutely stated. From this letter the following are points, that appear to be most unquestionably ascertained.
>
> First: That tame elephants will procreate in their domestic state, and perform the act of love without shame, and without feeling any sense of delicacy beyond other brute animals.

Secondly: That the period of gestation is about twenty-one months.

Thirdly: That they copulate invariably in the same manner as a horse with a mare, but with much less vigor. And,

Fourthly: That the female will again receive the male in five or six months after delivery.[29]

Mystery dispelled. Barrow also drubs poor Kolb 'who, although profess-edly sent out in the character of a naturalist, has described subjects that he never saw; retailed idle stories of the peasantry that betrayed his great credulity and imbecility of mind; and filled his book with relations that are calculated to mislead rather than inform'.[30] Similarly, Sparrman, who 'by his indefatigable labours, supplied a very extensive and satisfactory account of the natural productions, especially in the animal kingdom', but unhappily 'was credulous enough to repeat many of the absurd stories told of the Hottentots by his predecessor *Kolbe*' – and his map was 'miserably defective . . . jumbled together with fiction and romance'.[31]

Barrow supplies a fair degree of scientific observations of other animal species, drawing on Linnaean nomenclatures. Yet he remains aware that 'Nature, though regular and systematic in all her works, often puz-zles and perplexes human systems, of which [the elephant] affords an instance'.[32] For all his scientism, Barrow intriguingly sometimes echoes Hayley: 'The gigantic elephant is a harmless animal in comparison to the lion, the leopard, wolves, and hyaenas, and other beasts of prey which this wild and rugged part of the country abounds; and even these are much less dreaded than a nest of the most atrocious villains that ever disgraced and disturbed society, which these thickets conceal. The gang consists of seven or eight Dutch peasants.'[33]

Barrow notes indigenous depredations on elephant and buffalo, which fell 'in the woods by the Hassegai, but more frequently by deep pits made in the ground across the paths that led to their usual haunts'.[34] But the main culprit was the colonial expansion of the ivory trade, taking slaughter far beyond the locals' decorative requirements:

However abundant this article [ivory] might once have been in the southern part of Africa, it is now become very scarce, and, in the nature of things, as population is extended, the animals that furnish it, the Elephant and the Hippopotamus, must progressively disappear. Indeed, at this moment, except in the forests of the Sitsikamma and the thickets of in the neighbourhood of the Sunday River, not any elephants are to be found within the limits of the Colony. Of those few which the Kaffers destroy, the large tusks are always cut up into circular rings and worn on the arms as trophies of the chace. The small quantity of ivory that is brought to the Cape market is collected chiefly by two or three families of *bastaard* Hottentots (as the colonists call them) who dwell to the northward, not far from the banks of the Orange River. The whole quantity exported in the course of four years, as appears by the Custom-house books, amounted only to 5981 pounds, value 6340 rixdollars.[35]

If one surmises that elephant populations in the region were not huge in the first place, and one calculates a modest 30 pounds of ivory per elephant, Barrow's figures would indicate a significant toll of some 200 elephants in just four years. What this also indicates is the incremental monetisation of elephant presences, a dynamic that to this day continues to overwhelm and infiltrate the increasingly compassion-driven efforts of both science and romantic fiction to inculcate an attitude – nascent in Hayley's ballad – to preserve rather than destroy.

The year 1836 is an interesting one on which to end this chapter on the colonial travelogue. It was the iconic year that launched the Great Trek – a great disaster for hundreds of thousands of animals in the northern half of South Africa. It was the year Nathaniel Isaacs published his *Travels and Adventures in Eastern Africa*. As a teenager, Isaacs had spent time in the purview of Shaka, himself the 'Great Elephant' leader of the emergent Zulu. Isaacs's account is unreliable,[36] but he does relate how Shaka enjoined his earliest white visitors, sailors who had never hunted in their lives, to demonstrate their muskets on elephants:

We took our station about 200 yards from him [Shaka], under a smaller tree, waiting impatiently, yet dreading the result. Two hours had nearly elapsed, when a messenger presented to the king the tail of an elephant, at which they all appeared greatly surprised . . . It appeared that the natives drove the elephant from the forest to a plain, where the sailors placed themselves directly before the animal: the first shot entered under the ear, when it became furious: the other lodged near the fore shoulder, after which it fell, and soon expired. Had this affair turned out differently, we should, in all probability, have been held in a contemptible light by this nation, and awkward consequences might have resulted to the [white] settlement.[37]

Isaacs and his companions – notably Henry Francis Fynn – also began dabbling in the ivory trade. Even in 1824, Shaka had a stockpile of ivory from his own hunting operations; some of this became a political sticking point, particularly when Isaacs's mentor and father figure, James Saunders King, apparently purloined a gift of tusks from Shaka intended for George IV. Isaacs's account is mocking: '[Shaka] assured me he had a considerable quantity, that his people were still hunting the elephant . . . His idea of the capacity of a vessel was an extraordinary one, and remarkably showed his ignorance of their capaciousness. He conceived that one of his huts, filled with ivory or elephants' teeth, would be a sufficient lading.'[38] The intricate politics of the ivory trade, and the involvement of local populations therein, is often lost to sight; it was not as simple as white gunmen going in and extracting ivory unimpeded.

In the same area, the missionary Allan Gardiner had made contact with Shaka's assassin and successor, Dingane, whose praises were noted earlier, and also published his *Narrative of a Journey to the Zoolu Country* in 1836. He reminds one how difficult, in that period, it could be to actually hunt elephants, especially in the wooded Amapondo country west of Durban, in which the hunters only

> occasionally caught a glimpse of their huge bodies through the openings, and a few shot [*sic*] were fired chiefly to dislodge them from their retreat, as it was impossible, from the intricacy and tangled nature of the underwood, to obtain a proper aim. Tired at length by such fruitless attempts, we entered the wood by paths worn by the elephants themselves, and penetrated very near to the spot where they were standing, but still there was no possibility of obtaining a full view of them without being too much exposed.[39]

Further hazardous efforts to flush these elephants failing, the party retreated without a single elephant's tooth to show for it. In these two accounts, neither science nor compassion is in evidence.

Much more scientific was the medically trained English amateur naturalist and ethnographer, Dr Andrew Smith. Smith kept extensive diaries of his 1834–1835 expedition, sponsored by the Cape government, as far north as the Limpopo River. There he met the famous missionary Robert Moffat, as well as the itinerant Khumalo/Ndebele leader Mzilikazi, and made detailed anthropological notes on the Basotho, Barolong and Barotse peoples he encountered. Among the latter he noted the value of elephants and ivory to the panoply of political status: 'When they [the Barolong] killed an elephant one tusk was always sent to the king. When they kill an elephant they cut off a foot and the front of the trunk and bury the latter. The foot they eat.'[40]

Such long-standing mores would soon come under severe pressures from white invaders, not least because the elephants fell before waves of gun-bearing hunters. Otherwise, he had remarkably little to say of the increasingly scarce elephants, appearing much more interested in birds, lizards and snakes, which he examined and categorised in intimate Linnaean detail. Compared to the finesse and intricacy with which the Indian elephant, long domesticated, was already being anatomised, its behaviours delineated and managed, the science of elephant zoology in South Africa was barely in its infancy.

Smith returned to Cape Town in 1836 – which was also the year that Darwin, homebound after four years aboard the *Beagle*, made brief landfall. The visit was short and Darwin saw and said little of South Africa, beyond finding the edge of the Karoo rather bleak. That bleakness, he realised, however, did not necessarily translate into lack of biodiversity. He drew on Smith's experience to make the following comment:

> That large animals require a luxuriant vegetation, has been an assumption, which has passed from one work to another: but I do not hesitate to say that it is completely false, and that it has vitiated the reasonings of geologists on some points of great interest in the ancient history of the world. The prejudice has probably been derived from India, and the Indian islands, where troops of elephants, noble forests, and impenetrable jungles are associated together in everyone's mind. If, however, we refer to any work of travels through the southern parts of Africa, we shall find allusions, in almost every page, either to the desert character of the country, or to the large number of animals inhabiting it . . . Now if we look at the animals inhabiting those wide plains, we shall find

their numbers extraordinarily great, and their bulk immense. We must enumerate the elephant, three species of rhinoceros, and probably two others, the hippopotamus, the giraffe, the bos caffer [buffalo] . . . By the kindness of Dr Andrew Smith, I am enabled to show that the case is very different. He informs that, in lat. 24°, in one day's march with bullock-waggons, he saw, without wandering to any great distance on either side, between one hundred and one hundred and fifty rhinoceroses, which belonged to three species; the same day he saw several herds of giraffes, amounting to nearly a hundred; and that, although no elephant was observed, yet they are found in this district.[41]

Darwin would probably have been horrified by the eradication of those great herds, and he would have been fascinated by the modern debate over the relationship between elephants and vegetation density. Much of that debate would be governed by unquestioning repetition from one text to another, even as it was informed by the principles of natural selection that Darwin would in due course outline in *On the Origin of Species*. From this point onwards, the presence of evolutionary science would be increasingly inseparable from assessments of elephant ecology and well-being making its presence felt in the various literatures. Over the next century and a half, science would evolve in its aims, scope and methods, with commensurate shifts in its entanglements with compassion and related emotions.

Chapter 3

A Most Delightful Mania:
Hunters' tales and evasions

The hunt itself may be the least important and least gratifying phase of the sport, without the equally gratifying anticipation and recollection to complete the experience. [In the anticipation phase, your] imagination is your guide. You are in control. During the recollection stage, you are blessed with the gift that erases the bad memories and enhances the good ones, allowing the story to mature and improve much like fine Bordeaux wine. Reality is the root of the realisation phase, however. It comes on someone else's terms, and you must tackle it with storybook imagination or selective memory.
—Tony Sanchez-Ariño, *Hunting in Zimbabwe*

Why do men hunt? (It has almost always been men.) More precisely: why do men hunt elephants? More precisely still: why have men historically hunted elephants in southern Africa, and with what consequences? The nineteenth-century hunting literature suggests a slew of mixed motives, and they change further in the twentieth century when hunting becomes intricately, and still controversially, entwined with conservation efforts. Running beneath all the reasons hunters give, however, is the primacy of the *story*: in crucial respects, the telling of the tale, the lecture, the book, is as much the trophy as the dismembered tusk or the mounted head. So my interest here is how, among hunters in the pre-conservation era, the narrative contains and justifies all the other putative motivations: the egotistical addiction to the thrill and the power, the material gain, the masculinism and the temporary escape from constraining civilisation.

I am particularly interested in the emotions associated with the moment of killing. How is it that all other responses, including admiration and compassion, vanish at that moment, overwhelmed by the desire to *kill*? I was raised by a naturalist mother whose overriding *raison d'être* was to save animals from human depredation and to rehabilitate them to their natural condition. From her I learned all those skills so often adduced by modern hunters as justifications for the activity: tracking, stalking, getting close, understanding the intimacies of species behaviour and their environment. But instead of those skills culminating in raising the fatal rifle, we backed carefully, respectfully, compassionately away. I can understand the excitement of the chase, the intoxication of adrenaline and danger, the prideful marksmanship. I can understand the motives of impoverished Mozambican villagers induced to gun down elephants whose ivory will earn them some desperately needed cash, or those impelled to kill lethal crop-raiders. I can even understand that commerce, primarily for ivory in this case, can gain a momentum of its own that overrides compassion, apparently uncaring that it is extinguishing the very source of its profitability (modern capitalism is doing this on a globally destructive scale). But the triumphalism of the kill itself; the necessity of a *death*? That baffles me. When I did have to kill an animal, it was with regret, not exultation.

It is the gratuitous nature of so much of the slaughter by white men in Africa that intrigues and appals. Not infrequently, it could coexist with more admirable sentiments, enhanced to a grim piquancy by the very loss of the object of desire. H.A. Bryden put it this way in 1893:

> The decadence of game is hardly to be wondered at. Modern science has placed in the explorer's hands weapons of deadly power and precision. Fond though he be of nature in the abstract, in the veldt, in presence of great game, it is a hard matter indeed, even for the naturalist and lover of animals, to stay his hand. The unquenchable desire to pursue and slay leaps through his veins and will not be denied. I have known men, who in cool blood have held forth upon the sad and wanton destruction of game, quite unable to resist the attractions of the chase, when they

have encountered the same animals in the hunting veldt. The theory is so easy, the practice so very hard, as I can personally testify; and so the work of destruction goes on.

What wonder, if the naturalist and the moderate hunter find it so hard to control their primeval instincts of the chase when in the presence of game, that the Boer, the skin-hunter, and the native sportsman, who have no aesthetic sentiments or compunctions to hinder them, set no limits upon their powers of destruction, but slaughter by scores, by hundreds, and by thousands, whenever and wherever they find opportunity.[1]

'Primeval instincts'? The self-contradictions here constitute a persistent blind spot. There may well be something in hunter-novelist Stuart Cloete's opinion, voiced in his novel-memoir *How Young They Died*, that a sublimated sexuality is involved: 'Men's weapons had always been sexual: daggers, swords, spears, bayonets. All instruments of penetration, to make men and kill others. To force something that was part of you into something that was not part of you, and thus make it yours. Your woman, your corpse.'[2]

Sexual awakening modulates into an existential assertion. In attaining one's full humanity, one takes a paradoxical exultation in shedding it for the animal and instinctual. In a related vein, Friedrich Nietzsche argued that for Western men, reduced to a sick ineffectuality by the slave morals of Christianity and commercial overindulgence, the reason was almost metaphysical. Healthy men 'revert to the innocence of wild animals: we can imagine them returning from an orgy of murder, arson, rape, and torture, jubilant and at peace with themselves as though they had committed a fraternity prank . . . Deep within all these noble races there lurks the beast of prey, bent on spoil and conquest.'[3]

One can easily assimilate this view to the maverick hunters of nineteenth-century Africa, but it also seems to me an incomplete explanation. A close reading of their accounts reveals something rather more complex. William Cornwallis Harris, one of the seminal hunter-writers, opens his 1852 book *The Wild Sports of Southern Africa* with this recollection:

From my boyhood upwards, I have been taxed by the facetious with *shooting-madness*, and truly a most delightful mania I have ever found it. My first essay in practical gunnery was made at the early age of six, by the discharge of an enormous blunderbuss, known to the inmates of my paternal mansion by the familiar sobriquet of *'Betsey'*. A flock of sparrows perched upon the corner of a neighbour's pigstye, were the only sufferers; but information was maliciously laid against me, and I underwent severe corporal chastisement.[4]

Like François le Vaillant, Harris roots his adult behaviour in his 'natural' upbringing. Harris is facetious in tone here, but his self-portrait contains the serious seeds of this chapter's exploration. Hunting poses as the wild antithesis against which civilisation measures itself; each defines itself against the other. Yet hunting is also the acme of civilisation's technological power over the wild and unruly other. It is an unresolved ambivalence that takes on a particular tenor in nineteenth-century southern Africa. Within certain domesticated environs, Harris implies, hunting may be seen as irresponsible, perhaps ethically dubious, and even as a kind of madness. It is an activity outside civilised normality, subject to 'chastisement', whether corporal or verbal. Opportunity for sanctioned hunting certainly existed in Harris's native England, though within severe limits of legal hunting rights, land ownership and class dynamics. In the liberating spaces of (to Europeans) a widely unknown and lawless Africa, with its plenitude of helpless 'sufferers', the hunter could maximise the scope of his transgressive boyish verve, his self-confessed 'passion for *venerie*' (Harris's borrowing of the French word for hunting seems to carry connotations of indulgent and aristocratic excess). Africa provided freedom not only to hunt unrestrainedly, but also freedom from the debate about hunting. Far from being chastised, slaughter could be valorised; it could be projected as heroic. It could even be twisted, despite its maverick self-gratification, so as to be represented as actually *advancing* civilisation (as Europeans conceived it). While indulging in and recounting 'the emotions which the overpowering excitement of African wild sports naturally produced in his breast', Harris wrote, he was also aiding in the 'penetration of the interior', and was keen to 'contribute [his] mite to the Geography and Natural History of the countries [he] was about to explore' through close observation, cartography and artistic corrections to numerous misconceptions he perceived in the 'popular books' thus far produced.[5]

In reading the late nineteenth-century accounts, from Harris to F.C. Selous, it is hard to divine just what those emotions are – precisely because the laconic, self-deprecating style, which Harris did much to entrench, deliberately eschews emotionality. The jokey hardiness is part of the persona, and thus of the genre.

The effect on elephants was simply devastating. Perhaps 100 000 elephants wandered southern Africa before white settlement. Fairly large numbers of elephants were encountered by white travellers in the seventeenth and eighteenth centuries, but the simultaneous advent of monetary commerce, overseas demand for ivory and increasingly effective firearms rapidly spelled the pachyderms' doom. By the 1840s there were none left in all the Western Cape except for the remnant population in the Knysna forests. In the Eastern Cape in the 1820s, the poet Thomas Pringle was noting that 'the elephant had retreated since the arrival of the settlers, to the more impenetrable and solitary forests adjoining the Bushmans and Great Fish Rivers'.[6] Frontier wars further disrupted elephant safety; by the 1840s very few were left, and by 1900 probably none, bar the tiny fugitive group in the Addo bush. Boer trekkers carried the depredations north into the Free State and the Transvaal (most never recorded – in a way the literature serves to *mask* the reality). Harris recorded an abundance of elephants around the Magaliesberg in 1836, but they were rapidly diminished, not least by him. In 1881, a little further north, Selous exulted in the 'grand sight' of 'so many of these huge beasts moving slowly and majestically onwards', but by 1887 was aware that 'the magnificent fauna which was once abundant throughout the land' were 'day by day becoming scarcer whilst some, alas! are already verging upon extinction'.[7] Even in Zambezia (today's Zimbabwe), Selous wrote to his father in 1877, 'on this side of the [Zambezi] river elephant hunting is at an end, all the elephants being either killed or driven away', and by 1882, after ten years of hunting the region and collecting 'specimens', he lamented that 'it had become almost impossible to make a living by hunting at all'.[8] By the 1890s, hunters such as Bryden in the Protectorate of Bechuanaland (present-day Botswana) were noting that even in the remote desert regions around Lake Ngami elephants were hard to find.

A comprehensive and dispassionate history of southern African elephant-hunting literature apparently remains to be written, despite the wealth of material and the emotive intensity of the hunting debate today, though several works touch on the area.[9] The title of Jane Carruthers's article on southern African elephant hunting, 'Romance, Reverence, Research, Rights' (2010), hints at the complexity of the field.[10] (I would have added 'Rapacity' to that list.) For a literary approach more apposite to this book, we have to go back to Stephen Gray's pioneering chapter in his *Southern African Literature* (1979). Gray notes the self-consciously literary aspects of these hunting accounts and how, in the course of the nineteenth century, they came to constitute a distinct and self-perpetuating genre in which the self-image of the hunters 'hardly alters throughout, and their sentiments are virtually interchangeable'. This is partly because they *are* literary; certain rhetorical gestures are established and through repeated cross-fertilisation harden into conventions. Gray rightly points out that 'although each hunter emphatically claims for himself the right to have no literary pretensions, he makes no end of use of literary techniques . . . This pretence at being a literary hamhand, which is part of the hunter's acute self-defensiveness, is as cunning a technical ploy as any wielded by a Dickens or a Hardy.'[11] Gray, however, is not particularly focused on elephants. Here, I want to concentrate first on the literary intertextuality of the elephant-hunters' accounts, expanding on some of Gray's observations, and second on the role of compassion – or lack of it – in them. These threads can be drawn together by looking at some works related to an under-studied arena of elephant hunting – Mozambique.

Harris is the fountainhead of the hunting account genre – subsequent writers routinely listed him among their inspirations. These works include, most prominently, R.G. Gordon-Cummings's *Five Years of a Hunter's Life in the Far Interior of South Africa* (1850), F.C. Selous's *A Hunter's Wanderings in Africa* (1881) and *Travel and Adventure in South-East Africa* (1893), Samuel Baker's *Wild Beasts and their Ways* (1891), H.A. Bryden's *Gun and Camera in Southern Africa* (1893), Parker Gillmore's *Leaves from a Sportsman's Diary* (1893), W.C. Baldwin's

African Hunting and Adventure from Natal to the Zambezi (1852–1860) (1894), Arthur Neumann's *Elephant Hunting in East Equatorial Africa* (1898) and *The Recollections of William Finaughty, Elephant Hunter 1864–1875* (1916). The extraordinary flourishing of late nineteenth-century works would spill over into the twentieth century, and include C.H. Stigand's *Hunting the Elephant in Africa, and Other Recollections of Thirteen Years' Wanderings* (1913), James Sutherland's *The Adventures of an Elephant Hunter* (1912), W.D.M. Bell's *The Wanderings of an Elephant Hunter* (1923), and P.J. Pretorius's *Jungle Man* (1947). There are many others of lesser notoriety in between, but this is the conventional genealogy. Selous singled out 'Gordon Cumming, Baldwin and other authors' whose works 'had quite captivated my imagination, and done much to determine me to adopt the [hunter's] life of ever-varying scenes and constant excitement'.[12] Much later in the twentieth century American hunter David P. Prizio was still echoing him, naming 'Baldwin, Bell, Lyell, Manners, Stigand, Selous, Pretorius and Finaughty'.[13]

Even this select list of titles begins to give the flavour. More or less lawless 'wanderings' and 'adventure' are key, the structure likely to be reminiscent and episodic, the tone self-deprecating, even boyish. Though some are explicitly focused on elephants, all of them included brushes with numerous other animals (humans are generally of lesser interest). These foreign hunters' stays on the subcontinent were brief; many were 'on tour' from other parts of the world or of Africa, and this detachment aided their destructiveness. Only at the turn of the century would southern African-born hunters begin to make their literary presence felt, but by then much of the game in the region had been exterminated and – as Bryden's title *Gun and Camera* indicates – an aesthetic of observation was helping to stimulate an ethic of preservation rather than untrammelled slaughter. This would be embodied in the advent of the national park alongside animal rights discourses. The impress of these transitions makes the period one of fascinating ambivalence and conflicted attitudes, even within these apparently doctrinaire works.

The literary hunters' works were popular in Britain. Multiple reprints were amplified by lecture tours, exhibitions and excerpts in sundry periodicals – these, too, were part of the 'story'. They generally affected that rough-and-ready *anti*-literariness, though there could be marked differences between them. Baldwin employed an unadorned diary-entry style. Gordon-Cumming claimed to have 'almost literally transcribed' his accounts from his journals: 'Written under such circumstances, the reader will not look for grace of style. The hand, wearied all day by grasping the rifle, is not the best suited for the pen.'[14] Selous similarly claimed a 'plain, intelligible English', hoping 'that my shortcomings will be leniently judged when it is remembered that the last nine years of my life have been passed amongst savages, during which time I have not undergone the best training for a literary effort'.[15]

But evidence of literary knowledge, and not only of precursor's hunting accounts, litters these works. Harris, for example, having 'quitted civilisation', mentions some of his reading in his introduction (mostly popular works of natural history and cartographies), and notes that he is deliberately *not* reproducing a journal filled with minutiae he considers of no interest to the reader.[16] The narrative, in other words, is retrospectively *shaped* to suit the taste of a predetermined audience. Nor is Harris averse, in the style of many contemporary works, to inserting snippets of enlivening poetry of (to us now) obscure provenance. For all the avowed jungly roughness, the genre demanded such literariness. Harris's own style was far from as straightforward as he claimed. The following example is so ornate and deliberately archaic as to constitute self-parody:

> Cobus, who the morning before, when he dreamt not of the real state of the case, has ridden forth gasconading of his prowess in arms, now repeated several times emphatically that the contemptible spokesman had actually defied him in terms derogating him from his valour. 'Here,' said he, 'Here stand your oxen; come up if you're a man! Take them, ye poltroons, if ye dare!' Yet, although mounted, and abundantly supplied with ammunition, these hulking white-livered villains did not blush to acknowledge that their personal fears had induced them to decline the invitation.[17]

This is a long way from the sturdy plainness of, say, Baldwin's truncated (which is to say, not unedited) diary-entry style. Still, when it comes to the elephant-hunting scenes, certain similarities are evident. One is the manner in which the details of the approach to the intended target are laid out with the gratuitous precision of a military manoeuvre:

We had just descended a steep bamboo-covered hillside, crossed a mountain torrent, and were slowly climbing the steep opposite side of the valley when we heard a noise from the slope behind us. On looking back we at first only saw the bamboo moving by some unseen agency. Every now and again there would be a trembling in a clump of trees and the top of a stem would bend over and disappear with a cracking sound. On looking through my glasses I could distinguish here and there a black trunk soaring upwards to reach for a high branch, and occasionally a glimpse of part of a black body between the bamboo clumps. After watching for some time I made out what I took to be three bulls on the right of the herd. Knowing that I should not, in all probability, get another sight of them, once I left my vantage on the hillside, I took careful stock of their position and of any big trees on the way to serve as landmarks. Then I descended to the bottom of the valley again, crossed the stream, and began the steep toil up the slope. When I finally arrived at the spot at which I had seen them there was nothing but their spoor left; the whole herd had moved on and there was not even the noise of cracking bamboo to be heard. I followed the spoor a little way, and, as I could see or hear nothing of them, I returned to the porters and arranged a site for our camp.[18]

It is not surprising that the rhetoric and narrative structure of 'war' is endemic, given many hunters' military backgrounds. Harris was an army officer on furlough from India; Selous died fighting in the First World War. Colonel Richard Meinertzhagen was explicit: 'After all, the hunting of men – war – is but a form of hunting wild animals.'[19] A military fascination with both the armaments themselves (this grows increasingly sophisticated) and with what happens to the expended bullets, further helps to muffle emotional responses to the death of the animal. This is a moment I want to focus on. Adulphe Delegorgue wrote in 1847:

What paltry reason can justify the death and destruction of such beautiful, strong and excellent animals? What are a couple of hundred pounds

of ivory compared with the long service which such animals might ren-
der to man for generations? . . . I was perfectly conscious of the mischief
I was doing but I was a hunter first and foremost . . . I desired no other;
all the animals of creation, whatsoever they may be, are as nothing compared with the elephant.[20]

Delegorgue is fully aware that elephants may be regarded as beautiful, that greed for ivory is ultimately paltry, that killing them might be
regarded as mischief. Like many hunters, Delegorgue appeals to some
primordial essence of the *hunter*, the 'natural and apparently irrepress-
ible instinct' evoked by Bryden.[21] The edginess of remorse, the potential for compassionate feeling is there, troubling the surface – and is
instantly snuffed out. This psychological manoeuvre recurs throughout the period's literature. An early example is an account by the most
unabashedly rapacious of all these hunters, Gordon-Cumming, a passage often quoted precisely for its lack of compassion. He puts a bullet
into 'the tallest and largest bull elephant [he] had ever seen', failing to
kill it:

> Finding himself incapacitated, the old fellow seemed determined to
> take it easy, and, limping slowly to a neighbouring tree, he remained
> stationary, eyeing his pursuers with a resigned and philosophic air.
> I resolved to devote a short time to the contemplation of this noble
> elephant before I should lay him low; accordingly, having off-saddled
> the horses beneath a shady tree . . . I quickly kindled a fire and put on
> the kettle . . . There I sat in my forest home, coolly sipping my coffee,
> with one of the finest elephants in Africa awaiting my pleasure beside a
> neighbouring tree.
> It was, indeed, a striking scene, and as I gazed upon the stupendous
> veteran of the forest, I thought of the red deer which I loved to follow in
> my native land, and felt that, although the fates had driven me to follow
> a more daring and arduous avocation in a distant land, it was a good
> exchange that I had made, for I was now a chief over boundless forests,
> which yielded unspeakably more noble and exciting sport.
> Having admired the elephant for a considerable time, I resolved to
> make experiments for vulnerable points, and, approaching very near, I
> fired several bullets at different parts of his enormous skull. These did
> seem to affect him in the slightest; he only acknowledged the shots by a

'salaam-like' movement of his trunk, with the point of which he gently touched the wound with a striking and peculiar action. Surprised and shocked to find that I was only tormenting and prolonging the sufferings of the noble beast, which bore his trials with such dignified composure, I resolved to finish the proceedings with all possible dispatch; accordingly, I opened fire on him from the left side, aiming behind the shoulder; but even there it was long before my bullets seemed to take effect. I first fired six shots with the two-grooved, which must have eventually proved mortal, but as yet he evinced no visible distress; after which I fired three shots at the same part with the Dutch six-pounder. Large tears now trickled from his eyes, which he slowly shut and opened; his colossal frame shivered convulsively, and, falling on his side, he expired.[22]

The callousness of this protracted 'experiment' has prompted commentators to condemn its 'detached and unemotional language' and its self-delusion of grandeur and possession.[23] Phrases like 'take it easy' and 'resigned and philosophic' evade or mask the certainty that the animal was actually incapacitated by overwhelming pain. Yet the account *does* contain a turn towards the empathetic (recognising some form of cognate inner life in the elephant) and the compassionate (Gordon-Cumming finds himself 'shocked' at his own thoughtless prolonging of the 'noble' animal's 'sufferings'). There is no question that he regards the elephant as sentient, self-conscious and emotionally endowed, even demonstrating qualities he might well value in himself, including a 'philosophic air' and 'dignified composure', a kind of grace under pressure. This is in part self-serving anthropomorphic projection. Gordon-Cumming uses the same word, 'noble', to describe the sport of elephant-hunting – an early manifestation of the developing sporting ethic of the 'clean shot'. Ironically, the cleaner the shot, the less interesting and the more brusquely treated is the death itself; the story then has to be sought elsewhere, mostly in exaggerating the perils of the stalk and the glow of the aftermath. The philosopher José Ortega y Gasset also recognised the pattern: 'To the sportsman the death of the game is not what interests him; that is not his purpose. What interests him is everything that he had to do to achieve that death – that is, the hunt.'[24] This still feels to me somewhat disingenuous – the death remains central – as does his assertion that a good hunter does not hunt 'to enhance [his] personal status'.[25] These texts rather support Nigel Rothfels's observation: 'The kudos of the killing depends on inflating the status of the prey', and on a 'false estimate' of his achievement.[26] Still, Ortega y Gasset has also written: 'Every good hunter is uneasy at the depths of his conscience when faced with the death he is about to inflict.'[27] Not all hunters are 'good' by this definition – and that conscience still gets repressed at the crucial, lethal moment. In effect, the 'good' hunter is precisely he who has such pity, but is manly enough to crush it. In tandem, in claiming (in the passage above) to have been driven by the 'fates', Gordon-Cumming performs another typical shrugging off of responsibility.

The second example of emergent but suppressed compassion is from Harris. He wrote both his travel account, *Wild Sports*, and a lavishly illustrated, slightly more zoologically inclined survey, *Portraits of the Game and Wild Animals of Southern Africa*. The latter's chapter on the elephant is, however, scant on biological detail, dominated by narratives of Harris's 'campaign' against 'Nature's masterpiece' – this despite quoting a snatch of poetry describing the elephant as leading a 'quiet life' that 'offendeth none'.[28] *Wild Sports* supplies a vivid extended account of an elephant hunt in the 'Cashan mountains': 'Here, to our inexpressible gratification, we descried a large herd of these long-sought animals, lazily browsing at the head of a distant valley . . . Never having before seen the noble elephant in his native jungles, we gazed on the sight before us with intense and indescribable interest. Our feelings on the occasion even extended to our followers. As for Andries, he became so agitated that he could scarcely articulate.'[29]

Having thus rendered himself allegedly inarticulate as well, Harris turns instantly to the hunt, which consisted of the brave gunmen lying in ambush behind the remnants of a stone kraal as their underlings drove random elephants towards them:

We selected the finest, and with perfect deliberation fired a volley of five balls into her. She stumbled, but recovering herself, uttered a shrill note of lamentation, when the whole party threw their trunks above their heads, and instantly clambered up the adjacent hill with incredible celerity, their huge fan-like ears flapping in the ratio of their speed. We instantly mounted our horses, and, the sharp stones not suiting the feet of the wounded lady, had soon closed with her. Streaming with blood, and infuriated with rage, she turned upon us with uplifted trunk, and it was not until after repeated discharges, that a ball took effect in her brain, and threw her lifeless on the earth, which resounded with the fall.[30]

The animal may be 'noble', a 'lady', granted the capacity for feeling both lamentation and rage, but these are not enough to save her from this inefficient onslaught. Harris and Co. turn without delay to further targets 'majestically emerging into the open glades' whose background 'was filled by a limited peep of the blue mountainous range, which here assumed a remarkably precipitous character, and completed a picture at once soul-stirring and sublime!'[31] In opening fire on some of the animals, a scene of 'ludicrous confusion' ensues, 'ever coming upon fresh parties of the enemy'. One such offending party was 'attacked', several old females slain, and orphaned babies left behind. In self-mitigation, Harris claims: 'Much has been said of the attachment of elephants to their young, but neither on this, nor any subsequent occasion, did we perceive them evince the smallest concern for their safety. On the contrary, they left them to shift for themselves.'[32] (This is despite having observed precisely such attachment a page earlier, when the elephants were not panicking under unprecedented gunfire.) The following day the hunters return to the scene of the massacre to retrieve the ivory, resulting in one of the most often quoted – because gut-wrenching – incidents:

> Not an elephant was to be seen on the ground that was yesterday teeming with them; but on reaching the glen which had been the scene of our exploits during the early part of the action, a calf about three and a half feet high walked forth from a bush, and saluted us with mournful piping notes. We had observed the unhappy little wretch hovering about its mother after she fell, and having probably been unable to overtake the herd, it had passed a dreary night in the wood. Entwining its little proboscis about our legs, the sagacious creature, after demonstrating its delight at our arrival by a thousand ungainly antics, accompanied the

party to the body of its dam . . . The conduct of the quaint little calf now became quite affecting, and elicited the sympathies of every one. It ran round its mother's corpse with touching demonstrations of grief, piping sorrowfully, and vainly attempting to raise her with its little trunk. I confess that I had felt compunctions in committing the murder the day before, and now half resolved never to assist in another.[33]

This half-resolution is instantly suppressed by a return to practicalities and a discussion of the allegedly untameable nature of the African as opposed to the Indian elephant (on the backs of which Harris himself had fondly ridden on Indian tiger hunts). The fate of the little elephant, which 'voluntarily' follows them back to camp, is dismissed in a line or two. It dies after a few days 'in spite of every care' – and the hunting continues without any further inconvenient soul-searching.

This remains the pattern – hints of appreciation, touches even of anthropomorphic empathy, followed by the thrusting down of all sentiment. Thus do these 'inflated bullies',[34] with their ever-more efficient weapons, despite themselves, flirt with the compassion debate throughout the half-century. None does so more obviously than Arthur Neumann in the introductory comments to his 1898 book, *Elephant Hunting in East Equatorial Africa*:

Of course, I am prepared to be denounced as cruel. I admit at once that I am. This trait is part and parcel of the barbaric tastes which caused me, in my earliest years, to be stigmatised as 'a cruel boy' by tender-hearted members of my family, for my ardour in the pursuit of the harmless, necessary cat, in company with a couple of equally keen terriers . . . One cannot complain of the censure of kind-hearted people who object altogether to the taking of life – on the contrary, I respect them. But the attacks of such superior sportsmen as, while giving us graphic accounts of their exploits in pursuit of the harmless eland, giraffe and other defenceless creatures, write in horror of the cruelty of hunting elephants (having themselves not penetrated far enough into the wilderness to get the chance), are harder to bear. It is particularly cruel, they tell us, to hunt cow elephants . . . I wish one of these gentlemen would come and show us how to shoot bulls only, in the dense cover in which elephants have to be sought.[35]

This is a curious, even self-defeating argument. It does not, firstly, resolve his responses to real or imagined censure. Those he claims to respect – the kindly folk – he dismisses in a sentence. Disparagement from fellow hunters, however, rankles; these he derides as both cruel and cowardly. Yet the evidence of his own text exposes both his capacity to slaughter the 'harmless' *and*, at moments, palpable quivers of compassion in himself. Nor does he resolve the tension between being 'barbaric' and a 'sportsman'. In Nietzschean mode, Neumann embraces his fundamentally barbaric nature, implying that the elephants are as necessary to its expression as the cat of his youth, an admission most hunting 'sportsmen' would vehemently deny. The sportsman, wrote Neumann's contemporary Samuel Baker, distinguished the superior hunter from the 'merciless gunner' whose 'love is slaughter, indiscriminate and boundless'.[36] Baker also explicitly equated the latter with, what he claims, were the indiscriminate killings conducted by 'the African savage' who never exhibits 'any sympathy or pity, his nature being, like the gunner of the nineteenth century, to exterminate'.[37] The sportsman is by definition civilised, not barbaric. Neumann claims for himself many of the qualities of just such a sportsman: a man who, in Baker's words, 'studies nature with keen enjoyment, and shoots his game with judgement and forbearance upon the principles of fair play'.[38] Such protestations are always disingenuous, no matter what hardships the hunter claims to have (voluntarily) put himself through in his penetration of wild interiors: Neumann on his own account blazes away at half-concealed elephants of unknown value and loses a commensurate number of wounded animals in the bush. He justifies himself to the extent that he *once* got stamped on by an irate elephant, passing himself off as grimly laconic, even chivalrous: 'There is no need to describe my sufferings. That they were intense is self-evident . . . In following this pursuit one must reckon with the risks; and I always knew that there was a probability of an accident happening some day . . . Just retribution, perhaps you will say; and for my part, I harboured no ill-will against the elephant for avenging its kith and kin. It was the fortune of war.'[39]

Interesting here is the momentary lapse into an anthropomorphic mode – elephant as conscious avenger, as member of a family structure of loyalty. This is immediately dismissed by appeal to a higher ethical imperative, the 'fortune of war', which is to say an existential level on which an ethic of just retribution plays no role at all. Such lapses of logic, internal contradictions and evasions are, it seems, essential to the being of the hunter. The evasions have become necessary precisely because a societal debate has already been internalised – there are repeated muted addresses to an antagonistic or compassionate reader (the 'you' in the passage above).

Finally, Selous simultaneously displays the same awareness and evasiveness. Stalking elephants, he exults only momentarily at the 'grand sight' of 'so many of these huge beasts moving slowly and majestically onwards. However, as there was now but an hour of sunlight left, we could spare but little time for admiration, and so rode towards them, on murderous thoughts intent.'[40] The vocabulary of awe seldom goes beyond 'grand', 'majestic' or 'sublime'. The word 'murderous' evinces a touch of compassionate self-criticism, but it is swept aside by the transgressive excitement of a particular power relationship, that of diminutive bullet overcoming elephantine bulk. 'I have dragged forth *Behemoth*,' Harris crowed, and repeatedly, from then onwards, hunters express 'wonder that such a comparatively small missile as a .458 bullet could so easily kill the undeniable ruler of the animal kingdom'.[41] (Though, since that is what it is designed to do, and does regularly, this profession of wonder seems to me increasingly hollow.) This alleged incongruousness – the 'true monarch of the African forest . . . slain by the only living thing that could wreak him harm – ruthless man' – fuels the intoxicating excitement.[42] In effect, awed appreciation is essential to the triumph, even as it retrospectively mutes it. Hence, the writers habitually assert their congenital inability to convey it. This is William Tapp in 1914:

> The occurrences that happened today require a better pen than mine to give even a slight impression of them. The whole picture is so vast, made up of the great beasts with their trunks and ears swinging ever to and fro, and the huge forest with its mighty trees and glorious vegetation, and the contrast of the tiny little human being amongst it all is so great that I feel it is really hopeless for a person to try and picture it . . . *I will therefore leave my own feelings at once*, and . . . continue the facts of the diary.[43]

Pallid though this is, the evasiveness is inescapable. Suppression of feeling takes further forms. Having abruptly killed, the writer must linger over the aftermath. Selous again:

> Upon cutting out this elephant's heart I found that three bullets had gone clean through it, and that a fourth was still in it, whilst his lungs were riddled. I laid the heart upon the carcase, and made a drawing of it on the spot, showing the position of the four bullet-holes on the one side. This statement will, I am afraid, be looked upon with suspicion by the generality of my readers, though all those who have shot large game will probably be able to call to mind similar experiences.[44]

Here the self-affirmation of the accurate 'sportsman' offsets the self-conscious smugness in the implied gore. The boast of the trophy is suppressed by the preservation of a physical or artistic specimen, ostensibly for scientific or educational purposes. Several of these literate sportsmen claimed a place as amateur naturalists, following in the footsteps of earlier scientific travellers like Burchell and Delegorgue and used this as a defence for their massacres: 'Whatever damage he may have done in early years among the elephants, the magnificent specimens of great game sent home by Selous to the Natural History and other Museums, amply deliver him from the charge of mere wasteful slaughter' – thus Bryden in 1893, even as he lamented the disappearance of that very game.[45]

Again contradictorily, the accounts themselves undercut this denial of wastefulness. Selous shows that he was fully aware that his readership, extending beyond other big-game hunters, included people ethically opposed to the very basis for his adventures. Almost everything in their style is designed to outflank that implicit and anticipated critique. The studied flattening (excepting occasional clichés such as 'constant excitement') is more than just a habitual 'English suppression of emotion', as Gray puts it – it is the deflection of an ethical debate about animal compassion that underpins the texts' engagement with 'civilisation' itself.[46] Ultimately, the telling of the story is the thing. As Selous put it after one hunt: 'I soon had a piece of elephant's heart, nicely salted and peppered, roasting on a forked stick over the coals; and if I had but a white companion with whom to talk over the day's sport and fight the battle o'er again, my happiness would have been complete.'[47]

The literariness of the phrase 'fight the battle o'er again' emphasises the troubling but necessary presence of what some critics term 'the reader in the text' – signs of the writer's imagined audience. The phrase also functions to elevate grimy reality to the level of chivalrous war. Yet the debate is ever-present. Indeed, as Matt Cartmill's history of hunting shows, a guarded guilt had been pervasive in hunting literature from Renaissance manuals onwards.[48]

Whatever the generic commonalities of this era of hunting literature, the works are also transitional. As the turn towards protectionism and animal rights gained traction, the evasions grew even subtler, as in Gillmore's 'A Plea for the African Elephant', published in his 1893 book, *Leaves from a Sportsman's Diary*:

> The wealthy man anathematized the trader for shooting elephants for the sake of their ivory, yet the rich man does as bad, although he cannot plead that his subsistence depends upon his doing so. The professional elephant hunter is, as a rule, a rough and indifferently educated man, who adopts this very hardest of all businesses to obtain money to support him when age, exposure, and hardship has told upon his constitution, while the favoured son of fortune goes in for killing this game that he may boast of his prowess at his club, or exhibit his trophies to admiring relatives and guests. I leave it for the unprejudiced reader to judge which of these two types of men deserves the greatest amount of condemnation.[49]

However, Gillmore's appeal for this 'grand mammoth of brute creation', this 'noble, sagacious creature', then takes the form of another twist of the imperial screw: the ever-scarcer elephants must be preserved, but only by being assimilated into commercial profitability. They must 'repay' their protectors who, 'by domesticating [the elephants] and employing them in agriculture, in transport, in pageants, in destroying the carnivorous brutes, and, finally, as the instruments by which to explore every hole and corner in the unknown parts of the "dark continent"'.[50] This pipe dream is obviously modelled on the Indian example, but the exploitative mentality – *if it pays, it stays* – has gained even greater purchase over the subsequent century. Conservation itself, and the role of the hunter in it, has been widely commandeered to a mindset and rhetoric of monetarist exploitation that is almost more imperialistic, chilling and inhuman than anything Gordon-Cumming ever wrote. For example:

> The African elephant is a natural resource that lends itself to assignable ownership and that ownership, couples [*sic*] with benefits produced from hunting, provides an incentive for conservation . . . Hunting of the African elephant by foreign tourists has a long-standing tradition and is one of the uses of choice by many African nations today. Africans were hunting elephants before Eastern peoples or Europeans arrived in Africa . . . Hunting of elephants by tourists is cost effective, profitable and easily monitored . . . Foreign hunters are willing to convert [assignable ownership] from an asset capital in exchange for a cultural experience compatible with the history and use of the elephant.[51]

If the elephant could speak, would it accede to this wholly illogical appeal to tradition (the notion that foreign tourist-hunters are somehow seamlessly continuing an 'African' norm)? Would it agree that the kill is a valid cultural experience, that this is somehow compatible with the history of the elephant? Can the animal, which is hunted because it is both inferior and wild, be simultaneously farmed as a resource, be owned? Try substituting a persecuted human group – Rohingya, Jew, or slave – for elephant, cultural resource for natural resource, foreign soldiers for tourists – to see the ugly illogicality. For all the talk of conservation and choice, the evasions of responsibility remain, embedded in the language of immoveable systems, euphemism and the passive voice: the elephant allegedly 'lends itself' to its own entrapment and death. This reads as less a 'plea for the elephant' than a defence of free-market capitalism in 'the most tumultuous of times'.

The tumult reaches even the most remote of wild regions. 'Mozambique Elephants Obliterated' – a headline that could have come from the late nineteenth century. But it did not; it was from October 2014. Of all the subregions of southern Africa, Mozambique has been the longest subjected to depredations on its elephants, since Arab traders and their proxies hunted for ivory from the sixteenth century onwards. The volumes of ivory being exported from the coastal ports of Mozambique – Quelimane, Sofala, Delagoa Ba – increased steadily over four centuries. Hunters went far inland, as far as Monomatapa or Zambezia: E.P. Mathers's 1891 book, *Zambesia: England's El Dorado in Africa*, cites what he calls a 'very curious old work', dated 1600, 'A Geographical Historie of Africa Written in Arabicke and Italian by John Leo and More borne in Granada and brought up in Barbarie'. According to this account, Monomatapa's empire, 'which lyeth between the mouth of the Cuama [Zambezi], and the Cape de los Corrientes, is a very pleasant, holesome, and fruitfull country. And from the said cape to the river of Magnice [Limpopo], the whole region aboundeth with beasts both great and small . . . Here there are such plenty of Elephants, and it seemeth by the great quantitie of their teeth, that there are yearly slaine between four and five thousand.'[52]

If this is even roughly true the offtake was already unsustainable. As for the coastal areas, no area in Africa reveals more clearly the toxic mix of natural fecundity, centuries of global trade and slavery, colonial disruptions and corrosive poverty followed by devastating civil wars and unregulated multinational resource plunder. We know little about elephant populations until very recent times; at best, they fluctuated wildly as the animals migrated, were hunted and their habitats increasingly fragmented. After Mozambique was colonised, Portuguese hunters killed considerable numbers, too, for sport, for ivory, and because the elephants were so-called pests in tsetse-fly areas in the 1930s. The national park system in Mozambique has always been shakier than in neighbouring countries, especially during times of intense civil war (1964–1974 and 1978–1992). According to one study, an estimation of 60 000 elephants in 1974 had, by 2009, dropped to only 16 000, scattered over five national parks; according to another, some 20 000 inhabited Niassa National Park in the north in 2009, but these had been reduced to 13 000 by 2014.[53] Slaughter in other parts of the country appears even more damaging.

Naturally, English-language elephant-hunting accounts from Mozambique are rare, and are relatively neglected compared to the mainstream works examined above.[54] I glance at only two of them here.

The first, Harry Manners' *Kambaku!*, though written in the mid-twentieth century (published as late as 1986), echoes many features of the nineteenth-century accounts. The second is a magazine article by Stuart Cloete, better known as a novelist. Both carry further some of the transitional features, the new conservation aesthetics beginning to take hold.

In many ways Manners, regularly cited alongside the other mainstays of the hunting book genealogy, is a late manifestation of the irrepressibly restless hunting culture of the 1890s, though he was scouring the remoter regions of Mozambique between 1937 and 1953. The generally militaristic air, the half-concealed disdain for the numerous necessary local people, the slightly chummy humour of self-deprecation, the details of the kills and the pervasive nostalgia for the days of more abundant game are all there. But there are significant differences, too. The drawings and etchings of the previous century have been replaced by photographs: the cover jacket of the 1997 Rowland Ward edition shows a dapper Manners posing with two elephant tusks a great deal taller than he is.[55] The technology of hunting has been amplified in both weaponry and support – vehicles, lamps and all the other paraphernalia. Moreover, Manners' style is markedly different from that of his predecessors: it is more novelistic, including more detailed descriptions of the environment, and more emotively nuanced interiority to the hunting scenes:

> Yes, we were in the middle of nowhere and I thought of Carmen, now in a big city, surrounded by tall buildings and masses of people; a seaside holiday centre contrasting sharply, solidly, with the loneliness of our present primeval surroundings.
>
> Except for the occasional wanderer, such as I with my black comrades, this was a mountain-studded, profusely wooded *terra incognita*, pathless, roadless, the streams unspanned by bridges. Had the signs not shown that we were slowly reducing distance still separating us from our objective, my mind and spirit would have given way to the gloomy prospect of final defeat. How much longer Big Fish, Big Elephant, do I have to go on keeping my line in the water? I chuckled mirthlessly, a little crazily, at the comparison. Chisulo looked back at me over his shoulder, his eyes slightly glazed. I gave him an inane grin and touched my temple with my forefinger.

Then, at last, we heard a distant rumble, followed by the thump of
something solid against a tree trunk. Weariness evaporated from me
and the old, old thrill of contact with those forest monsters took over.[56]

There is much of this kind of narrative, with details of emotional states,
body movements and, most interestingly, shifts into present-tense interior monologue – a narrative technique that collapses the distance of
recollection. The influence of fiction here is clear. In addition, there
are extended passages of fiction-like dialogue – not least of all with his
love interest, Carmen. The parallel of a love-romance with the romance
of hunting-in-Africa ('white ivory and black men, the old romance
through bygone times', he calls it), with all its admissions of more tender feelings towards women, is unprecedented in this most masculine
of genres, though it was becoming a staple of the popular novel.

Some dialogues are utilised to air arguments about the ethics of
hunting. (The contrivance of this device reminds us that Manners the
man is not necessarily identical to the narrator of the book – an important distinction.) Carmen directly questions Manners' 'conscience',
demanding at one point: 'But you, the ivory hunter, tell me this: is there
much difference, basically, between fashion, trophy hunting and the
ivory trade? I say that the interests correlate . . . Do we really need
them?' Manners inwardly admits to some truth to this, but his voiced
response is of a different order: '"Let me put it to you this way. It's
a necessary evil, like prostitution. Since time began, since the sexes
became a way of life and without which, somewhere in society, there is
something missing . . . Again, since the beginning of time, there have
been hunters. That's why I have never had any such qualms. In retro-
spect, I think it has always been the call of the wild – and adventure."'[57]

Here is that old evasion, the simplistic appeal to some uncon-
querable (and masculinist) force beyond the individual will. There is
that word 'necessary' again, which we recall from Neumann, writing
three-quarters of a century before. But Manners does eventually have
qualms. His book *Kambaku!* (meaning 'tusker') culminates (as do most
hunting novels) in a search for a particularly spectacular elephant bull.
According to the *Oxford English Dictionary*, the word 'tusker' was first
used by one J.E. Tennent in Ceylon in 1859, merely to distinguish elephants with tusks from those without. In 1893, Selous wrote of looking

for 'good tuskers'.[58] So in the twentieth century, even as they become rarer, the word becomes attached to bulls with exceptional tusks. The goal becomes less a commercial weight of ivory than a duel, a highly personalised combat. Manners feels he is 'treading in the direction of what might prove a lifetime experience, an appointment with prehistory, a meeting with mammoths . . . I felt myself being swept into the Stone Age by a time machine but, instead of a club and a flint-tipped spear, I still gripped a modern, high-velocity rifle.' He goes on to make much of how puny his rifle is in comparison to the gigantic elephant bull he finally confronts, 'the Great One': 'in my blurred, fevered mind I saw him as a super-giant, ten times that height, a nonpareil dwarfing the very trees from which he fed, reducing me to less than nothing in the presence of that monstrous bulk'.[59] Manners is unusually frank about the influence of his own inflationary imagination, though it ultimately remains in service of inflating his own ego. He takes the tusker down. The death itself is, as usual, perfunctory, but the rumination that follows is not:

And then we found him, magnificent in solitary grandeur, even in death. And I was overcome by a strange feeling as, with those present, I admired the colossal elephant from various angles, staring incredulously at those super-thick, super-long poles of ivory, 187 and 185 pounds, when later weighed. There was something still majestic, unreal, in the recumbent form as I looked at him silently . . . Yet, as I gazed at him, the colossal prize stretched out before me, I felt remorse instead of elation. How could it be thus, at the supreme moment of my whole hunting career, the moment I had conjured, in fantasy, through years of hunting?

I had killed the king of them all. I sank down beside him and, though I did not weep openly, remembering my companions and their lack of emotion (barring excitement or fear) when hunting, I nevertheless felt the tears on my cheeks and a lump in my throat. Yes, I had killed the king and, beside him I was the repentant murderer.

Could this be me, acting this way?[60]

Surprise at his own remorse wrestles with the traditional manly suppression of emotion. More oddly, when he shortly afterwards learns that Carmen has been drowned off Durban's South Beach, he wonders if this is not that same elephant's form of vengeance, 'decreed by fate'. Does this anguished, almost paranormal speculation extend the evasion of personal remorse for the *elephant*'s death, or intensify it? This moral struggle lays the grounds for Manners' somewhat reluctant transition to hunting guide and ironic protector of animals in wildlife 'concessions' in South Africa: 'I accepted this as inevitable, though my gradual mental metamorphosis still did not quite favour the hackneyed cliché of gun being abandoned in favour of the camera. Hunting had been practised since the dawn of time, through the ages, and now controlled hunting was a viable solution for securing the future of game animals within the concessions.' But this new life, as he says in his closing sentence, 'is another story'.[61]

And it seems there is always another 'last ivory hunter', as in the story of Wally Johnson, a partial contemporary of Manners. The much-acclaimed hunter-writer Peter Hathaway Capstick – narrating as if he is Johnson – relates Johnson's hunting exploits in Mozambique and elsewhere in a still later period, until Johnson flees from the civil war in 1975. *The Last Ivory Hunter* is all quasi-fictional derring-do and near-death experiences – except for the hundreds of lions and 1300 elephants Johnson killed, in the interest, he claims, of 'thinning out' the 'destructive' herds. The nostalgia for the 'old Africa' is fully in place, the dearth of elephants to hunt is blamed on poachers, and the background politics are updated to a diatribe against communism 'and its surrogates'. The prose is both purple and at times jarringly inappropriate – a cover for the same evasion of either compassion or responsibility.[62]

Cloete hunted elephants in Mozambique in the same period as Manners and Johnson, his experiences forming the basis for his novel, *The Curve and the Tusk*. For now, Cloete can have the final word on the transition, in an article published in the *Saturday Evening Post* in 1949. It is, significantly, titled 'We Never Fired a Shot'. In Mozambique's Maputo reserve Cloete confines himself to photographing the elephants; he has become a tourist 'on safari'. The article itself, largely devoted to detailed naturalistic information about the elephant as a species, is at once nostalgic for a less confined past and guardedly optimistic that the elephant will never be hunted out. Here, palpably, a

different aesthetic is taking hold, romanticised, coloured in a style alien
to the hunting forerunners:

> It is hard to describe the effect that the elephant country has on a per-
> son. In this wild land the tortured trunks of great ghostly trees assume
> fantastic shapes in the evening light – shapes like the faces of rhinos,
> pigs and baboons that grin at you as you wait for night to fall in the hour
> the natives call 'the time when everyone is beautiful' – that mauve glow
> that suffuses all Africa for half an hour before the shadows suddenly
> grow long. Nothing at this time could be more sinister or mysterious
> than an elephant water hole reflecting a circle of yellow-barked fever
> trees. There you stand alone in the silence . . . The country is untamed
> and untameable.[63]

'Tortured', 'ghostly', 'sinister': it is a strange phantasmagoria that
Cloete indulges in here. This untamed land is, it turns out, a regulated
reserve, simultaneously populated with villages; the most threatening
adventure is encountering 'thirty-six scorpions'. Hence, it is not ethical
reconsideration so much as a succumbing to necessity, saturated with
weary nostalgia, with which Cloete looks back on more lethal days:

> During my three months in the elephant country I had five guns with me
> and was licensed to hunt. Yet I never fired a shot, although I always car-
> ried a rifle and often had game under my sights. Once I loved hunting,
> but now I do not want to kill anything. Perhaps this is because it seems
> a sacrilege to eliminate any of the game still left in the world; perhaps a
> man reaches a time when he is no longer the hunter and warrior; per-
> haps there has just been too much killing in the world of late. Anyway,
> now I want only to see and watch, live and let live.[64]

Cloete's generalised regret, it seems, is not about killing per se, only
that there has been too much of it, and that the hunter's racy wander-
lust has been reduced to the shadow of the 'safari bug'. The hunting
accounts of this period are not, evidently, designed to bring us much
closer to explaining *why* some men enjoy killing elephants, let alone
whether it is moral; their whole *raison d'être* is to close off even thinking
about motive and culpability.

Chapter 4

Not Very Good at Remorse:
Elephants in fiction

If self-serving non-fiction hunting accounts are congenitally reticent about motivations for killing animals, perhaps novels will reveal more about the tension between murderousness and compassion. After all, fiction is traditionally a primary medium for the exploration of emotional inwardness and human motivations. Hunting remains a central question in this chapter because, without exception, southern African elephant adult novels are about hunting them. The chapter asks, then: what does fiction bring to the question of compassion towards elephants?

Distinctions between fiction and non-fiction are not always easy to make. From Thomas Mayne Reid to Wilbur Smith, generic novelistic features can be seen both to feed off and leak back into the travelogues, hunting accounts and game-ranger memoirs. Reid, because he never came to South Africa himself, drew heavily on the late eighteenth-century and early nineteenth-century travelogues for *The Bush Boys* and its sequel *The Young Yagers*, but laid down some of the structures for later fiction. H. Rider Haggard, who did have some local experience, was even more influential in his adventure tales – *King Solomon's Mines, Allan Quatermain* and *She*, in particular. Both writers hover between young adult and adult audiences, an ambiguous pitch retained in many subsequent novels. Haggard dedicated *King Solomon's Mines* to 'all the big and little boys who read it', and the narrator states that he is writing it for his son.

At least one late nineteenth-century hunter turned his hand to fiction. H.A. Bryden's *Tales of South Africa* (1896) are all set on the turbulent fringes of imperial advance. Its main characters are trekboers compulsively escaping state control, or English hunter-traders searching out still-untouched lands. These readable stories are historically knowledgeable and rich in appreciative natural detail – more camera than gun. One character articulates a view of the natural that is perhaps closest to the author's: 'One comes out here in the veldt and looks at Nature, and one finds *everywhere* the most ghastly war, and murder, and suffering incessantly around one. Birds, beasts, insects, reptiles, fish – all hard at it . . . You may have epochs of civilization and calm, but only for a time. Nature tells us that plainly.'[1] In this crudely Darwinian view humans are also ultimately part of the natural cycle of ferocity and death – a neat way of evading personal responsibility or remorse, especially in the context of Empire. An idealistic streak within imperialism 'posits a metaphysical conception of causality . . . understood to be working out the design of some transcendental force'.[2] This is to ignore the decidedly undesigned and untranscendental outlaws who in practice extended the frontier precisely by trying to escape it – men represented by the highly individualistic and elusive hunters who populate Bryden's stories. These characters express scarcely an iota of compassion for the wild animals being exuberantly slaughtered on a massive scale – only repeated regret that the good old days of teeming targets have gone. The scarcity of elephants is especially regrettable. The description of an elephant hunt in 'The Story of Jacoba Steyn' follows the conventional hunting account:

> At half-past twelve they came suddenly upon the elephants in some troublesome thorny bush. There were eighteen in all, and some good bulls among them. Meredith quickly got to work and slew two magnificent bulls, carrying long, even teeth, after a hot and most exciting chase. He next tackled a big cow, furnished with a capital pair of tusks. After a sharp gallop he got alongside and put a four-ounce ball, backed with seven drachms of powder (those were the days of smooth bores and heavy charges), behind her shoulder. But stricken though she was, the

cow was by no means finished. She turned short in her tracks and, spout-
ing blood, came with a ferocious scream straight for her tormentor . . .
It was her last effort. The heavy bullet had done its work. Thrice she
lifted her blood-dripping trunk as if for air. Then she swayed softly to
and fro, and suddenly sank down upon all fours, as if kneeling, and so
yielded up her fifty years of life.[3]

Is there, in the faintly religious gestures, and despite the gore that foreshadows later pulp fiction, just a hint of empathy? No more than a hint. As
for the hunters' motives, they are no more complex than that 'most exciting
chase', euphemistically called 'work'. Meredith, despite being badly pum-
melled by the dying elephant, gives her not another thought. He is one of
those self-styled 'Englishmen' for whom, as part of their national identity,
'the constant spice of danger adds greatly to the charm of sport in Africa'.[4]
Part of the persona, too, is the euphemistic use of 'spice' and 'charm'.

For the four or five decades after Bryden, there appears to be little
substantial adult fiction centred on elephants – a curious gap. Elephant-
centred fiction resumes abruptly in the mid-twentieth century, at which
point it devolves to variations on one particular motif: mortal combat
between a hunter and a special tusker. This exaggerated duel governs
Stuart Cloete's *The Curve and the Tusk* (1953), T.V. Bulpin's *The Ivory
Trail* (1954), Colin Burke's *Elephant across Border* (1968), John Gordon
Davis's *Taller Than Trees* (1975) and probably others. Yet these are
also novels that transition between unfeeling destruction and conservation; the duel is questioned, and ultimately abandoned. Wilbur Smith's
Elephant Song (1991) exploits the ethic of modern conservation, the
role of the 'game ranger' and his ecological consciousness, and the
problem of 'culling' (albeit with little real contribution to the deployment of compassion). Dalene Matthee's eco-sensitive novel *Circles in
a Forest* (1984) seems genuinely to feel *for* elephants and to lament
their destruction insightfully; and in Keith Meadows' *Sand in the Wind*
(1997) the hero is a ranger heroically battling to save particular named
tuskers from human predation. Here, fiction meets game-ranger memoir, and the non-fiction/fiction divide blurs once more.

To return to the beginning, Captain Thomas Mayne Reid (1818–
1883) is often cited among the earliest South African writers, but his

contribution has not been closely studied – partly because there is no evidence that he ever visited South Africa (he spent most of his life in North America, deriving his title 'captain' from his Civil War involvement); and partly because his work now feels stilted and laborious. Still, Reid is often cited as a pioneer in the 'boys' readers' genre, of which there was very little prior to the 1850s, and as a formative influence on Arthur Conan Doyle, Rider Haggard and others, not excluding the Polish Nobel laureate Czesław Miłosz, who read him in one of many translations. A reviewer for *The Spectator* in December 1856 thought *The Young Yagers* was rather good, singling out one or two crucial points – one is its appeal not only to children, but also to 'sportsmen who are still young' and a second is a tension evident in subsequent elephant literature: 'When art or practice rather than science is the "fundamental feature" of the fiction, we fear that the accuracy is equally sacrificed to effect.'[5] Nowadays, one may be more inclined to agree with a vividly scathing reviewer in the same newspaper in 1883, who found Reid's characters 'not a little tiresome. They have qualities, but not characters, and move like marionettes . . . The stories, too, are not very exciting, being devoid of plot, and made up of a succession of violent scenes, in essence stagey . . . Nevertheless, Mayne Reid did possess one literary faculty of a very rare and noticeable kind. He could create atmosphere as very few but the greatest story-tellers have ever done.'[6]

Reid rested heavily on earlier travelogues and on naturalists' accounts: his books are little more than reworked didactic expositions on a long series of different animal species, awkwardly juxtaposed with clumsy dialogue. In *The Young Yagers* (1857) he includes an intriguing meta-comment on his sources: 'Much of the information here given was furnished by Hans, who of course had gathered it from books; but the Bushman contributed his quota – perhaps of a more reliable character.'[7] He mentions the French naturalist Georges Cuvier by name, particularly in relation to what was becoming a standard comparison of African and Asian elephants.

Surprisingly perhaps, the elephant appears only twice in the two sequential novels, *The Bush Boys* and *The Young Yagers*, both of which feature the journey of a group of young friends into the remote southern African interior. This penetrative probe into strangeness would constitute the narrative structure of much later fiction. In *The Bush Boys* (1856), the death of an elephant is described – but not, unusually, at the hands of the human protagonists. The 'boys' are certainly all set to pepper an elephant bull with bullets, if only he would turn to an advantageous position, but it is to the wound inflicted by a rhinoceros that the elephant succumbs. Far from any compassion being evinced towards the elephant, it is immediately turned to commercial and gastronomic ends. One of the adventurers, the field cornet and father to the youngsters of the party, is overcome by awe at the financial worth of the fallen elephant's tusks, pointing to the undertow of commerce and exploitation already in place. Indeed, the well-being of the party depends on ivory sales. The field cornet notes that ivory was then selling at 'four shillings and sixpence the pound weight', and the group begins to dream of spending 'even years' hunting and trading in more ivory (this despite the fact, as Reid notes, that Dutch ivory hunters had already made the elephant scarce to non-existent south of the Orange River.[8] A full chapter is then devoted to 'jerking the elephant', that is turning it into 'bill-tongue' (biltong, or jerky), and to the method of cooking the feet in buried makeshift ovens: 'Although not equal to either beef or mutton, or even pork, the flesh of the elephant is sufficiently palatable to be eaten. There is no reason why it should not be, for the animal is a clean feeder, and lives altogether on vegetable substances – the leaves and tender shoots of trees, with several species of bulbous roots, which he well knows how to extract from the ground with his trunk and tusks.'[9]

In a second incident, the party tracks a single bull elephant, a 'rover or *rodeur*', or 'rogue'. This massive animal leads them on with footprints (exaggerated to 24 inches long) and a trail of vegetative destruction. Reid is concerned, in passing, to tackle myths such as that elephants do not lie down, or that it is best to shoot them in the forehead. In the course of a confrontation that stretches over a dozen tedious pages, that tactic fails – the Bushman tracker Swartboy is chased and treed, and eventually the wounded elephant, as 'frightened' as his rather hapless human would-be killers, races away into the 'jungle'. Any twinges of empathy with the injured animal are swamped by the 'feeling of disappointment' that they could not obtain the tusks. With its insertion of dialogue and excessive detailing of movement and gesture, this fictional extrapolation of the more laconic incidents of the earlier travel accounts also foreshadows the hunter-tusker duels of later novels.[10]

Despite this particular failure, the party's hunter, Von Bloom, still manages to accumulate a 'pyramid' of ivory, which secures all their futures – even though elephants had now retreated so far from the hunters' reach that ivory hunting was no longer profitable.[11] And this was being written in 1856.

Plot and character exert a more coherent and alluring presence in later adventure fictions. Haggard carries the motif of the 'venture to the interior' (to use Laurens van der Post's title) to the extremity of fantasy: the Gothic absurdity of some of his plots was precisely what generated his popularity, significantly at a time when in reality there was little interior left to be penetrated, at least in southern Africa. Like F.C. Selous and other traveller-hunters before him, Haggard has his white protagonists venture to the Zambezi River and beyond in search of treasures, animals and peoples weird enough to be thoroughly 'othered', if not yet eliminated or explained away. Very like his model, Selous, the narrator of *King Solomon's Mines* (1885), Allan Quatermain, asserts his lack of writing professionalism in phrases so close to those of Selous as to border on plagiarism.[12] 'And now,' he writes in an introduction designed to look like those of the predecessor travel accounts,

> it only remains for me to offer apologies for my blunt way of writing. I can but say in excuse of it that I am more accustomed to handle a rifle than a pen, and cannot make any pretence to the grand literary flights and flourishes which I see in novels – for sometimes I like to read a novel . . . 'A sharp spear,' runs the Kukuana saying, 'needs no polish'; and on the same principle I venture to hope that a true story, however strange it may be, does not require to be decked out in fine words.[13]

Very clever – not least in its canny inducement to take the 'strange' as 'true', the pretence at *not* writing a novel, and the commandeering of a proverb of the non-existent Kukuana.

It is far from the focus of the story, but the journey northwards of Sir Henry Curtis and his fellow adventurers necessarily, it seems, incorporates an elephant hunt – an assertion of the superiority of European firepower and of the fundamental masculinity of the whole enterprise. Indeed, Quatermain almost boasts, 'there is not a *petticoat* in the whole history'.[14] Quatermain regards the elephant hunt episode as a 'treat', for he does 'dearly love a hunting yarn'. To a degree, Haggard can cast a naturalist's eye on the landscape:

> About a fortnight's march from Inyati we came across a peculiarly beautiful bit of well-watered woodland country. The kloofs in the hills were covered with dense bush, 'idoro' bush as the natives call it, and in some places, with the 'wacht-een-beche', or 'wait-a-little thorn,' and there were great quantities of the lovely 'machabell' tree, laden with refreshing yellow fruit having enormous stones. This tree is the elephant's favourite food, and there were not wanting signs that the great brutes had been about, for not only was their spoor frequent, but in many places the trees were broken down and even uprooted. The elephant is a destructive feeder.[15]

Following Reid, Haggard reinforces the perception that the elephant's feeding patterns are 'destructive'. The aesthetic lenses that would govern later 'parks' are already present in Haggard's conception of what makes a landscape beautiful. The possibility that – as most ecologists now acknowledge – these very habits are beneficial in equal measure for other species and ecological cycles hidden to the casual eye, does not occur to Haggard.

Nor does the possibility of simply leaving the elephants alone (though Haggard elsewhere, in his 1877 piece 'A Zulu War Dance', would express unease at the rate of slaughter). In this 'paradise of game', Sir Henry Curtis elects to pause and 'have a go' at the elephants, and Quatermain admits that 'it went against my conscience to let such a herd as that escape without a pull at them'.[16] Only to *kill* would satisfy the man's 'conscience'. Such is the weight of the imperial 'tradition'. So the hunt unfolds, economically told and with next to no interiority or psychological insight; these are not features of the genre. As in the hunting accounts, the actual killings are dismissed in a sentence or two.

> Boom! boom! boom! went the three heavy rifles, and down came Sir Henry's elephant dead as a hammer, shot right through the heart. Mine

fell on to its knees and I thought that he was going to die, but in another moment he was up and off, tearing along straight past me. As he went I gave him the second barrel in the ribs, and this brought him down in good earnest. Hastily slipping in two fresh cartridges I ran up close to him, a ball through the brain put an end to the poor brute's struggles.[17]

That word 'poor' seems to indicate at least a quiver of remorse behind a self-confessed 'burning for slaughter', and this strengthens slightly as the narrative continues. Eight dead elephants later, the herd flees in 'mad confusion' and the hunters find themselves 'too tired to follow them and perhaps also a little sick of the slaughter'.[18] And perhaps there is a hint of remorse in the episode's denouement, which is virtually a summary of a corresponding passage in Selous: one elephant, wounded earlier by Good, returns and tears one of the African retainers, Khiva, limb from limb, before being cut down in a hail of bullets. Khiva is only momentarily mourned, his loss mitigated, apparently, by the perception that 'he died like a man!'[19] There remains much self-congratulation at the haul of ivory from that very animal – 'one hundred and seventy pounds the pair'.[20] Those tusks remain the key trophy, as Curtis writes to Quatermain after returning to his Brayley Hall home in England: 'P.S. – The tusks of the great bull that killed poor Khiva have now been put up in the hall here, over the pair of buffalo horns you gave me, and look magnificent.' In a way, the elephant hunt and its concrete banal trophy constitutes the anchor of reality for the almost paranormal qual- ity of what Quatermain calls 'the strangest trip I ever made'.[21] This fib, or cover, was already an acceptable feature of the 'imperial Gothic': *King Solomon's Mines* 'may be a manifestation of a vast colonial net- work which interconnected all parts of the known world during one era of history, but it is also . . . a work that derives its strength and its assuredness from thoroughly tried predecessors'.[22]

An ageing Quatermain is the narrator of the later, somewhat more elephant-centred novel *The Ivory Child* (1916). Regret at the retreat of the elephants before European gunfire has already become a trope, even as the death of yet another pachyderm remains the ultimate goal. The adventurer advances the reach of rapacious imperialism while denying its core drivers, casting himself as the marginalised maverick

attaining unprecedented access to the inner lives of previously undiscovered tribes. In this story it is the 'Kendah', who happen to incorporate the elephant as a totem. So Quatermain faces the unexamined
paradoxes in the sunset of his life:

> Commerce in all its shapes I renounced once and forever. It was too
> high – or too low – for me; so it would seem that there remained to
> me only my old business of professional hunting. Once again I must
> seek those adventures which I had forsworn when my evil star shone
> so brightly over a gold mine. What was it to be? Elephants, I supposed,
> since those are the only creatures worth killing from a money point of
> view. But most of my old haunts had been more or less shot out. The
> competition of younger professionals, of wandering backveld Boers and
> even of poaching natives who had obtained guns, was growing severe. If
> I went out at all I should have to travel further afield.[23]

So he is led by the elephants to discover the 'Black Kendah' whose
Lord, Jana, 'is an elephant, or at any rate his symbol is an elephant, a
very terrible beast to which sacrifices are made, that kills all who do
not worship him if he chances to meet them. He lives farther on in the
forest yonder, and the Black Kendah make use of him in war, for the
devil in him obeys their priests.' Quatermain indulges in a kind of early
anthropological conversation:

> 'Indeed, and is this elephant always the same?'
> 'I cannot tell you, but for many generations it has been the same,
> for it is known by its size and by the fact that one of its tusks is twisted
> downwards.'
> 'Well,' I remarked, 'all this proves nothing, since elephants certainly
> live for at least two hundred years, and perhaps much longer. Also, after
> they become "rogues" they acquire every kind of wicked and unnatural
> habit, as to which I could tell you lots of stories. Have you seen this
> elephant?'
> 'No, Macumazana,' he answered with a shiver. 'If I had seen it should
> I have been alive to-day? Yet I fear I am fated to see it ere long, not
> alone,' and again he shivered, looking at me in a very suggestive manner.
> At this moment our conversation was interrupted by the arrival of
> two Black Kendahs who brought us our breakfast of porridge and a

boiled fowl, and stood there while we ate it. For my part I was not sorry, as I had learned all I wanted to know of the theological opinions and practice of the land, and had come to the conclusion that the terrible devil-god of the Black Kendah was merely a rogue elephant of unusual size and ferocity, which under other circumstances it would have given me the greatest pleasure to try to shoot.[24]

After this imperious and reductive dismissal, Quatermain in fact sets off to find the rogue, discovering as he does so the fabled 'elephant graveyard'. The passage is worth quoting at length for the many ways in which it sets precedents for later elephant-hunting fictions:

Ten minutes or so more brought us to the eastern head of the lake, where the reeds whispered in the breath of the night wind like things alive. As I expected, it proved to be a bare, open space where nothing seemed to grow. Yes, and all about me were the decaying remains of elephants, hundreds of them, some with their bones covered in moss, that may have lain here for generations, and others more newly dead. They were all old beasts as I could tell by the tusks, whether male or female. Indeed about me within a radius of a quarter of a mile lay enough ivory to make a man very rich for life, since although discoloured, much of it seemed to have kept quite sound, like human teeth in a mummy case. The sight gave me a new zest for life. If only I could manage to survive and carry off that ivory! I would. In this way or in that I swore that I would! Who could possibly die with so much ivory to be had for the taking? Not that old hunter, Allan Quatermain.

Then I forgot about the ivory, for there in front of me, just where it should be, just as I had seen it in the dream-picture, was the bull elephant dying, a thin and ancient brute that had lived its long life to the last hour. It searched about as though to find a convenient resting-place, and when this was discovered, stood over it, swaying to and fro for a full minute. Then it lifted its trunk and trumpeted shrilly thrice, singing its swan-song, after which it sank slowly to its knees, its trunk outstretched and the points of its worn tusks resting on the ground. Evidently it was dead.

I let my eyes travel on, and behold! about fifty yards beyond the dead bull was a mound of hard rock. I watched it with gasping expectation and – yes, on the top of the mound something slowly materialized.

Although I knew what it must be well enough, for a while I could not see quite clearly because there were certain little clouds about and one of them had floated over the face of the moon. It passed, and before me, perhaps a hundred and forty paces away, outlined clearly against the sky, I perceived the devilish elephant of my vision.

Oh! what a brute was that! In bulk and height it appeared to be half as big again as any of its tribe which I had known in all my life's experience. It was enormous, unearthly; a survivor perhaps of some ancient species that lived before the Flood, or at least a very giant of its kind. Its grey-black sides were scarred as though with fighting. One of its huge tusks, much worn at the end, for evidently it was very old, gleamed white in the moonlight. The other was broken off about halfway down its length. When perfect it had been malformed, for it curved downwards and not upwards, also rather out to the right.

There stood this mammoth, this leviathan, this *monstrum horrendum, informe, ingens,* as I remember my old father used to call a certain gigantic and misshapen bull that we had on the Station, flapping a pair of ears that looked like the sides of a Kafir hut, and waving a trunk as big as a weaver's beam – whatever a weaver's beam may be – an appalling and a petrifying sight.

I squatted behind the skeleton of an elephant which happened to be handy and well covered with moss and ferns and watched the beast, fascinated, wishing that I had a large-bore rifle in my hand.[25]

The fabled devil-elephant (more Eastern in mien than African) is later despatched, with what would become a standard lack of ceremony. Notwithstanding all those exaggerated projections – which arguably speak to the imperial venture's profound anxieties, and of their denial – the destruction of the elephant echoes with its own emptiness.

In the early 1920s, the writer-conservationist Laurens van der Post, working as a rookie reporter for the *Natal Advertiser*, had had some contact with Scandinavian whalers working out of Durban, possibly even going out to sea with them. From these contacts he eventually spun a novel, *The Hunter and the Whale*. Its young protagonist strikes up a deal with a Norwegian whaler, to exchange an elephant hunt for a whale killing: two leviathans of ocean and savannah aligned in both magnificence and – in the hunter's world – attractiveness to the harpoon and the rifle. The duel-like allusions to *Moby Dick* are inescapable. The

agreement may have had its germ in an actual conversation, albeit retrospectively embellished:

> In the cabin he meets the terribly formidable Norwegian captain, ready
> to write him off as a newspaper nobody. But hearing that Van Der Post
> came from the Interior, he asks, 'Then you shoot and know elephant?'
> Van Der Post hesitated in answering because of the captain's 'expres-
> sion of profound longing, for which hope of fulfillment had evidently
> been long deferred.' At length he replied, 'I don't know that I know
> elephants. But I love and respect them more than any other animal in
> Africa.' This reply does not put the captain off. So he goes on to men-
> tion a hunter who had shot 999 elephants but then stopped because he
> wanted to know what an elephant really was, but could not. Again this
> does not put off the captain. He says, 'I, Thor Kaspersen, would give
> all my season's bonus and more to meet such a man. But, please to go
> on.' Whereupon Van Der Post answers the other half of the question:
> 'I have had to shoot elephant myself.' That did it. 'This admission was
> the turning point in the relationship. In the short time it took to utter so
> short a sentence, I had emerged no longer a stranger and intruder, but a
> member of the company that was elite to him.' Then came the question,
> 'And when you have shot your elephant, what is it then that you yourself
> feel? Good? Yes – no?' And the resolute reply: 'I hate myself for it, not
> only at the time but for days afterwards.'[26]

In the 1920s such ethical qualms were just developing, but they emerged
much more strongly in Van der Post's lifetime, in no small part through
his own (still largely unstudied) literary works. How distant is the following from Selous and Haggard?

> [There was] a great, lone elephant bull, a profound imperial purple
> in that light, standing not thirty yards away, sound asleep on his feet
> from the heat of the day. Although asleep, his great sensitive ears were
> never still but fanned his head so constantly and rhythmically that at
> one moment they seemed part of the breathing of some strange vast fish
> lying there, head upstream, in an amber current. His long broad brow
> was corrugated with furrows of age, his knees limp with his hunger for
> sleep, his eyes were shut in abandon, and the great arch of his shoulder
> was but the curve of the purple magnet of longing which clasped his

supple legs so firmly to the warm African earth. His long trunk hung straight down in front of him with a heavy, sagging immobility until it began to curl over ever so faintly at the utmost tip and to glisten with a light rhododendron pinkness as it began to search the air in our direction. Both Tickie and I couldn't help smiling at the expression which then came over that monumental face as the heavy skin of his great trunk, with wonderful butterfly flutter puckered like the nose of a baby about to sneeze. Then our scent, faint as it was, won. One moment he was sound asleep, the next wide awake, eyes open, trunk out, ears still tense on the alert. Lone old elephant bulls are notoriously uncertain characters. As his trunk flew out searching the air strenuously in our direction, I slipped the safety catch of my gun. But that sound, slight as it was, added to the agitation already beginning to boil in him. He took one delicate step in our direction, curling up his trunk under his chin as if about to charge, then undoing it with a quick, heavy swish, to bring it once more to bear on us. At that moment, however, a new sound arose; the noise of animated bearers' conversation back in camp. That decided him. Head proudly up and ears daintily fanning, he slowly turned his back, like that of some fine old Patrician reduced by revolution to a pair of outsized trousers, and marched off with a long, nimble stride and immense disdainful Mandarin dignity into the eurythmic bush.[27]

So detailed, admiring and, for once, non-fatal depiction of an elephant in southern African fiction is almost unprecedented. It comes from *Flamingo Feather*, Van der Post's 1955 thriller set in what is now KwaZulu-Natal, that region's features not quite mythologised beyond recognition. Though obviously indebted to Haggard in his adventure-tale structure – the penetration of a neo-Gothic interior landscape, the invented African tribes and rituals – Van der Post incorporates certain elements of modernity, as well as a wholly different view of the natural world. Even at the height of the action, Van der Post could not resist interpolating long passages of exuberant appreciation of animals, birds and landscapes, in prose often lyrical to the verge of the purple. If this makes for somewhat unsatisfying fiction, the admixture of adventure and natural appreciation is symptomatic of a new and influential aesthetic.

Also striking is Van der Post's sensitivity to changes to the elephant's face – the recognition of a face at all, to which one might *respond* and then (following Jacques Derrida's pun) feel *responsibility*. Furthermore, he repeatedly emphasises aspects of extreme delicacy in this massively bulky animal, bordering here on the comical, there on the aristocratic (it is a quirk of his to invoke the Far East, as in 'Mandarin'). In addition, we are close here to according the elephant a complex interiority. Finally, the elephant is – for once – released to depart, not with disappointment that the kill has been thwarted, but as a lyrical, observant eulogy to life and respect. One might not guess it from *Flamingo Feather*, but this aesthetic was already deeply entangled with the politics of conservation in its 'national park' guise, as subsequent literature attests.

Even by the end of the nineteenth century, almost nowhere south of the Zambezi River seemed remote enough for a committed adventure story protagonist to exercise his skills of survival among exotically unintelligible tribesman and vicious natural predators. A cluster of writers therefore elected to set their elephant-hunting tales in the wilder areas of Mozambique which, at least to the English-speaking world, appeared satisfyingly unexplored. Mozambican wilderness certainly attracted real-life hunters such as Harry Manners and Stuart Cloete.

Cloete has been conventionally rated – and denigrated – as a pulp-fiction writer of no great literary merit, a Wilbur Smith for his day. While he certainly produced some genuinely purple potboilers among his fourteen novels and numerous short stories, at his best he is a vivid and arresting stylist. The complexity of his depictions of the natural world and its ecologies has been almost completely ignored, and deserves more detailed exposition. In his elephant-centred novel, *The Curve and the Tusk*, for example, both human and elephant are seen as embroiled in a complex if vicious dynamic in which dominances can change from moment to moment, from scale to scale:

> In the forest there are many worlds. The world of the tree-tops and the world under the tree-tops in the canopy of shade. The world of the bushes, and the world under the bushes, in the holes in the ground and under the stones; and each of these worlds is subdivided into numberless little worlds so that each is a solar system in miniature, revolving slowly with the force of the seasons . . . And each thing, great or small, in these manifold worlds in which they move, sees a different world. For the world of the elephant is different from that of the ant . . . To an elephant, a tree of medium size is a blade of grass to be swept aside. To

a man, all living things are things that should be made to live, because of the meat that clothes their bones, or skins that clothe their meat, or just for the sport of it. The sport of killing, so that his spears shall drink blood, or his bullets smack with a pleasant sound against the bone and flesh of a beast.[28]

Within interlocking envelopes of Darwinian predation and exploitation, humans become merely another species wrestling for a material and existential edge – though Cloete stingingly critiques the human as 'greatest of all parasites' who 'consumes his own kind in war'.[29] This view raises a certain difficulty in explaining the rise of human morality, and especially of compassion towards other creatures. Through fiction, Cloete draws a little closer to the central problematic I raised earlier: the emotional content of the kill itself. *The Curve and the Tusk* is predicated on the duel for supremacy between a human hunter and a particular tusker. First published three years before *Flamingo Feather*, Cloete's depiction of man-in-nature is less lyrical than Van der Post's, but still more nuanced and complex than that of his contemporaries. He has several protagonists working in parallel: not only the aged white hunter Carew, out for his culminating challenge, but also a somewhat reluctant young Portuguese hunter, Maniero; a local African, Mashupa (whose story, unusually, absorbs a large proportion of the text); and, most innovatively of all, the elephant himself. Cloete makes it abundantly clear that they are all enmeshed in a common natural fate. Repeatedly throughout the novel, Cloete draws parallels between the being and destinies of elephant and humans. For perhaps the first time in adult southern African fiction, the novelist gives almost as much space to the 'biography' of the elephant protagonist as to his human counterparts, amplified by biological detail and divagations into his ecological milieu. Indeed, an educative impulse at times threatens to overwhelm the narrative, and Cloete includes an appendix of naturalistic observations, a short cultural history of the elephant and a list of interesting plants, complete with Latin names. The inner world of the elephant is evoked: at first 'happy', later making 'mock love' and beginning to 'feel different' as puberty sets in, later still fleeing in 'pain, fright and fury' when attacked by a Portuguese 'brigand' and his ivory hunters.[30]

Throughout, Cloete depicts a tenderly communicative relationship between the tusker and his tuskless brother; they collaborate to protect one another, to evade and to ambush pursuing hunters. In a psychologically coherent if starkly drawn manner, Cloete explains the vengeful mindset of these elephants, shot at and harried all their lives until they are among the last of their kind – as are hunters like Carew, and the late Pretorius, who is flattened by these very elephants near a huge, equally iconic, baobab tree. Pretorius's blood has been absorbed into the surrounding fever trees, upon which the elephants return periodically to feed, defecating and fertilising the soil there and so perpetuating the endless cycle. At this spot, the climactic confrontation unfolds, as in a stage drama (a word Cloete often uses).

It all happens against a backdrop of lamentable nostalgia – the novel was published in 1952, a year before Harry Manners stopped hunting in this very region:

> 'Ah, the old hunters,' Maniero said. 'There are none like them left.'
>
> 'There are no times like the old times either,' Carew said. 'The days when the nyala swarmed, the buffalo ran in great herds, and wildebeeste were found in every flat . . . and men, as I knew them, have gone too. Both white and black – they are less than they were. But come, Maniero, we must convince them that we are still great. Greater than a couple of spook elephants.'[31]

The elephants are spooks – ghostly legends – partly because of their elusive longevity and also because in local lore they are somehow imbued with the spirits of the famous kings T'Chaka (Shaka – Zulu) and Moselekatse (Mzilikazi – Ndebele).[32] This is to invoke a warrior ethic no longer deemed possible in modernity, its unavailability encapsulated in the tragic fate of a somewhat hapless Mashupa. Equally ambivalent is Maniero, who once shared Carew's atavistic primal urge but, like Manners, finds himself doubting:

> 'Is this me, Maniero, talking?' . . . this was no ordinary hunt. It was a final conquest and if he killed the elephants, he would have conquered the greatest beasts of the forest. After that, anything else would be

an anticlimax. But there was more in it than that. From his heart, his soul, the depths of his personality, had come the command to stop, the feeling that he had killed enough . . . His sword he would beat into a ploughshare . . . All that stood between him and this ambition was the lame one. Hatred for this elephant welled up in his heart. Never before had he hated an animal. He knew, suddenly, that he feared the lame one. That he had feared him all his life.[33]

There remains in Maniero a romantic urge to live on in the forest, for all its savageries. For him (and probably for Cloete himself), legislated civilisation has become a 'cushion that comes between man and reality', and the loss of wilderness occasion for a deep nostalgia: 'the countless herds of game . . . all were gone now, replaced by the sludge of the mines, the grassless kopjes of dead pulverised rock – rock crushed beyond recognition and poisoned with the cyanide of extraction'.[34] For the ancient Carew, too, a final hunt with the ultimate antagonist promises an authentic connection with life and its essential rhythms and vividness, a chance to attain 'the maximum speed of which his ancient organism was capable, into the fury of the hunt, the last expedition . . . That must end, as it had been lived, in the forest, amid the explosions of his guns, the trumpetings and screams of elephants, the wild cries of his men . . . Only thus, on the chariot of his art, could he attain the freedom he desired.'[35]

So the final confrontation occurs, quickly related in under ten pages. The inevitable deaths of the elephants is as brusquely described as in the old hunters' accounts. The contrast with the overblown language of the anticipation is vividly apparent. Ironically, the unwilling Maniero dies, while the gung-ho Carew survives, thus failing to reunite with his dead love Esther (the entwining of all the male characters with their female loves is another element new to this strand of fiction). And in this irony lies also some of the futility of the whole enterprise, hinted at, but not quite openly expressed. Carew does once say to Maniero, 'In all the world, Maniero, there are no two men who know more of elephants than you and I, but they remain a mystery. We have killed many hundreds of them, but that is all.'[36] The heightened vivacity of the encounter is all, then:

By the miracle of being again in the great forest, these old men had gained new strength . . . The hum of the insects in the air, the croaking of the frogs at night, the feeling that the world about them was palpitating with unseen life and with death, threatening each creature, excited them. The twin laws of nature, the law of life and increase and the law of death and putrescence, that would lead to more life, never ceasing for an instant, all added to their feelings.[37]

There is something of the familiar evasiveness here, the appeal to one or another kind of law; they all succumb not to inner personal urges (let alone choices) but, rather, to something labelled the 'aphrodisiac of war', 'destiny', or 'possession' by 'Kaffir superstitions'.[38] Elephants and humans alike partake of an inner drive, which is by definition both inexplicable and beyond moral judgement:

But when a beast has been hunted as the great elephant they called the lame one, and his brother, had been hunted, and when they have reached an age that is incomprehensible to man, and when they find, on their trail, and following it, on several occasions over a period of years, the same smell, that of a white man, the scent finally gets registered in the convolutions of their ancient brains, and produces a peculiar effect – an effect of show-down, of furious resentment against the monotony of a peaceful old age being broken into, pierced by the irritation of interference. So, when the elephants found the man there, on their spoor again, remorselessly attached to them by his will, the intermediate bond between them being his traces in the bush and their footmarks, their dung, the fallen branches they had torn down, the twigs they had chewed, they planned to make an end. The elephants as much as the man. All now were planning, not as they had been before on other occasions, one to follow and the other to escape, but all to kill.[39]

When it comes to the killings themselves, there is no pleasure after all in hearing the smack of bullet on flesh. One suspects that Cloete himself cannot escape the sense of futility and emptiness in the gargantuan slaughters that have led to this point. At the same time, because elephants and men have been equalised throughout under depersonalised natural law, open expressions of individual compassion or remorse are also excluded. Carew feels 'ashamed', in the end, only in still 'being alive'.[40]

Cloete's great tusker may be a fictional incarnation of Dlulamithi, apparently a real elephant – or more than one. Anthony Hall-Martin, the late doyen of elephant studies, claimed to have named a Kruger tusker Ndlulamithi (Tsonga: Taller Than Trees) in 1980.[41] However, such a tusker had already had his story told in Allan Wright's *Valley of Ironwoods* (1972), and John Gordon Davis had appropriated it for his novella, *Taller Than Trees*, three years later. Even before that, Bulpin had written of a Dlulamithi roaming the border region in the 1920s – the possibly fictional prey of his hunter protagonist. There may have been an original Dlulamithi, along with unconfirmed claims that he was shot in the early 1930s, in present-day Zimbabwe's Gonarezhou (place of the elephant) region. But as hunter Richard Harland has pointed out, Dlulamithi had become a generic or hereditary name for any great tusker.[42] Crucially, this Dlulamithi developed a textual presence of legendary proportion, a wanderer and breaker of boundaries – a rogue in some appellations – an elephantine corollary to the vagrant, raff-ishly criminal men who hunted him. Elephant movements across the region's artificial boundary did occur, and still do, volitionally and oth-erwise. Many of the newly designated park's first elephants, including some large males, came in from Mozambique, as the founder-warden, James Stevenson-Hamilton, noted in 1947.[43] The divide between the legally bound protective Kruger National Park and the relatively law-less Mozambican forests east of the Lebombo hills provides a central geo-cultural tension, fruitful material for the novels discussed below.

The first of these, Bulpin's *The Ivory Trail* (1954), relates, 'somewhat romantically', the life of one Stephanus Cecil Rutgert Barnard, widely known as Bvekenya (translated as 'one who swaggers as he walks').[44] Barnard was born in Knysna in 1886, encountering as a child the tales of the elusive Knysna forest elephants. After his parents' farming ven-ture near Schweizer-Reneke collapsed, he gravitated towards a fugit-ive bush life in that area of the conjunction of Kruger Park with the Mozambican and (then) Rhodesian borders known as Crooks' Corner. For some 20 years he hunted elephants and smuggled both ivory and illegal recruits for the mines of the highveld, becoming one of the most successful of these 'blackbirders'. He consistently managed to evade the law in all three countries, shot (in Bulpin's estimation) over 300 ele-phants, and eventually settled and married on a farm near Geysdorp in the North West, dying in his bed in 1962, aged 76. Bulpin's treatment of an undeniably extraordinary life is delivered in unpretentious, even pedestrian prose, a readable enough admixture of fact and imagination, of travelogue and novel, a genre he made his speciality. In *The Ivory Trail* he imagines himself more into Bvekenya's headspace. Not that one can expect much psychological complexity from a book more interested in adventure and daring exercised, even valorised, against a backdrop of historical change and a panoply of similarly shifty and debauched bushwhackers. Those passages outlining Bvekenya's motivations for hunting elephants are simplistic – but initially, as always, derived from literature: 'Hunters' stories of hairsbreadth escapes and almost incredible adventures were his normal bedtime portion; and in his dreams he saw himself on the ivory trail, in search of the fortune and the excitement which he supposed to be the normal daily life of the elephant hunters . . . He heard, too, strange stories of the wisdom, strength and ferocity of the elephants, and of that legendary hunters' pot at the rainbow's end – the elephants' graveyard.'[45]

It turns out to be less than easy and not so glamorous. When it comes to shooting elephants, Bvekenya seems subject to some of the same ambivalences of his predecessor hunters, but is as incapable as they were of acting on his 'scruples'. There is, for example, one moment when he is content to watch elephants living out their natural rhythms, 'protected by a kindly Providence' in their 'sanctuary', so peaceable that 'never once had he felt any inclination to kill'.[46] This bucolic symbiosis cannot last, however: the implication is that the human is as subject as the rest of nature to 'the grim, primeval theme of all the wilds – the endless duel between life and death'. Necessity for meat drives him to hunt again. The old evasions are in place here. Similarly, when Bvekenya shoots a young male elephant, he initially merely wounds him and has to chase him down, and he is 'sorry he had to kill him'. The regret is only, however, because 'given another ten years, the elephant would have been a worthwhile shot. Now he just represented a poor substitute for the tusks of Dhlulamithi.'[47] The mitigation of being sporting – being prideful of the clean shot, of not leaving wounded animals behind – is slight.

Appearing sporadically through the sundry episodes of the story, the hunt for Dlulamithi provides the ultimate narrative thrust. The circumstances are becoming increasingly tricky: 'there were very few of the old professional hunters [read "poachers-at-large"] still left':

> Times were changing; and civilisation, with its advance guard of the policeman and the game warden, was gradually making the life of the bushranger too precarious for either comfort or profit . . . The Portuguese and Rhodesian authorities were making it more risky to poach game; and the Transvaal police were making it difficult to smuggle the tusks and whips back to any profitable market. As a final difficulty, the Kruger National Park was being properly organised and a ranger's post had recently been established at the site of old Sikokololo's kraal. Admittedly, the pioneer ranger at what was first called *Punda Maria*, Captain '*Ou Kat*' Coetser, was more of a poacher than a conservationist: but he was obviously the thin end of the wedge.[48]

Nothing about compassion for the elephants themselves here; nothing except concerns for profitability. He continues 'to hunt with his habitual skill and fortune; but if the truth be told Bvekenya was growing weary, and a trifle uneasy about his restless and destructive way of life . . . The first thrill of hunting had long since gone.' It appears that a loss of excitement, not unselfish empathy or compassion, then, turns the tide of feeling. Bulpin only has Bvekenya express a kind of generalised condemnation of human depredation, which still does not quite transcend self-justification:

> He had no illusions about himself or his fellows in the bush. From the very beginning, mankind has been a parasite on the sunburned back of Africa. The Bushmen, the Negro and the Bantu killed everything on sight, whether it was animal or lizard. The Dutch Voortrekkers and the host of British gold diggers and hunters passed over the country like a swarm of locusts: shooting, cutting down trees and destroying. Of all of them, not one single racial group ever tried to understand or love Africa for herself.[49]

Yet Bvekenya himself seems incapable of expressing this love in terms other than how delicious certain animals taste when eaten!

Only in the story's denouement does – perhaps – a certain compassion show itself. Bvekenya does in the end track down Dlulamithi; he almost gets killed by the elephant, but finally lines him up in his sights.

> They found Dlulamithi at last, standing wearily in the shade of a tall thombothi tree. Bvekenya studied him long and silently. He stalked the elephant slowly and skilfully. He found his range and his ideal target. The elephant seemed weary and heedless. Bvekenya lifted his gun. He found his favourite shot: the most deadly mark of all . . .
>
> He saw the elephant's eyes: its weatherbeaten face, the wrinkles in its skin, the tremors of its body, the waving of its ears with the ragged ends where the thorns had torn them. He saw the scars of ancient battles and the slight wound of his own bullet. He saw the elephant in its wisdom, its savagery, patience and courage. He saw Africa, and he knew that he loved it.
>
> He put down the gun.[50]

But what does this love really consist of? The elephant is still an 'it', primarily symbolic, denied interiority. Nevertheless, this moment of restraint will be picked up repeatedly by future commentators as iconic of a more general shift in attitude from the grim coldness of poaching for profit to a conservation ethic. The elephant is at least seen as something more than a lump of potentially profitable meat and bone. Importantly, it is *named*.

The tusker of interest in Burke's ponderous thriller *Elephant across Border* is not named as Dlulamithi, but might easily be – an animal whose great age and tusks are a result of the protection afforded him by the Kruger National Park. However, the animal does venture into Mozambique from time to time, as announced by the telegram forming the novel's title. The telegram draws into the six days of the plot the various characters, each of whom represents the constituencies involved in the elephant's welfare. There is Joe Lorenz the photographic tourist, being guided by Hendry, ex-ranger turned professional guide, a crack shot who does not like to kill unnecessarily. There is Gomez, another ex-ranger turned hunter-poacher who, like the hastily summonsed

British trophy-hunter Allard, wants to kill the elephant and claim the great tusks. On the other hand, protective forces are represented by Major Murray, a conservationist who wants to herd the elephant back into the protective custody of Kruger's rangers. Murray captures in his personal history some of the prevailing tensions:

> I was brought up with hunting. In the early days when I was a warden at Wankie I was really more of a full-time ranger and part of my job was culling animals. I've shot thousands of them, but it was a spit in the ocean compared to what poaching accounted for . . . There are over fifteen hundred [elephant] in the Kruger Park. Too many for the available grazing. If they could get rid of a few of them it would more of a blessing than hardship. But this elephant we are talking about – there is something far more important about it than the size of its tusks . . . Forty years of battling to conserve game. You can say that this animal with its tusks are an example of the success of that work, a veritable symbol of what I worked for.[51]

Allard scoffs that it is equally a symbol of his own selective trophy-hunting, which he compares favourably to conservationists' indiscriminate 'culling' – though he himself is portrayed as egotistical and potentially unethical. He might even stoop as low, so to speak, as to kill the elephant from a helicopter. Gomez exemplifies a parallel argument: 'Gomez had little time for the conservationists, who lead a sheltered, do-no-wrong existence. He maintained that they destroyed professional hunting no matter how selective it was and, at the same time, culled vast numbers of animals to suit their theories which were generally proved wrong.'[52]

Like Cloete, Burke underlines the restriction upon old-style hunters of new protective legislation and boundaries, but unlike his predecessor he is thin on evoking the elephant's nature and habitat; he is more interested in the human characters' tussle among themselves, laid out in laborious dialogues. The elephant really is more symbolic than actively present. Only towards the novel's close does action predominate – as Hendry vies with Gomez, Allard and Murray to get to the elephant first. In the process, the animal is badly wounded, shot in the leg as it appears to be heading back towards Kruger. Even Hendry, the guide lacking the true hunter's instinct (as Gomez opines), takes pity on it: 'The elephant is old, pathetic and half-demented,' he argues to Murray, 'the kindest thing to do is put it out. If you stop Allard from doing it now, you'll be torturing the animal unnecessarily.'[53] Murray's stratagems to allow the tusker back into Kruger ultimately prevail, but the novel ends with the sad and heavy irony that the wounded, thus possibly dangerous animal might well have to be shot by Kruger's own rangers. Hendry, probably closest to voicing the author's views, divines a certain absurdity in all this, a confusion surrounding 'Major Murray's rather batty attitude about the beautiful old elephant on the one side, and Joe's save-all-the-poor-animals-in-Africa on the other . . . two very decent old chaps, feeling like mad about something that could normally be done without any great feeling one way or the other and with no noticeable effect on the lowveld elephant population . . . or something like that'.[54] But it is precisely such feelings (suitably masked in manly cursing) with which Burke closes the story as Hendry, watching the elephant disappearing into the Kruger bush, says to himself: 'Don't shoot it, damn you. Damn Allard, and damn old Murray. Damn bloody elephant. Go on, elephant, keep going. Get into cover and keep away from them and die in your own way. Go on, you old bugger, keep going.'[55] It is, in its clumsy way, an appeal for all elephants.

The cover of the Corgi edition of Davis's *Taller Than Trees* illustrates the duel motif that governs these novels: the huge elephant looms over the diminutive khaki-hatted hunter with his even more diminutive rifle. It is an image derived from Selous, and has been repeated ad nauseam on subsequent book covers. It exemplifies humans' primary fear of the elephant, no doubt – the head-on, unstoppable charge. Very unlike the deliberately restrained and homespun Selous, however, *Taller Than Trees* is clamorously overwritten, its concentration on swift and brutal action emphasised by a saturation of present participles ('screaming' is used four times on a single page), concatenations of conjunctions, and numerous italicised prayers to an apparently heedless God. If the other novels tend towards emotional reticence, this one overindulges its focus on the hunter Jumbo McGuire's feelings as he pursues his equally aged elephant quarry – the inevitable Dlulamithi himself. In this duel, man and elephant fight and mutilate one another to a bloody standstill, ultimately fatal for both, though the ending pulls up just short of actually describing

111

Jumbo McGuire's death. They are portrayed, in the end, in a kind of macabre partnership of suffering, thirst and pain. When Dlulamithi will, it appears, finally succumb to lions, Jumbo McGuire (Davis insists on the full name at almost every instance) expends his last shell not on committing suicide, but on putting the elephant down, as if this 'act of mercy' might excuse the man's role in his demise. Almost all his predecessors retained a certain brusque aloofness from the details of shooting and death, usually keeping it short and militaristic, at most a brief post-mortem description of the path of the bullet through the elephant's body. Davis, in contrast, wallows in gratuitous gore. The feelings are mostly of that shallow variety that accompanies action, rather than of reflection; only in one instance does the text openly approach our theme:

> Jumbo thought about the book he was writing, that was waiting back at his house unwritten, and he was shamed and remorseful for mistakes he had made, and particularly for the agony he had caused the elephant through his mistakes, and he grunted: 'I am very sorry, Elephant' and he meant it. Jumbo McGuire was not very good at remorse, but it had always seemed to him to be worse to make an animal suffer than a human being because an animal does not properly understand, it only reacts, knowing it is in pain and having to endure; somehow it always seemed worst of all for an elephant, because if its great size to suffer with, and its great soul – its majesty. Jumbo was not sufficiently good with words to write it in his memoirs, but to him the elephant was wonderful, a kind of monument to nature, to Africa, the greatest beast, the king of animals, so independent and confident it did not hurt anybody and yet so strong it can smash up a whole village just like that: the most intelligent, the most gentle and the most dangerous. Jumbo McGuire had shot over ten thousand elephants, and he had admired every one. He had killed them for their ivory for that was the law of the jungle of which the elephant was king, and he was excited and sad and impressed each time: but he had never shot an elephant in the mouth before and let it go a full day with that agony, and he felt very sorry; he also felt a little bit remorseful for all the other elephants he had shot in his life: that was how Jumbo was feeling, and he snorted out loud to stop himself feeling it.[56]

In this self-contradictory mush we find once again an echo of Selous's and others' disclaimer of eloquence, and hence the retreat into cliché;

the same appeal to sporting accuracy; the same evasive shift of responsibility onto 'the law of the jungle'; the same rigorous and deliberate
suppression of empathy or compassion. He is in the end just 'a little bit
remorseful' – not enough to deter him from this or any other hunt, and
hardly enough to save him from the 'disgust' he finally feels at shooting
Dlulamithi.[57]

If there is anything that can rescue this novella from its own turgid-
ity, it is that at least Jumbo McGuire is being somewhat satirised. He
is – or in old age has become – a parody of the insouciantly dangerous
elephant hunter: he is bumbling, disorganised and hapless to the verge
of slapstick, generally 'terrified shitless'.[58] There is a certain refreshing
honesty in that.

Wilbur Smith's popular thriller *Elephant Song* is perhaps better
written than *Taller Than Trees*, but equally contrived, even deceitfully
exploitative of the plight of the elephants. Though it is impossible
to gauge the novel's societal impact, certainly many people will have
learned from it something of the science and ethics involved in the
periodic southern African elephant 'cull'. In its favour, the novel economically if didactically lays out the parameters of that dilemma in the
modern era. On the one hand, prior to the publication of the novel, the
Convention on International Trade in Endangered Species (CITES)
decided provisionally to downgrade southern African elephants'
endangered status and allow for limited trade in ivory. On the other
hand, contrary to trends elsewhere on the continent, southern Africa's
elephants were increasing at an estimated rate of 14 000 a year, so many
argued that they were outstripping the resources available in the limited areas humans had allocated them. They needed to be culled – the
most ironic outcome of what seemed to be southern Africa's greatest
conservation success. At one level, then, 'poaching' should not appear
to be a problem; it becomes less an issue of population size than one
of managerial and political control, of who gets what fiduciary benefits,
and (to a secondary degree) of ecological balance.[59]

Smith sets his story in Zimbabwe – the pioneer in culling as a management technique. *Elephant Song* (a title promising some sort of anthropomorphic empathy?) opens with a gory and manipulatively emotive
culling scene. The rationale for culling is rather gauchely explained for

the benefit of an attendant film crew (and thus for the reader), by the black warden of the fictional Zimbabwean Chiwewe National Park, Johnny Nzou. The name 'Nzou' – 'by coincidence'! – means 'elephant' in Shona; in this crude manner Smith attempts to present the justification for culling in an 'authentic' African voice.[60] During the course of Johnny Nzou's explanation, a number of tensions fundamental to the problem emerge.

One tension is between, roughly, science and emotion. While Nzou explains that the cull his department 'is forced to undertake' is necessitated by hard ecological science, and is further justified by the commercial income the cull generates through the sale of ivory and skins, he is portrayed as having a deep emotional repugnance to the slaughter. On the one hand, then, Nzou replies to his provocative interlocutor, the hero Daniel Armstrong, in purely pragmatic terms. 'Your management of your herds of elephants has been too good,' Armstrong asserts; 'Now you have to destroy and waste these marvellous animals.' Nzou replies: 'No . . . we won't waste them. We will recover a great deal of value from their carcasses . . . The proceeds will be ploughed back into conservation, to prevent poaching and protect our National Parks. The death of these animals will not be a complete abomination.'[61] When Armstrong presses, 'But why do you have to kill the mothers and the babies?', Nzou accuses him of cheating and using the 'emotive, slanted language of the animals rights groups . . . Let's rather call them cows and calves.' On the other hand, in virtually the next breath, Nzou is shown displaying deep emotional attachment to the animals he is obliged to kill. As the cull itself comes to an end, Nzou pays a quasi-religious tribute: '*Hamba kahle, Amakhulu* . . . Go in peace, old grandmothers. You are together in death as you were in life. Go in peace, and forgive us for what we have done to your tribe.'[62] We are evidently required as readers to approve of this maudlin nonsense (delivered, anomalously, in Zulu, not Shona). The word 'tribe' betrays the anthropomorphism that underlies Smith's emotiveness; he also has Nzou deliberately substitute the word 'herd' for 'target', a shift in the opposite direction to that displayed earlier. In this linguistic awareness, Smith perhaps inadvertently points up the extent to which our attitudes towards the natural are dependent on fundamentally imagined

linguistic categories and values – a concern echoed by at least some
alert conservationists. (To cite one example, John Hanks, a prominent
wildlife researcher, notes: 'It is strange that biologists seem reluctant
to use . . . that simple and unambiguous verb [to kill]. The literature
is full of ponderous euphemisms such as "elephant population reduction programmes" and "elephant capital removal programmes".'[63]
'Cropping' and 'harvesting' have also been used in the elephant culling context.) Up to a point, Nzou will try to justify the dynamics of the
cull in terms of scientific observation, in appropriate language: 'We
have to take out the entire herd. It is absolutely essential that we leave
no survivors. The elephant herd is a complex family group. Nearly all
its members are blood relatives, and there is a highly developed social
structure within the herd.'[64]

This reflects, in fact, the impact that empathetic understandings of
elephant trauma *have* had on the mode of culling, contrary to all the
protestations of scientific objectivity. So Nzou's foray into scientific language immediately breaks down: '"The elephant is an intelligent animal
. . . They know – I mean, they really understand . . ." He broke off, and
cleared his throat. His feelings had overcome him.'[65]

Smith builds on this aspect in an authorial venture into the elephant's perspective, immediately preceding the cull and thereby posi-
tioning the reader to sympathise with the elephant's fate: 'The elder [of
two sisters] had been weaned at the birth of her sibling and had helped
to nursemaid her as tenderly as would a human elder sister. They had
shared a long life, and had drawn from it a wealth of experience and
wisdom to add to the deep ancestral instinct with which they had been
endowed at birth.'[66] 'They had seen each other through'; 'They had
shared'; 'They knew'; 'They had played': in these phrases Smith captures the empathetic dimension. But he seems uncomfortable with it,
and steps away into authorial contemplation: 'Perhaps it was fanciful to
endow brute animals with such human emotions as love and respect, or
to believe that they understood blood relationships or the continuity of
their line, but no one who has seen the old cows quieten the boisterous
youngsters with raised ears and a sharp angry squeal, or watched the
herd follow their lead with unquestioning obedience, could doubt their
authority [or] question their concern.'[67]

Exactly who is doing the fancying is not narratologically clear: the 'was' suggests it is not the author, but no other character is present at this point. It is a telling ambiguity. Smith goes on to outline more of the family structure, in semi-scientific generalising style, before returning to the more 'personal' focus on the two sisters. This deployment of the empathetic, however, is symptomatically fragmented and superficial: the narrative shifts abruptly to the point of view of the approaching human killers and their lethal technology. Smith is as fascinated by the details of rifles, bullets and the placing of shots as any old-style hunter, and relates the unfolding of the cull in the kind of tediously tactical language of Selous or Neumann. Smith, like Davis, however, injects a voyeuristic strain of overblown gore, which becomes part of the particular emotionality of the description: 'The bullet sliced through her head as neatly as a steel nail through a ripe apple. It obliterated the top of her brain.'[68] At the same time, Smith is concerned to distance himself from the attitudes of the old hunters, and takes pains to historicise the new ethic in politically correct terms. Johnny Nzou explains this as a diametric contrast between the attitudes of 'primitive man, living with nature, [treating] it as a renewable resource', whose beneficent 'balance with nature' was destroyed when 'the white man came with explosive harpoon and Sharpe's rifle, or here, in Africa, came with his elite game department and game laws that made it a crime for the black tribesman to hunt on his own land'.[69] Smith here raises crucial issues about the articulation of racial domination with conservation policies – but in the novel the implications, as of most aspects of its opening scene, are rapidly lost to view. That Smith actually finds this idyllic view of the 'primitive' impossible to sustain is evidenced on the very next page, where the indigenous peoples are said to have lost 'control of nature' – not *balance with* nature – to the whites.[70] An unacknowledged white superiority, now exercised through conservation ethics, is maintained.

The ecological debate with which the novel opens is little more than a pretext for a very conventional helter-skelter thriller of manifold violence and cardboard villains. The very real problems *for elephants* raised by the opening are not worked through, the empathies never translated into profound relationships *with* elephants. The stance is, in sum, what Josephine Donovan has termed a 'dominative transaction', in which the depiction of violence 'requires the sacrifice of the animal as an independent being to human aesthetic interests [but] to no redemptive purpose'.[71] Still, *Elephant Song* shows with particular sharpness the empathy-pragmatism debate that pervades other genres of conservation literature, including the game-ranger memoir and what I will call the 'field-research memoir'. Indeed, the empathy-pragmatism debate pervades Western society and its self-conceptions, and it takes on particular nuances in the postcolony. As Mary Midgley has put it, 'Fear and contempt for feeling make up an irrational prejudice built into the structure of Western rationalism.'[72] That such feelings are permitted to emerge primarily in fiction, especially juvenile fiction, and hardly at all in other non-fiction prose genres, raises a final disturbing issue. As John Cawelti has argued, popular fiction is a means of displaying issues of violence or distaste while making them psychologically safe.[73] It is questionable whether such fictions enhance our ecological engagement or muffle us against it – or provide a substitute for it. The emotionality found so lavishly displayed in and evoked by literature does not necessarily translate into commensurate action in the world.

Chapter 5

A Tear Rolled down Her Face:
Teen fiction and elephant mind

Although adult fictions build plots around the potential conflicts between hunters, poachers and the new dispensations of protective legislation and national parks, they have remained locked largely within the hunter-elephant duel paradigm. Some representations of elephant interiority from Stuart Cloete and Wilbur Smith notwithstanding, no southern African adult novelist has ventured anywhere near Canadian author Barbara Gowdy's dense and sophisticated fable of elephant life, *The White Bone* (1998), set in East Africa. Fiction for the young, by contrast, has been much more adventurous, unabashedly courting the empiricist's devil of anthropomorphism; it is willing to accord the elephant what legislators are only now beginning to recognise as 'personhood'. At the same time, such fiction establishes itself as a primary vector for environmental education. The early travelogues, hunters' accounts and even novels often included a didactic element – explaining the exotic elephant to the armchair traveller-reader. The late twentieth-century teen (in current parlance, young adult) fictions continue and update many of the features of those earlier works.

Southern African elephant books are dominated by publications for the young. Many are boiled-down versions of African folk tales, with titles like *How the Elephant Got His Trunk* and *The Rabbit and the Elephant*; others are adventure stories, or domesticated scenarios of the

118

'Dumbo' variety. These numerous texts have received little critical attention, though they are arguably as important as any in disseminating and
affecting people's attitudes towards animals, science and ecosystems –
children being self-evidently both the most impressionable of readers
and those most needful of an ecologically sound education and future.[1]
Hence, I am raising the question: how do – how should – we educate
our children about ecological and animal concerns? In this chapter,
I focus on the pedagogical values embedded in a selection of southern
African novellas aimed at teenagers. The first is an early one written,
unusually, by a devoted woman hunter: Agnes Herbert's *The Elephant*
(1917). A second, somewhat similar story is H.W.D. Longden's *Goliath:
The Tale of a Rogue Elephant* (1943). Then I will leap to a clutch of fictions from the near-present. Two novellas – Dale Kenmuir's *The Tusks
and the Talisman* (1987) and John Struthers' *A Boy and an Elephant*
(1998) – are partly set in Zimbabwe's Zambezi Valley. A third is a kind
of Herbert for today, Howard Blight's *An Elephant Bloodline* (2007),
and I close with Lauren St John's *The Elephant's Tale* (2009), written by
an ex-Zimbabwean but set in Namibia and South Africa.

One way of assessing the potential value of teen fictions is to set
them against southern African educational practice within schools. In
both South African and Zimbabwean secondary-school textbooks and
syllabuses the emphasis is on systemic ecology or environmental issues:
weather systems, water security, agriculture and forestry, health and pollution, land use and soils, biodiversity, urbanisation and climate-change
science, which emphasises the global and statistical above the local and
individuated. Zimbabwe's Grade 7 Environmental Science textbook
makes no mention of animals or wilderness conservation. At the junior
level of South African syllabuses, the Life Skills courses do incorporate
sporadic attention to animal welfare, but this component disappears at
more senior levels, which are dominated by the now commonly labelled
'sustainable development' and 'ecosystem services' models. There is, in
short, no room made in the syllabuses at present for consideration of
an ethical or compassionate response to the individuated animal, and
none whatsoever to the possible role of imaginative literatures in the
development of compassion or related ethics. Even at tertiary level,
the infiltration of ecological concerns into humanities studies remains

embryonic – and even more so in animal studies. So there is a further question for consideration: what is the role of the humanities, particularly imaginative literature, in promoting ecological and animal ethics?

A second important area of contextualisation is the historical practice of conservation in southern Africa, the features of which inform and literally structure these novellas. It was seen in the previous chapter that this aspect inflects the adult novels. The allocation of natural resources was, and largely remains, skewed by racialistic elitism, allied with an internationalist philosophy of 'fortress conservation'. Globally, this preservation of notionally pristine wilderness in enclosed areas, effectively exclusionary and instrumentalist, is now recognised as deeply problematic. Kenton Miller notes: 'Existing reserves have been selected according to a number of criteria including the desire to protect nature, scenery and watersheds, to promote cultural values and recreational opportunities. The actual requirements of individual species, populations and communities have seldom been known, nor has the available information always been employed in site selection and planning for nature's reserves.'[2]

Nowhere is the problem more obvious than in Zimbabwe: at present, economic mismanagement, corruption, land hunger, political uncertainty, international ivory-poaching and other factors have meant that, in the decade or so after 2000, 90 per cent of white-owned private conservancies were obliterated, and most national parks placed under severe strain from illegal human settlers, subsistence hunting, commercial-scale poaching and government-approved mining operations. Most distressing recently are incidents of the poisoning with cyanide of dozens of elephants in Hwange National Park by impoverished villagers in the employ of ivory syndicates. Mana Pools, the north Zimbabwean setting for two novellas studied in this chapter, is one of the few national parks still relatively untouched. Yet much public discourse in the region continues to valorise wilderness reserves as a self-evident good. These novellas emerge against this backdrop and, indeed, grapple with some of its difficulties.

A third necessary area of contextualisation is the ongoing debate concerning the precise quality of elephants' consciousness and emotions. All the novellas explored below offer imagined states of 'elephant mind' greater in speculative and empathetic reach than anything we have seen so far. The debate about elephant mind or psyche, and its effects on management and conservation, have now been intensively discussed by environmental ethicists, biologists, philosophers and animal-rights advocates.[3] To oversimplify: on the one hand, zoological scientists and some philosophers eschew such imaginings as empirically vacuous and unproveable, relying instead on species-specific, repeatable behavioural patterns or neurological evidence. On the other hand, are those who insist on animal sentience broadly, and in particular on elephants' emotional sensitivity, communicative intelligence and culture, assuming individual subjectivity and agency? These roughly antithetical positions can even be entertained by a single person: Gaye Bradshaw writes, in *Elephants on the Edge*, 'I have felt wedged between two worlds and struggled to bridge the chasm between the collectivity of science and the personal nature of suffering – between my role as objective scientist and the subjective experience of a living, feeling, sentient member of the animal world.'[4] Ostensibly objective thinkers also run into problems. For example, in his book *Wild Minds* behaviourist Marc Hauser discusses elephants' response to the death of a family member, often interpreted 'as evidence of empathy and an understanding of death'. He is suspicious of such an attribution, but almost inadvertently shows that in fact the various behaviourist experiments he describes are intrinsically incapable of demonstrating anything useful about 'what animals really think', as his book's subtitle proclaims.[5]

All this has made anthropomorphism 'one of the great anxieties of the modern age' in Marian Scholtmeijer's view.[6] The critical literature on the anthropomorphism issue is now extensive and contested, roughly between those who argue, with Charles Snowdon, that it is 'possible to explore the cognitive capacities of non-human animals without recourse to mentalistic concepts such as consciousness, intentionality and deception'; and those who, with Eileen Crist, argue that such rigorous behaviourist models and discourses mean that 'animal behaviours can appear automated as a consequence of a descriptive technology that is generic and thin'.[7] Mary Midgley argues that there is not much – if any – difference between the ways in which we attribute states of mind and motivation to other people and to animals. She cites a passage from Konrad Lorenz's *King Solomon's Ring*: 'You think I humanise the animal? . . . What we are wont to call "human weakness" is, in reality, nearly always a pre-human factor and one which we have in common with the higher animals . . . an enormous animal inheritance [which] remains in man, to this day.'[8] There is now a much greater tolerance for soft versions of anthropomorphism, which can serve to express this commonality, enhance a variety of animal research projects and support animal rights legal challenges.[9] The questions concerning the notion of animal thought or mind have featured in such mainstream media publications as *Time* magazine and *National Geographic*: children's literature is no longer so alone in acknowledging and imaginatively embracing that animal inheritance.[10] In the end, we can only *imagine* what is going on in an individual elephant's brain. Fiction manifests precisely that imagining, providing, in ways unavailable to all other discourses, a tool for representing such subjectivities, and thus opening up at least the potential of intersubjective communication and compassion.

Nevertheless, much recent southern African debate on the elephant problem has remained divided between writers who valorise scientific objectivity and statistically based ecological studies, and those who valorise the beauty, intrinsic rights and subjectively experienced sentience of other beings – witness Zimbabwe's Tony Ferrar fulminating in 1992 that the Convention on International Trade in Endangered Species (CITES) was 'in danger of being completely hijacked by the media who are promoting politically expedient, emotionally-charged decisions based largely on the animal-rights philosophy [as opposed to] decisions based more on factual scientific information'.[11] I once overheard a prominent advocate of elephant economics complaining about the animal rights lobby's influence and snapping to a fellow manager, 'Ag, just kill the fuckers!' (I was unsure for a moment whether he meant the offending 'excess' elephants or the animal rightists.)

An early example of a young adult elephant-centred fiction is by Agnes Herbert (*c.*1875–1960), who is all but forgotten today, despite a solid list of publications. Along with a cousin, she wrote accounts of three major hunting expeditions to Somaliland, Alaska and the Caucasus; they dubbed themselves the 'Two Dianas'. Despite being a hunter of some competence and notoriety in her day, she does not appear on even the most extensive website listing women big-game hunters.[12] Her accounts were condemned for being 'heartless', and one reviewer found her 'tone of bravado and devil-may-careness . . . irksome'. In large part she mimicked the style of her predecessor's hunting accounts – so much so there were subsequent accusations that the books were written by a man despite their 'feminine' flourishes. She was not above shooting recklessly at a rhino or clubbing a lynx to death as it chewed on her cousin's leg, but *The Elephant* offers something quite different. A contemporary review considered it 'a volume not intended to be fiction, yet in its detail so attractive that the text reads like a story'.[13]

Like Thomas Mayne Reid, Herbert never visited southern Africa. *The Elephant* is set on the southern bank of the Zambezi River, in the fictional 'Shupanga Forest', and is very much a story. The novel begins, in perhaps the first substantial effort of the kind, as a 'biography' of a particular elephant. A baby is born to a blind mother, and its development is knowledgeably tracked with a blend of interiority and authorial commentary. The influence of the huge elephant literature out of India is evident in her comparisons with the 'Indian prototype', as she calls it, and a rather odd invocation of Ganesh, the Hindu elephant deity. Rudyard Kipling's presence may also be felt in Herbert's relating of an elephant-crocodile altercation, and in her observation that 'the lore of the African jungle, as the elephant now retailed it, was just as romantic in its way as any of our human fairy tales, its philosophy as deep, its legends as miraculous'.[14] This attribution of something like a culture to elephants is thus achieved more through anthropomorphising folklore than through biologically founded speculation on elephant mind. The admiration seems heartfelt: 'It was not strange that a consciousness as of some long-gone epoch should move, phantom-wise, beside the stately moving creatures. Sense of age and immortality is co-existent with elephant life.'[15]

But Herbert's hunting propensities reassert themselves, and she introduces that now-familiar trope: the ageing hunter in pursuit of big ivory. Jock is rather more multifaceted than your regular hunter, 'cyanide worker in the Rand mines, typist, postmaster in Pondoland . . . a veritable

Admirable Crichton in the adventure line, and something of a philosopher, too, as a world roamer must be who drives an ox-team today and plays Shakespeare tomorrow'.[16] Part of the 'philosophy', it seems, is the usual version of a fundamentally unfeeling Nature, its 'law of necessity, the balance of economy', in which 'oblivion is the remedy for all ills, and there is nothing permanent but change . . . In the endless mystery of the utterly unknown each day has a sweetness and a greatness of vaguest hazard.'[17] If the first part of that sounds like the usual justification for blasting elephants into oblivion, the last part, albeit more vacuous rhetoric than substantive philosophy, drifts into an antithetical, more compassionate mode. Her love of the hunt notwithstanding, Herbert seems to place the responsibility where it belongs: 'The grown elephant was in the happy position of having no jungle enemies whatever, save two-legged human ones . . . The white ones were most to be feared, but the brown have their dangers, with their pitfalls and spears and knowledge of the ways of the jungle people. With the white ones came the strange scythes of death which speak destruction and torment. They were despoilers who were ever abroad, hunting without intermission.'[18]

Jock is one of the despoilers, though when he comes to the point of actually shooting the elephant, he suffers some doubt: 'For a moment he held his fire, and all sorts of curious thoughts tumbled over each other in his imaginative brain. He was safe and might walk away as though no elephant existed! What an insanely stupid adventure it was to try to hustle out of this world that mountain of solid flesh with a tiny bullet not so big as a man's little finger!'

As we have seen so often, though, this quiver of honest self-reflection is instantly repressed: 'Jock pulled the trigger.' He is, after all, just another 'pitiless Achilles'.[19] Not only is compassion repressed; so is the imagination. It has to be, in order to kill.

Herbert's sympathies do seem ultimately to lie with the elephant, however. The track of the bullet through the elephant's flesh is described as 'cruel', the elephant hunt as a 'disaster'. And later in the story, when Jock shoots the blind mother elephant, Herbert again adopts her point of view: 'She did not want to die. She clung to life, for all her blindness, for life's sake.' Jock captures her calf, a 'prize' upon which he gazes 'complacently', even as the calf evinces 'a world of pathos in his always sad-looking eyes'.[20] Then, in somewhat unlikely fashion, the calf is rescued and freed by a phalanx of female elephants – an expression of just those family loyalties from which most hunters seemed to want to exclude themselves.

Herbert's novel takes to a new extent those tiny hints of compassion or empathy, the gestures towards admiration and ecological under-standing that we saw in the hunting literature – without quite leaving behind its ambivalences. She was ahead of her time, but it is both unfortunate and significant that this more empathetic mode is confined to the younger reader.

Herbert's book was published in the middle of the First World War (in the year F.C. Selous died); Longden published *Goliath* in the middle of the Second World War, in 1943. In their essentials, the two works are very similar. Goliath is, obviously, the giant, pursued by diminutive man, the armed David. The tusker is born, grows uniquely massive, is tracked by the hunter, kills the hunter and is vengefully pursued once more by the hunter's son, David van Heerden. Longden's language speaks volumes about the classical, not to say imperialist, tenor of his reading and metaphoric burden: 'Through the darkness flickers of white fire ripped from the drifting battlements of clouds like forked flame, till it seemed as if Jove himself had forsaken the Olympian heights to visit those earth-bound kopjes of Africa, for over the parched bushveldt and through the hills rolled the deep tattoo of distant thunder like a fanfare heralding the reign of the boisterous god.'[21]

Goliath is portrayed migrating over much of the subcontinent, from the lower Limpopo River to the Kalahari, and witnessing a great deal of its history, from Arab slaving through the legendary violence of Shaka and Mzilikazi to the invasion of the north by the whites who rapidly 'thinned their ranks'.[22] This larger-than-life, preternaturally ancient animal, whose scale, size and wisdom becomes a literary trope, is again granted both a biography and interiority. For example, Longden imagines Goliath's experience of being hit by an elephant-gun's shell – 'as if a sledge-hammer had dealt him a terrific blow on the forehead. Flames danced before his dazed eyes.'[23] And when it comes to the inevitable final confrontation, interiority switches between elephant and man.

The story must conform to its founding myth; David van Heerden, the 'silent lonely man', must kill his Goliath – but the final note is one of tragedy and grief: 'And the little black and white plover with the cry like a beaten anvil, as he piped his lament over a dying monarch – Goliath of the Silongwe Hills.'[24]

Of the four late twentieth-century novels I examine, three are structured as journeys by the human protagonist in conjunction with an elephant; each journey breaches the borders of the human/animal divide, the civilisation/wilderness divide, the local/international divide, and to some degree the racial divide. Elephants are almost always cast as boundary-breakers, embodying a wildness that defies, and thereby critiques, the human propensity to impose such boundaries between geographical areas and species. Such didactic values as the novellas evince, however, remain securely attached to the ideals of fortress conservation, both in the manner in which 'wildness' is described and in the outcome of their plots. In their dating, though – 1987 to 2009 – they do manifest some shifting in attitudes and the progression of broader knowledge.

Kenmuir's *The Tusks and the Talisman* is the earliest, most realistic and most unremittingly masculinist of the novellas. It is in many respects the established hunting account turned to conservationist ends, reminiscent of Colin Burke's *Elephant across Border*. Kenmuir offers a book-length contest between a ranger turned ivory poacher named Dirk Cronjé and an incumbent ranger, Cronjé's erstwhile pupil, Tom Finnaughty, over the fate of one particular tusker named M'tagati (meaning 'bad magic – the Devil').[25] While Cronjé, cutting increasingly illegal deals with an obnoxious and incompetent American hunter named Sneddecor, tries to kill the tusker, Finnaughty strives to save it. The two bushwise men battle it out as M'Tagati is harried, wounded, radio-collared and shot at all the way from Mana Pools on the Zambezi River, past the settlements alongside Lake Kariba and across it to the mountains of the final haven of Matusadona National Park. The final stratagem Finnaughty employs to outwit Cronjé is a little implausibly elaborate, but the contest, with its plot twists, technologies, bushcraft and hand-to-hand combat, is well designed to appeal to the youthful male reader, and on the whole competently achieved. The description of

Finnaughty is archetypically heroic, indeed archetypically 'Rhodesian': 'bare ankles, worn veldskoens, khaki shorts, a shirt with the sleeves cut away, no hat . . . cool, relaxed'.[26] While Cronjé is a tough and worthy but unscrupulous opponent, the reader is unquestionably meant to identify with Finnaughty and his ideals. Conservation values are a given.

If actual *sympathies* are invoked, they are for the elephant: Finnaughty is admirable but aloof. We learn more about M'tagati's birth, youth and early traumas – many violent contacts with humans that explain why he is so aggressive a loner, 'branded a rogue and a crop raider, dangerously intractable', than we do of Finnaughty's.[27] The two are nevertheless inextricably linked: both are highly independent rebels with 'lone wolf ways', and Finnaughty symbolises his passion for the animal by making a wrist bracelet of M'tagati's tail hairs in indigenous quasi-magical fashion – the 'talisman' of the title.[28] He muses on this charm's non-lethal nature, in contrast to taking tusks as trophy; it forms a 'tangible bond' even as he hears Cronjé's mentoring voice in his ears: 'Don't be a sentimental fool.' This is as close as Finnaughty gets to corporeal companionability, however: though M'tagati becomes habituated to his constant presence and Finnaughty acknowledges his own 'strong sense of affection', he does not seriously think it might be mutual, however intelligent with 'some very human traits' elephants might be.[29] The narrative situation is also complicated by a discernible gap between author and character. Though Kenmuir's free indirect style of narration allows him and his reader access to both Finnaughty's and Cronjé's inner thoughts, it is to M'tagati's consciousness that the reader is given the greater access. The elephant is portrayed possessing fears, pleasures, pain, confusion, anger, revenge, thoughts, desires, inchoate intuitions and embedded urges. Kenmuir is particularly strong on the centrality of scent to the elephantine *Umwelt*, but the narration is shot through with authorial judgement (wounds become 'hideous scars', for example) or information (a companion elephant is blown up by a landmine).[30] Although it is not overtly sentimentalised, when M'tagati is felled by Sneddecor's bullet we are undoubtedly meant to feel the shock – and the relief that it is not fatal.

Nevertheless, the empathy is of a somewhat distanced kind, congruent with the story's generic strategies and literary antecedents. Among

those antecedents are the nineteenth-century hunting accounts, including the *Recollections of William Finaughty, Elephant Hunter 1864–
1875*, whose name Kenmuir is presumably echoing. Kenmuir draws
on such narratives, centralising the near-masochistic derring-do that
distinguished the hardy, resourceful, cool, bushwise, plain-speaking
and self-deprecating adventurer at the maverick fringes of Empire and
civilisation; but *The Tusks and the Talisman* also evokes the particular
dilemmas of modern conservation, and so constitutes a kind of filial
obverse of the hunting account.

A number of those dilemmas and issues are explicitly broached in
the novella (one does not expect a story for younger readers to explore
them more thoroughly). International commerce and American
hunter pride is pitted starkly against locally loyal conservation values.
Sneddecor's egotistical prancing about on M'tagati's recumbent body
and insistence on his triumph being filmed is portrayed as repugnant
even to the unscrupulous Cronjé. As for Cronjé, he is now labelled a
traitorous 'poacher' – a particularly judgemental term in the context –
and, as Kenmuir states in his author's note, is of that ilk who believe
'if I don't take it, someone else will'. In contrast, Finnaughty embodies
the philosophy 'once gone, gone forever'.[31] His ethic is refined later in
the tale, as he gazes across the Zambezi Valley: 'A wilderness paradise
lay beneath his gaze, where animals roamed in freedom as they had
done for thousands of years. It was a remnant patch of wild country in
a shrinking world. He knew that if the valley was to be preserved in a
land-hungry country it had to pay for itself, and animals like M'tagati
were the drawcards that that helped the valley pay protection money
to society.'[32]

Though mavericks like Cronjé and Sneddecor 'threatened the whole
system', hunting is not excluded as a legitimate revenue-earner, bringing in 'hundreds of thousands of dollars on hunting safaris'.[33] There
are nascent ironies and irresolutions here; indeed, Kenmuir is careful
to show that Finnaughty's own views are not universally accepted even
within his own Wildlife Department. His boss, Sutton, insists, 'It's not
just looking after wildlife anymore. We're not zoo-keepers, Finnaughty.
People are involved. It's a people business, too.'[34] Among those people
are tourists; others are neighbouring farming and fishing settlements

vulnerable to elephant crop raids – and also capable, as the novella depicts it, of exaggerating such losses to the authorities. Although these complexities are not fully worked through in the story, at the very least the young reader is being alerted to their existence. On the whole, however, the language of emotion is suppressed beneath both the manly ruggedness of Finnaughty's persona and the rhetoric of pragmatic economics.

One prominent feature of *The Tusks and the Talisman* is the descriptive and educative display of natural knowledge. A typical passage: 'With the coming of the annual rains the game had dispersed, and for a while he saw only a few scurrying mopani squirrels. Then he saw a knot of impala rams who snorted and pranced away defensively. A little further on a troop of baboons shambled and cantered off as he approached. There must be water nearby, he thought.'[35]

If such detail seems a touch gratuitous at times, anyone who has spent time in the Zambezi Valley (as I did just a few years before *Tusks* was published) will recognise the accuracy and indeed affection of the descriptions of independent animal, plant, bird and insect life. The idealism of that wilderness paradise, free of human influence, is easily disparaged; nevertheless, it still holds powerful symbolic currency, even as its limits and vulnerabilities are obvious, as this novella shows – and Kenmuir is careful to depict the dangerously predatory nature of that world, what he calls (as his hero hears a leopard taking a baboon in the night) its 'awful pathos'.[36] Ultimately, Kenmuir's values are evident in the poachers getting their legal comeuppance and in the tusker's final survival and move to the safe confines of Matusadona National Park. Fortress-conservation values are not left entirely unquestioned, but they certainly are preserved.

In Struthers' *A Boy and an Elephant*, aimed at rather younger readers than Kenmuir's text, the lineaments of compassion are based more fundamentally on a boy-elephant relationship of unquestioning fidelity. To summarise: the young elephant (named, childishly, 'Gerry') is left alone and bewildered by an authorised cull in the Zambezi Valley; the boy is left alone and bewildered when his father is killed by ivory poachers. Having found one another in mutual vulnerability, the two forge an intimate communicative relationship, and walk some

200 kilometres to the capital Harare (and back again) to talk to the president himself about the whole elephant plight: *response breeds responsibility*. The novella does raise a number of issues such as the reasons for ivory poaching, the justifications for culling, the suppression of traditional modes of respect by modernity, human overpopulation and government corruption. Again, plot constitutes authorial sympathy: the elephant and his boy disappear happily back into the jesse bush of the more or less safe Zambezi Valley.[37]

The novella's plot is clumsy and its style even clumsier, but it is of particular interest for my purpose because it incorporates several levels or vectors of explicit education. First, the elephant, a very 'human-ised' narration of whose interiority also opens the story, learns how to live from the other members of his herd – and as he grows becomes a mentor himself. Second, this is obviously paralleled with the educa-tion Jamie receives from his father and from a series of hard knocks, including the loss of his mother in a car accident and a brain-damaging or mind-altering fall, which (it is hinted) ultimately makes it possible for him to communicate with the elephant. Third, the boy and the elephant learn a great deal of and from one another in the course of their journey. Fourth, Jamie's uncle Lou, who turns up from England to find the lost boy, instructs him in the evils of the modern world as he escorts him back to the haven of the bush. This character is most obvi-ously a mouthpiece for Struthers' own feelings, including this state-ment: '"Educators everywhere," Lou spat out, "they think knowledge is everything! Teach the people, and all will be hunky-dory . . . fine! Education, our last, best hope? Pah!" ". . . [Rather] every individual has his or her reason for being. No less than does every species have a place, ecologically justified, on this earth. Fathers. Mothers. We don't need education – learning – to understand such things."' [38]

As Jamie begs not to be sent back to school, Lou responds, 'No, you'll be teaching us.' Somewhat incongruously, Lou's own educative interventions are laden with scientific language and a global perspective, which could only have been acquired by book-learning, yet it is evid-ent to Jamie that this man 'cared just as deeply about all living things as he himself did'.[39] This dissonance – or attempted reconciliation of modes of learning and caring – sharply points up the questions: what does this 'caring' actually consist in, and what is it that Jamie, the 'unlearned', can teach us?

Clearly, Struthers wants to counter the government's stated doctrine of 'use them or lose them' with what Ralph Acampora calls 'symphysis', that is 'cross-species compassion . . . mediated by somatic [bodily] experiences'.[40] In his tightly argued book *Corporal Compassion*, Acampora suggests that 'bodiment is submerged in status and topicality by the dominant intellectualist mainstream of Western philosophy'.[41] However, he argues, effective compassion arises from actual physical contact, a sense of somatic or bodily affinity. This is easily understood in relation to humans, even to a companionable dog or cat, but it is not so easy to forge a safe and efficacious physical connection with an elephant, even with those orphaned calves and semi-domesticated cast-offs who have become increasingly common in the region's elephant sanctuaries. Acampora does allow for a 'secondary symphysis' – compassion at a distance, as it were – and perhaps even compassion as a more clearly imaginative construct, as one sees in this fiction.

Struthers similarly seems to suggest that actual bodily connection offers the sturdiest foundation for the generation of compassion, and provides several concrete examples. In the following passage, the first encounter between boy and elephant initiates a crucial confluence of bodily presence, communication and compassion:

> When Jamie awoke, he thought it was his mother's soft hand exploring his face. Already so shocked, his system was slow to grasp the fact of it. This was the tip of an elephant's trunk exploring the contours of his head. Moving down the body, slowly, to scent the groin area.
>
> Only gradually did his eyes focus beyond this rough, dark, sinuously-bending thing, upward. To a curving white tusk and the long lashes of an eye, behind. A great ear lifted, cutting out even more of the early morning light. And, into his newly aroused consciousness, the giant seemed to be soundlessly speaking.
>
> 'Doing here, what, little brother?' he thought he heard the elephant say, 'Happened, what?'
>
> 'My father . . .' Jamie began.
>
> Then, realisation of what had happened hit. And, with it, the agony of it all began to flood through his system.

Instantly, Gerry's exploring trunk stilled, as his senses absorbed these new messages of the boy's distress.

'Yes?' he seemed to ask solicitously.

Jamie put a hand up. Heedless of what he was doing – somehow, without fear – he grasped the roundness of it, pulled himself up onto his feet. For a moment, he rested his forehead against the wrinkled skin. Then, his arms went around Gerry's long, immobilised nose, and he clung to it tightly, sobbing.

'Little one, right, all,' Jamie heard in his mind, after a while. 'Too, loss, know I . . .'[42]

This mental telepathy, if it is that, which Struthers tries to capture in this sort of stuttering pidgin, is developed through the novel until they communicate more easily. Yet it is *not* depicted as English language as such, though this must be the manner in which Jamie utters his thoughts; it *seems* to be such words, but is more akin to the infrasonic rumbles and waves that are received by the boy's whole body, rather than by any conscious thought pattern or translation. As a narrative device, this is awkward and ultimately unworkable. However, locating the basis for compassion in *some* form of communication (including, crucially, the trustfulness of touch) is I think a profoundly important conjunction. It also seems to me – having myself been raised in bodily contact with innumerable animals, wild and domestic – blindingly obvious that such contact potentially generates a form of compassion quite different from one that might develop in its absence. Struthers seems to be indicating that caring for animals in some kind of distant, abstracted sense, however scientifically, ecologically or economically supported, is deeply inadequate. Uncle Lou comes to this realisation late in the novella, when he in turn is tenderly touched by Gerry's exploring trunk, and experiences a near epiphany of companionability. The somatic commonalities between man and elephant are seen to be greater than their differences, though difference and communication are ever in a kind of paradoxical dance.

Is the act of reading itself a gesture of compassion, or at least a potential prelude to compassionate 'action-at-a-distance'? That Struthers writes a novella at all shows at least some faith that an *imaginative* identification with Jamie's experience might be conveyed, such that compassion in other ways (financial support for parks or rescues, or just leaving the animals alone) might be stimulated in his readers. We necessarily approach the physical encounter with our imaginings already partly formed, our expectations of it moulded by previous experience, our learning, our reading – and how the encounter confirms or modifies that basis will help determine our future behaviour and ethics. When Jamie relates to the president 'the empathy that started to flow, when he learned Gerry's own *story*', it is surely a flow Struthers hopes the book will carry beyond the confines of its covers.[43] What Struthers' and other novelists' efforts imply is that this imaginative element is as important as and is already involved in even the most intimate levels of the somatic. Throughout the novella, Struthers is insistent that an elephant's mental and emotional life is no less complex than the human's: indeed, the crucial questions *he* wants to address to humanity he places in Gerry's mind: 'People. Killing animals, so many. Why?'[44]

Blight's *An Elephant Bloodline* came weighted with approving blurbs from alternative scientist Lyall Watson and the doyen of so-called elephant whisperers, the late Rory Hensman. This novella develops and updates so many tropes of previous works that it cannot help feeling derivative. It follows a now-familiar plot of an elephant's biography, its growth into the bush world of the Kruger Park and its bordering territories, its natural trials and its conflicts with humans, both agricultural and more predatory. Like Cloete, Blight unrelentingly narrativises information about the broader natural ecology, the behaviour of its creatures and its vegetation, an urge that similarly spills over into informative appendices and diagrams. As in *The Curve and the Tusk* there is an iconic baobab, mystical in its antiquity. Blight – as if picking up on Herbert's passing reference to the Indian elephant-god Ganesh – works up a whole chapter on one Lord Rijhna, imagining this already invented figure inventing in turn a successor African elephant-goddess – Mma Thohoyandou – who is at once 'the daughter of *ubuntu*' and 'the goddess of biodiversity, the goddess of gender diversity and the goddess of reason'.[45] Although this is evidently an effort to persuade readers that the African elephant ought to be as revered as the Asian, such a foray into pure fantasy lies awkwardly alongside the naturalism of other parts of the story. It feels both politically correct and bordering on the absurd.

As with a number of his predecessors, Blight attempts a presentation of elephant interiority, but comes still closer to the representation
of elephantine culture:

> Mafunyane turned his attention to the Matriarch. She had left some
> damp evidence of her condition in the forest. The bull touched the
> urine patch with the tip of his extended trunk, leaving it in position for
> only a moment.
>
> He then lifted his trunk and inserted it into the upper level of his
> open mouth. On his palate was his Jacobson's organ, the gland that
> would, in the flash of an elephant's eye, confirm his suspicions.
>
> Yes, this cow was his.
>
> She too meant business and would be receptive to his amorous
> advances.[46]

This is empathetic – an attempt at closing the gap between human and
elephant mind worlds. Naming the elephant protagonists is another
part of the strategy (and here the pretence is that the elephants have
named themselves, rather than the author/omniscient narrator). That
achieving true interiority is ultimately impossible is evidenced by the
uncertainties or wavering in the narrative voice. Forays into elephant
interiority are constantly interrupted by the authorial voice, particularly
the injection of scientific jargon ('Jacobson's organ') and zoological
observations. Elephant actions are explicated at one point by a kind
of psychosomatic emotional model, at another by appeals to notions
of 'soul', at yet another in terms of floods of chemicals in elephantine
organs. If this fails to cohere, perhaps the text's very flaws exemplify
the philosophical problems involved in imagining elephant mind at all.
Ultimately, it is an *imaginary*, even when bolstered by modern science.

Blight is by no means the only writer to wrestle with the problem – a
distinctively modern one. One might mention briefly here, for example, David Paynter's beautifully produced book *Elephant, Me* (2006).
The bulk of this large-format coffee-table publication is devoted to colour photographs, of the clarity and intimacy one has come to expect of
the contemporary long lens. The photographic section is preceded by
a short narrative similar to Blight's, titled 'From the Memory-Diaries of
Tembo the Elephant'. The first-person perspective possibly promised

by the book's title is not fulfilled: parts of the narrative are related from the perspective of Tembo, from birth to death, but as in Blight, the omniscient, authorial voice interpolates swathes of generalisation about elephant species-wide behaviour. Individuation thus vies with ethological normatives, and the didactic purposes of the narrative blur with those of the periodically inserted boxes of factual information. Paynter will not go as far as Blight in spiritualising the elephant mind, but in a prologue somewhat oddly titled 'In the Spirit of Fact versus Fantasy' he enters the 'heated debate' about anthropomorphism, coming down on the side of according elephants a complex and rich emotional life not unlike that of humans – though he asserts categorically that they have no sense of the future (on what grounds is unclear).[47] Volumes like this, for all their contemporary gloss and colour, are the clear descendants of the more educative elements in travelogues of the previous century, and the desire of writers to explain the intricacies of elephant behaviour seems inexhaustible. For all the repetitions, however, even Paynter, not unlike John Barrow commenting on Peter Kolb, feels a need to disburse certain myths about elephant behaviour. Even the typographical layout of this title is deployed to this end, with 'IN THE SPIRIT OF FACT' prominently capitalised on the first line, 'versus fantasy' diminished on the next.

Blight made a fashionable gesture towards gender equality, but St John's The Elephant's Tale is the only one of the novellas discussed here that features a female protagonist, the bold and vivacious Martine. Having lost her parents in a fire, she and her grandmother are trying to save the family's wildlife sanctuary in South Africa's KwaZulu-Natal province from commercial acquisition by a sinister buyer named Reuben James. The sanctuary, Sawubona (Zulu, 'health'), bears some resemblance to the late Lawrence Anthony's Thula Thula, as he relates in his memoir The Elephant Whisperer (see chapter 7 of this volume). Both sanctuaries house orphaned and traumatised elephants; in St John's case, a particular elephant named Angel shows her vulnerability to abuse and her elephantine memory by attacking Lurk, James's nasty assistant who (it turns out) once hurt her. Following James and Lurk's disconcerting visit, Martine smuggles herself and her friend Ben Khumalo aboard James's plane and ends up stranded in the Namibian desert, but is rescued by a young Bushman named, appropriately, Gift. Gift is himself something of an orphan, his father having inexplicably gone missing. It turns out that the latter is the archetypal elephant whisperer and has been blackmailed by James, who has created an artificial Eden in a desert crater, using water diverted from local communities. There, he is experimenting on Namibia's desert-dwelling elephants in order to develop an animal that will better resist looming climate change. This partially laudable ideal is, however, being manipulated by nasty commercial forces bigger than James himself, who emerges a more ambiguous figure than first suspected: for instance, he, along with Gift's father, had originally rescued the elephant Angel from starvation and abuse and transported her to faraway Sawubona.

This short but rich novella conforms to thriller-adventure conventions more than the other examples addressed above, including some rather stereotyped characters, some unlikely coincidences within a swiftly moving plot and little in the way of heavy description or didacticism. Such didactic elements as there are – information on elephant behaviour, climate change or the petroglyphs of Twyfelfontein – are neatly and naturally delivered via conversations between characters. In the end, Martine wins, of course: Angel is reunited with her elephantine twin and Gift with his father Joseph; James and his thoroughly evil backer are rumbled and arrested – and the sanctuary and its animals are saved.

An Elephant's Tale economically raises a number of issues and dimensions crucial to a twenty-first-century ecological sensibility. These issues overlap with those raised by Kenmuir and Struthers, but also update them. One aspect involves water shortages exacerbated by global warming, with species extinction a tragic corollary. As pollution eventuates in more extreme weather, James states, 'more wars will be fought over water than have been fought over oil or religion throughout history . . . The people who control the water supplies will control the earth.'[48] As Martine accuses, such control is all too easily commandeered to self-serving international capital, becoming more 'about money and power' than about conserving wildlife or water. James's defence that 'it is possible to do both' is not borne out by St John's portrayal of the suffering of elephants trapped in James's efforts to engineer drought-resistant animals in his artificial oasis. When Martine intervenes to help a fallen elephant, the portrayal of suffering is thoroughly humanised, and focused on the eye: 'The elephant's thick lashes lay flat against her rough grey-brown cheek. Her whole body trembled. When Martine touched her tenderly, a tear rolled down her face.'[49] Here, as in Struthers' novella, the advent of corporeal touch, the implication of eye contact and the recognition of a *face*, is culmination and confirmation of more conceptual reasons for compassion. The face is a kind of cipher for the recognition of elephants' complex communication abilities, or the notion that they are 'supremely evolved beings – far smarter than people, in Martine's opinion'.[50]

A second contemporary aspect, then, is the portrayal of a particularly self-humbling empathetic sensibility, one historically contingent upon a long development – scientific, philosophical and legal – of human responsiveness to animal mind and *Umwelt*. This sensibility is embodied primarily in Martine, who 'couldn't bear to see any animal suffer', but also in her friend Ben, and in the Bushman elephant whisperer Joseph.[51] St John is careful to fend off possible charges of oversentimentalising this attitude by educating Martine into recognising the dangerous quality of independently wild animals, and by deliberately flagging some of the issues. Ben, for instance, notes how he himself wants only to protect animals 'cute and cuddly and small, like a Labrador puppy', or gentle like a dolphin or a giraffe, but finds it more awkward to respond in this way to the radical alterity of an elephant: 'They're so big and their hides are so thick that it's never occurred to me they might be able to reason like us or have similar emotions.'[52] And it is Ben who has to prevent a distraught Martine from wanting to intervene in a vicious fight between two oryx: 'You shouldn't interfere with nature.'[53] It seems clear from St John's overall presentation, though, that neither complete non-interference nor its opposite, James's experimentation, is realistically possible any longer; perhaps Sawubona exemplifies a kind of halfway solution, a necessary sanctuary for whatever is left behind after human depredation.

In the service of this 'solution', St John develops in Martine a sensibility of communicative empathy deeper even of that of Jamie in *A Boy and an Elephant*, one that spills over into the mystical. Martine has an unquestioned gift for healing and communicating with animals: she has connections with her white giraffe Jemmy and with a rehabilitated leopard (both characters in parallel novellas by St John) that can only be termed spiritual. At points, her gift for communication resembles Jamie's: 'Martine had a strong feeling the animals were trying to tell her something. She put a hand on Angel's trunk and the elephant's unspoken words came to her as clearly as if they'd been written on her soul with indelible ink: "Bring me my sister. Bring me my sister."'[54]

This kind of messaging may of course be regarded as intrinsically implausible, but it obliges the reader to *consider* non-rational modes of living with animals as essential to holistically ethical behaviour. St John takes this further than the other writers in this chapter by incorporating elements of indigenous mysticism or magic that are not just additive local colour, but essential to the plot's progression. Among Martine's several surrogate-mother figures is a part-Zulu, part-Haitian woman named Grace, who provides potions, *muti*, that Martine can use to near-miraculously heal a buffalo or an elephant. Grace also supplies cryptic prophecies, which Martine has to unriddle and act upon at crucial points in the story. The sage's ambiguous presence allows St John to effect simultaneously a critique of scientific realism and its lack of ethical content, and a resolution to the plot in a manner consistent with the norms of fantasy-adventure. This is, indeed, the (so to speak) bewitching persuasive power of fiction.

Importantly, this mystical element is inseparable from a valorisation of indigenous knowledges missing or merely nascent in the earlier novellas, though it is not oversimplified. The Bushmen have been regularly romanticised for their supposedly more ecologically sound life ways, but Gift defies the archetype by being a rather poor tracker and a thoroughly modern career photographer. Joseph is, nevertheless, the 'elephant whisperer', the result of a strange childhood abduction, as Gift relates:

When my father was four years old, the San camp was raided by desert elephants. There was a drought and they were looking for food. During the raid, he was snatched by one of the elephants. My grandparents assumed he'd been dragged away and killed, but three months later he was found alive and well and living with a herd of elephants. They rescued him with great difficulty, and were shocked to find he was reluctant to come home.

Ever since, he has been able to communicate with elephants.[55]

Elephants are, Joseph explains, 'family' to him, 'brothers and sisters and uncles'. He represents compassion in its deepest form: 'Do you know what it's like to watch them die slowly in their hearts because the freedom of the desert winds has been taken from them; because they are confined? Elephants lose their minds in such a situation. They become so desperate to be free of captivity that they have been known to take their own lives.'[56]

Sentimental and idealistic, it may be, but the novella suggests that some such manner of empathetic engagement is necessary to saving not only the elephants, but ourselves as well. Ironically, the 'elephants need us', as Martine says; but, in the words of the sangoma Grace, it is also they who might lead us to 'the truth'. In her canny admixture of narrative realism and fantasy elements, well judged to appeal to younger readers, St John gives fictional expression to what anthropologist E.N. Anderson has termed 'ecologies of the heart': 'Human society – specifically, as a resource-managing institution or set of institutions – depends on the ability of people to provide ways *correct empirical knowledge, emotionally involve therein, and educate children in the tradition.* To the degree that this is accomplished, the society succeeds. To the degree it fails, the society fails.'[57]

Chapter 6

Bosses of the Bushveld:
Game-ranger memoirs

Can the creation of a national park or a game reserve be regarded as an act of compassion? The answer may differ from case to case. Some of South Africa's earliest parks, including the Kruger National Park, were conceived in order to protect and prolong hunting opportunities for an elite – the very opposite of compassion. It is easier to discern compassion at a personal, emotional or somatic level than at the communal or once-removed level. In practice, most reserves have been established for and maintained by a mixture of reasons and methodologies ranging from profit-driven hunting preserves, which may be good for wildlife and the ecology on a broad scale, but are scarcely touched by sentiment, to the various animal orphanages primarily motivated by the desire to save individual animals. In the bigger national parks, governmental legislation, management imperatives (including the culling of various species) and tourism earnings and motives may all serve to modify or clash with expressions of empathy or compassion felt by the individual.

John Cairns has usefully delineated a tension between 'targeted compassion' (as for individuals or for 'keystone' species) and 'multidimensional compassion':

> Targeted compassion is highly selective, emotionally based, and enormously variable from culture to culture, or even from individual to individual. Diffuse compassion for abstractions such as the interdependent

web of life, for species unseen or about which little is known, and for future generations is an extremely difficult task. Yet, if sustainable use of the planet is the goal and if humans are dependent on the interdependent web of life (as I believe they are), then such compassion must be developed, even if it is only enlightened self-interest for oneself and one's descendants. Sustainable use of the planet requires an emotional commitment or it will not endure; however, it also requires enlightened environmental compassion for other species or ecosystems [to ensure that they] are not sacrificed because there are no emotional ties to them.[1]

This passage also points to the ways in which certain modes of compassion towards wild animals are a relatively modern invention, whereas other modes merely revisit old problems in a newer socio-political and environmental context.

The responses and textual expressions of some individual participants, namely, the 'game rangers', evidence many of these tensions within themselves, and no creature brings out those tensions more powerfully than the elephant.

The advent of national parks and the 'game-ranger memoir', for obvious reasons, developed in tandem; they were and are almost essential to one another. As shown earlier, the game ranger as the protagonist of elephant-centred fiction gradually overlapped the hunter. The unsporting hunter of the nineteenth century became, in many stories, the villain, aligned with the poacher and the heartless ivory capitalist. Harry Wolhuter, warden of Kruger, writing in 1948 in *Memories of a Game Ranger*, exemplifies the early stage of this compassionate shift: 'Henceforth I was to protect game, instead of hunting it. My long, subsequent experience has taught me that, thrilling though the pleasures of shooting undoubtedly are, infinitely greater and more lasting pleasure and interest can be obtained from the observation and study of wild animals, unafraid and uninterfered with, in their natural haunts; and I have never regretted my metamorphosis from hunter to guardian!'[2]

Just five years later, C.S. Stokes trenchantly wrote in his Kruger overview, *Sanctuary* (a book prefaced by James Stevenson-Hamilton):

Man possesses no moral – even though he may hold the physical – right utterly to obliterate wonderful and beautiful types of creatures which Nature has placed on earth with him: types which it may have taken millions of years to perfect. It is not as though destruction were invariably dictated by necessity. However thickly clothed in specious pretext, more often than not the pursuit to annihilation of the creatures of the wild is prompted by motives of sordid temporary and usually insignificant financial gain, sometimes by the mere lust for slaughter . . . Even today the spirit which prompts ruthless slaughter is far from dead; it requires indeed but a little encouragement, even a mere easing of restraint, to recall it to active and malevolent life . . . Properly organized and controlled national parks are, in fact, the chief instruments whereby destructive interests . . . are resisted and defied . . . It is becoming realised that a live animal is more interesting and attractive than a dead one.[3]

Killing an elephant as a game ranger became a matter for regret, whether it was a so-called problem animal or rogue, or a necessity driven by the philosophy of population-control culling.

There are nevertheless evident continuities in style and narrative modes between the old hunting accounts and the game-ranger memoirs: generally, the air of laconic derring-do and protestation of literary shortcoming, the mix of narrative adventurousness and natural history didacticism (as if every memoir is addressing a novice reader). However, the late twentieth-century game-ranger memoirs also become intricately involved in the politics and economics of fortress conservation. The 1980s witnessed a toughening critique of fortress conservation globally, the recognition that 'uninhabited wilderness had to be created before it could be preserved' and that national parks were in many ways an artificial aesthetic and political construct of doubtful sustainability.[4] This critique is paralleled by a slew of fragmentations and coalescences (private-land conservancy enterprises, community conservation efforts and transfrontier parks among them), largely governed by a globalised and neoliberal commoditisation of wildlife and wilderness.[5]

In this context, understandably, most rangers' accounts are quite conservative: their frequent defence of the fortress-conservation philosophy, the ways in which they deploy their expertise and tales of wildlife encounters vis-à-vis comparatively naive, cossetted and ignorant tourists, become crucial to the entire project. The difference between ranger and tourist is like that between soldier and civilian: the armed and the unarmed, the uniformed and the civvies, the participant in as against the voyeur of the tough struggles of the natural world. (Positioned somewhat between them is the non-governmental, so-called 'professional hunter' or 'professional guide'. This is a figure who has emerged with the late twentieth-century growth of private hunting reserves and allied wildlife enterprises, involving a whole new economy of animal trade and ownership alongside a more traditional trophy-collecting ethos, as well as different dynamics concerning poaching. I largely ignore the professional hunter figure here, though memoirs by such are also emerging.)

Though there is a sufficient number of ranger memoirs to constitute a distinct genre, there are marked differences among them. Some were written by hunters turned conservationists, some entered the profession as callow youths, others are scientifically trained ecologists – hence stylistic flair and philosophical slants vary quite widely. All, however, are aimed at the general public and, especially in the recent period, at once concerned to educate and to entertain, to distinguish the ranger from the common herd while insisting on a certain ordinariness, and to address the ethical problems known to exercise the minds of that public. These writers are very conscious of their intended readership.

I begin with some memoirs of the Kruger National Park, one of the earliest wildlife reserves and ultimately South Africa's flagship. Two early memoirs remain among its most celebrated, those of Stevenson-Hamilton and his successor, Wolhuter. Neither, however, has much to say about elephants, as there were very few in the park at the time. Wolhuter recorded only that he was excited by his first sighting, but was 'rather scared of them'.[6] Within a few decades it would, ironically, be very different, with elephants the centrepiece of overpopulation concerns and Kruger the centrepiece of the culling debate. Then – at the cost of ignoring several other areas of importance to elephant conservation, notably Botswana and Zimbabwe's Gonarezhou – I focus on memoirs set in the Zambezi Valley.

Jane Carruthers has comprehensively studied the troubled, stop-start history of the establishment of the Kruger National Park – proclaimed as such in 1926 after protracted, often neglectful, stages of carving out a series of game reserves along South Africa's border with Mozambique. She summarises:

> National parks fulfil an important cultural function in that they are the tangible embodiment of those elements of the natural environment which citizens consider worthy of state protection. They therefore evoke a love of the country for its intrinsic, rather than for its political, worth. Thus a national park is not merely a physical entity, a geographical area, or a suite of ecosystems and species, but a mirror of society and a vigorous symbol.
>
> The Kruger National Park is one of South Africa's most famous symbols, both nationally and internationally. Indeed, for many people, South Africa is epitomised by two concepts: its former political philosophy of apartheid; and the Kruger National Park. However, unlike the political evils of apartheid, the symbolism of the Park is powerful because conservation is thought to be intrinsically 'good' and the park has come to represent values which are generally considered to be morally sound.[7]

As Carruthers explains, the 'morally sound' values espoused are intricately but problematically tied to the broader history of the country, including the hardening of apartheid, subtle aesthetic histories and progressions in international wildlife protection law. Ostensibly objective, 'scientific' values are espoused essentially by a privileged white middle class, but they are not shared by impoverished black people whose ancestors were evicted from the area, or who suffer depredations by the wildlife the park protects. Carruthers thus reveals the historical fragility of the fortress-conservation philosophy, how its emergence was dependent less on ecological principles than on the contingencies of national politics, racially motivated land distribution and preservation of elite privileges.

The rangers' sundry accounts played an important part in purveying to the public this complex admixture of influences. Bruce Bryden expressed it succinctly: the parks 'are invaluable to scientific research [and] can make significant contributions towards social upliftment . . . but at the end of the day they are first and foremost safe havens for the "first people" of the bushveld, and open-air classrooms where human beings can renew the ancient interaction between man and animal that has progressively disappeared in an increasingly overpopulated and technologically advanced world'.[8] The new ranger, thus, is both somewhat misanthropic educator and uniquely placed guardian of a certain primordial authenticity, by definition privy to experiences denied to carefully marshalled and monitored tourists. He is purveyor of another myth of sorts, the emergence of which can be traced in the memoirs of the earliest wardens.

Stevenson-Hamilton (1867–1957) was not only the first appointed warden of Kruger and indeed of its predecessors, Singwitsi and Sabie; he was also its first chronicler in book form. He was energetic, politically astute and a more than competent writer. Indeed, he was more competent than most of his successor ranger memoirists, even as his two important books *South African Eden* (1937) and *Wild Life in South Africa* (1947) in many ways set the textual patterns for them. The first provided the template for the narrative of memoir, the second for the educative, more scientific survey of animal species.

The very title of *South African Eden* hints at one mythic framework for the Kruger National Park: the self-contradictory forging of a putatively pristine wilderness – this despite its having been hunted and inhabited for centuries, and from the beginning entangled in legislation, local politics and forced removals. Stevenson-Hamilton initially revelled in the solitude and relative wildness that the park afforded, and resented outside interference and management pressures thereafter. At the same time, he called the park project the 'Cinderella' of government policy, initially neglected but, in its eventual proclamation, a story with a similarly happy ending – another mythic framing. Stevenson-Hamilton's overall project was, in Carruthers' words, 'to change attitudes in favour of game protection, to provide an understanding of natural history, to legitimise the colonisation of Africa in terms of conservation efforts, to entertain and also to record his own version of events'.[9] Moreover, though not himself scientifically trained, he read and corresponded widely, and was determined to open the public's eyes to the realities of wildlife. This also meant, to his chagrin, increasing influxes of tourists, so that his Cinderella shifted from her 'former rustic simplicity' to resembling a 'sophisticated town lady', and the 'Spirit of the Wild' would flee from the dusty crowded roads. Yet, without those visitors, he knew, his Cinderella would have been 'swept into oblivion, unregretted and unrecorded'.[10]

Of the few elephant references in *South African Eden*, one is worth repeating. Stevenson-Hamilton recorded the testimony of another early assistant, Ledeboer, then living north of the appropriately named Oliphants River:

> Ledeboer said that about seven bull elephants, singly or in pairs, fre-
> quented the neighbourhood, and so tame were they that they often came
> quite close to his quarters, becoming truculent only if the dogs barked
> at them or attempted to drive them off. Once an old male had pursued
> his terrier almost up to the house. Natives complained that if mealies
> were stored in a sleeping hut, the elephants sometimes at night would
> remove the thatch, and insert their trunks, so it was difficult not only to
> raise any crops but to keep the grain when reaped. Unfortunately for the
> sufferers, in a game sanctuary the only remedy was to move out of the
> patrol area of the animals.[11]

These dynamics and priorities are repeated across the subcontinent, only exacerbated as protected elephants burgeon and threaten even faster-growing human populations.

In *Wild Life in South Africa*, Stevenson-Hamilton records the grad-ual migration of elephants westwards out of Mozambique, where they were severely persecuted, until by 1938 he estimated not fewer than 400 animals scattered throughout the park. Despite many having suf-fered distress at human hands, such was their intelligence, Stevenson-Hamilton notes, 'that they were able within the park to recognise a changed spirit' in the humans they encountered, and to behave with equanimity and trust.[12] He is nevertheless able to intersperse remarks about the biology and history of the elephant with anecdotes of encounters with an occasional recalcitrant or aggressive pachyderm, with a touch of humour that would become the hallmark of such ranger accounts. If there is no overt sign of targeted compassion for elephants evident, it is perhaps implicit in the whole philosophy of leaving them be as much as possible. Stevenson-Hamilton did remark on the feeding habits that would become the centrepiece of later culling debates: 'The elephant is a browser, and probably among the most, if not the most, wasteful feeders in the world. He is one of the checks used by nature to ensure that the growth of forest vegetation is kept within due bounds.' This ecological insight would at times be overridden by the rhetoric of wasteful, 'destructive' behaviours leaving nothing but 'wreckage'.[13] This entails, of course, the imposition of human-centred conceptions of what landscapes and vegetations ought to look like, the aesthetics of a manufactured balance of nature, and an impossible ideal of neat and sanctified stasis. Ironically, elephant culling becomes the acme of such management, central to later Kruger memoirs such as Bryden's.

Bryden was a ranger – or 'nature conservation officer', as he is termed – in Kruger for most of his career between 1971 and 2001. His attitude towards elephants is embedded in his own justifications for protecting wildlife, and for the national park itself:

> The retreat of the game herds and the shrinking of their habitat is a matter beyond pity or regret; in the end, as it is everywhere in the world, it is part of a greater cycle of change that is driven by the struggle for resources (not unmixed, of course, with depredations inspired by sheer greed, and compounded by silly or short-sighted actions), and inevitably the animals have lost, so that they have become prisoners in the land where once they teemed in great numbers almost wherever the eye could see. But game reserves like the Kruger National Park and many others have ensured that although a relatively pristine southern Africa has disappeared, most likely for ever, most of the veld creatures in all their enormous diversity have survived.[14]

Awkwardly nested within a broadly Darwinian and amoral 'struggle for resources' is an ethical stance that condemns animal slaughter, greed and short-sightedness, combined with a qualified nostalgia for the teeming past. The ranger's closeness to natural cycles not only makes him 'master of life and death' (as he titles one chapter), it also excludes the sentimental. Modern ecological science tells Bryden that a static and pristine wilderness is an impossibility, but it also valorises diversity as a fundamental good. The tensions between these entangled aspects inevitably resurface in depictions of relations with elephants.

In one rumination, Bryden (echoing Stokes) encapsulates the shift from the hunt mentality to that of the ranger:

> In my mind, elephants are the bosses of the bushveld, and if you have hunted an elephant and won, then you have earned your spurs. But it must not be forgotten that a game ranger's version of elephant hunting is not the same as a hunter's. The hunter seeks the elephant that suits his aims; the game ranger is much more focused because of his greater conservation task, so he culls members of a herd (when this could still be done) or kills specific individuals that have become a problem, particularly along the boundaries, where the fences and our neighbours' crops had to be protected.[15]

Here is the ranger's habitual recourse to the bigger picture, a conservation task, in terms of which an elephant, or numbers of elephant, become a problem. Three problems are ironically consequent on conservation's own successes. One requires protecting neighbouring humans from marauding elephants. The second is the increased attraction to ivory poachers of tuskers whose numbers and heavy tusks have grown under park protection. (Bryden devotes a chapter to backstories about the 'magnificent seven' tuskers illustrated in Anthony Hall-Martin's coffee-table book of that title.) The third spin-off of success is the perception that growing elephant numbers harm biodiversity or the aesthetic appeal of the landscape. Elephants, a century into the park's history, have become the primary determinant of its health. Culling was for a time the resultant strategy, with sometimes wrenching ethical situations for the rangers. Bryden nevertheless defends culling, and expresses confidence in the future of the Kruger National Park 'provided they work out how to keep the elephant population under control'. Bryden enters the debate on an assumption that the public is ill-informed; rangers and other parks staff and scientists are the experts to be deferred to:

> People can be educated and convinced about certain basic necessities, but an elephant destroying a 100-year-old baobab tree to fill his guts is going to continue doing that and other far worse things to the environment if something is not done very soon. My gut feeling is still that

culling is the quickest and easiest solution, apart from the fact that it could provide a sustainable income which could be used for many good purposes. As I write this, the latest news on culling in Kruger is that everyone now believes that there are far too many elephants in the park except the ultra-greens, who are totally opposed in principle to the killing of any animals at all – although one can't fail to notice that their compassion doesn't seem to require that they should all be vegetarians or use shoes and bags made of something other than leather.[16]

It is notable how flawed Bryden's argument is here. The first sentence contains an odd non sequitur; the last simplistically dichotomises a complex spectrum of views. Scientists have always been far from in agreement on the issue; many ecologists and scholars now no longer support culling – and not only on compassionate grounds. The zoologist Dan Parker has compiled a thorough overview of some 200 scientific studies of elephant impacts on vegetation throughout Africa, and concluded that there is, all told, much less to worry about than previously believed.[17] As it is, Bryden resorts here to a 'gut feeling' – his gut interestingly (perhaps inadvertently) juxtaposed with the guts of the baobab-destroying elephant. This individualised encounter, deployed symbolically to stand for all 'destructive' elephant behaviour, echoes Bryden's condemnation of 'greed' noted earlier. It hardly seems fair on elephants. Note also the resonant use of the '100-year-old' motif, often used for aged elephants, and perhaps not coincidentally matching the age of the Kruger National Park itself.

Bryden does go on to support his gut feeling with figures – the 2.81 per cent per annum increase in the elephant population, the then apparent failure of the transfrontier park initiative to spread that population significantly, and the ongoing threat to rare botanical species. 'Emotionalism that refuses to confront the facts', he asserts, 'will not cut the mustard', and culling remains the only viable option to maintain a 'proper population equilibrium' – a 'tough decision' that just has to be made.[18]

Although the ecological big picture provides a resource whereby emotions can again be suppressed, those emotions are not absent from Bryden's world view: 'When you have worked with these magnificent, highly intelligent creatures for as many hours as I have, there is no way to avoid developing a deep affection for them.' He eschews anthropomorphism while recognising elephants as 'unique in appearance and personality'. Hence, culling, 'especially elephant culling, was traumatic for any ranger, and the best way to limit the stress factor on both the shooters and the animals was to do it as clinically and rapidly as possible'. Textually, then, Bryden dwells at length not on the trauma, but on the technology of its avoidance: discussion of weapons and cartridges and aiming spots. His reference in the course of this to W.D.M. 'Karimojo' Bell, whose brain-shot techniques 'we all knew', shows how the literature continues to exert its influence. Still, at one subdued level of all this, a certain compassion for the elephants emerges: the quick-fire method of eliminating whole family groups is one designed to avoid the suffering of abandoned family members and of unnecessary wounding. What was a matter of pride among the professional gentleman hunters – taking down the elephant with a single clean shot – is now extended to the culling teams: 'The first time the R1 [rifle] was used for culling it took just one minute and twenty-one seconds to kill 19 elephants.' This in time becomes even a matter of competitive record-keeping – the operation of slaughter becoming game-like, another tactic to rebuff compassionate engagement.[19]

Emotionally loaded, too, are the more individuated encounters Bryden relates. Where the dynamics of the cull largely preclude individuation, incidents involving recognisable elephants invoke rather different sympathies. Among his early tasks, Bryden is sent to put down (kill) some particular problem elephants. Some of these have come in from Mozambique, traumatised not by the hunter figures we saw in the fictions of that region, but by civil war, sprayed with ineffective AK-47 fire, or damaged by anti-personnel landmines, and maddened with pain and rage against humans. 'It was a terrible business', writes Bryden; 'my blood boiled every time I heard about or came across one of these landmine victims. Try as I might to forget them, I retain a fund of sickening memories.' With difficulty he brings himself to relate one case, an elephant barely alive and so odorous with putrefying wounds that Bryden throws up. The ranger approaches the tottering animal:

> I got close enough to see that his eyes, which should have been brown and shiny, were the dull red of old blood. I was sure now that he was

blind, and I walked directly towards him without any attempt at concealment. About 10 metres away I stopped and spoke softly to him. His only reaction was to flap his ears feebly; he didn't even move his trunk, an elephant's all-purpose tool and weapon. So, with a heart full of sadness I lifted my rifle, jacked a cartridge into the chamber and gave him the only thing I had that could help him out of his agony – a swift and painless death.[20]

Speaking softly is not an option most of the time, however. The next incident involves an elephant raider who was beginning to endanger tourists, and therefore had to be hunted down. The chase is related as 'a mixture of high drama and low comedy', as Bryden puts it, spiced with the 'friendly insults and robust humour [that] were characteristic of the way we operated'. At one point the ranger takes a tumble, 'derrière-over-teakettle', landing 'on [his] head with [his] backside in the air', occasion for much ribbing later. There is the obligatory charge, and humans scattering for cover. He does despatch the offending elephant, celebrating the victory with a massive braai: 'Meat is meat, and a man must eat', he quips. The triumph is modified, however, when a massive abscess is discovered on the elephant's rear, doubtless the cause for his aggression: 'So there was some satisfaction in knowing that he had not died simply because of a clash with human intruders; I had performed an act of mercy.'[21] Compassionate though this act is, it remains another human intrusion into the natural order – possibly an inescapable dilemma now.

As a coda to the foregoing, I want to glance at a book that takes some cues from the game-ranger memoir, and begins its story in the Kruger National Park, but is also more multi-generic in its form. This is Richard Peirce's *Giant Steps*, the story of two elephant orphans, baby survivors of a Kruger cull, and their eventual lives of constrained security in the Tankwa Karoo. In some ways it echoes elements of what in the next chapter I call the 'field-research memoir'. It is, centrally, a story of compassionate rescue, a narrative of individuals with a concomitant ethical drive generally missing from the game-ranger memoir. Trading to a degree on the cuteness factor of the baby elephant, it can border on the cheesy, especially in its advertising: the front cover proclaims it as a 'true story from Africa about exploitation and the meaning of freedom'. This belies both the richness and ambivalence of Peirce's narrative, however; given what these abandoned, imprisoned and exploited young elephants eventually had to endure, Peirce wonders at one point whether it was right to let them survive at all.

Peirce generates sympathy for the elephants through a number of narrative strategies, borrowed from fiction, which the game-ranger memoir usually denies itself. He intertwines several subjective narrative threads, alongside boxes or sidebars that list objective facts about elephants generally. The first narrative thread is that of a fictionalised interiority of the elephants themselves – the baby, the mother; seeing the world; and the mounting panic as a cull develops, from the elephants' point of view. A second strand concerns John Booker, a man who had participated in culls, but is now designated to attempt the rearing of the orphans. Again in the manner of imaginative fiction – with sometimes a touch of Wilbur Smith – Peirce portrays Booker's feelings as he observes the body of one orphan's mother:

> No matter how tough they are, real men with hearts and souls cry, and tears streamed down John's face, making clear streaks through the dust on his cheeks. He almost wanted to tell the butchers to leave this primal mother alone, not to touch her because it didn't seem right or fair that she should be mutilated. Almost paralyzed with grief himself, he just sat there and absorbed the scene, the tragic waste of life, and he feared for the future of elephants in Africa.
>
> An experienced bushman and a pragmatist, he knew and understood all the arguments around culling. As he stared at the dead matriarch, more than ever he wished for open spaces large enough for animals like elephants to live in viable ecosystems that regulated themselves without needing interference from humans.[22]

Here Peirce encapsulates a relatively new confluence of attitudes: a more open emotionalism modifying the pragmatics of park management; the new 'real man' alongside valorisation of the matriarch; and the winsome, probably unobtainable Edenic ideal of independent and self-regulating ecosystems. *Giant Steps* goes on to chronicle the triumphs and the plights of elephants in varying states of captivity and domestication: the necessary constraints of elephant sanctuaries, their exploitation for touristic revenue, their subjection to veterinary science, court cases over alleged cruelty, the occasional killing of a handler by an elephant, and so on – the parameters of a wholly new situation for increasing numbers of elephants. An unsettling combination of compassion and entrapment.

From being a playground for great white hunters like F.C. Selous, what was then Rhodesia developed wildlife policies similar to those of many colonial countries. Land was divided on racial grounds, Africans were abruptly transformed from organic inhabitants, using wildlife as a resource in their own fashion, into poachers excluded by law from new regions devoted to wildlife preservation. A number of game reserves became world famous, not least for their elephants. Indeed, so successful was elephant conservation that it was Rhodesia's national parks that pioneered culling in the region.[23]

The attainment of liberation from white minority rule in 1980 coincided with more widespread challenges to the philosophy of fortress conservation. David Hulme and Marshall Murphree sum up:

> Conservation policies and agencies in Africa came under heavy fire in the 1980s. The charges against them were both empirical and conceptual. Evidence from many countries indicated that conservation goals were not being achieved. Increasing rates of illegal offtake on many mammals (most obviously elephants, rhinoceros and gorilla but also many less charismatic species) were interpreted as bringing many species 'to the edge of extinction'. At the same time the pushing forward of the agricultural and grazing frontiers into 'wild lands', ranging from savannas to moist tropical forest, was characterised as irreversible loss of habitat.[24]

In Zimbabwe, new efforts at community conservation, exemplified by the Communal Areas Management Programme for Indigenous Resources (CAMPFIRE) initiative, radically changed much thinking about relations between humans and wildlife. However, these initiatives have had mixed success. Overtaken in some respects by the post-2000 land redistribution movement, the havens of the national parks – while under increasing threat from various quarters – remain in place, staunchly defended by a dwindling and under-resourced coterie of rangers, government officials (often in opposition to intrusive government agencies or individuals) and largely white concerned citizens. Though reduced by national political turmoil and economic downturn, tourism of the established 'return to the wild' sort remains a drawcard. As we have seen, young adult fiction set in the region tends to be quite conservative (in more senses than one) in its underpinning defence of fortress conservation, and the same can unsurprisingly be said of game-ranger memoirs.

In many areas, elephants have always been, and remain, central to the identities of the country's parks. Hwange (formerly Wankie) is home to wide-ranging herds that drift into Botswana and Zambia. Its fringes around Matetsi are home to the avowedly specially protected 'Presidential Herd' of elephants, which (as documented at book length by Sharon Pincott) have come under increased, government-colluded threat. (Former president Robert Mugabe raised international outrage, characteristically brushed off as neocolonial sour grapes, by eating elephant meat on his ninetieth birthday.) Hwange elephants have also made headlines after a spate of poisonings by cyanide, obtained from invasive mining concerns and used by impoverished locals to get ivory more easily. Ironically, Hwange was also the venue for pioneering implementations of a culling policy to control perceived overpopulation. Other major parks, notably Gonarezhou (*zhou* is Shangaan for elephant) in the south-east, and the Zambezi Valley parks of Mana Pools and Matusadona, are historically well known for their elephant populations. It is on the Zambezi Valley that I concentrate in the rest of this chapter.

Elephant Valley, subtitled *The Adventures of J. McGregor Brooks, Game and Tsetse Officer, Kariba*, is largely set on the northern, Zambian side of the Zambezi River. It boasts three black-and-white photographs of elephants. The frontispiece shows the rifle-wielding author-protagonist standing next to a 'rogue elephant just shot'; another is of an elephant in front-on charge mode; and a third is of peacefully browsing elephant families, apparently undisturbed by the photographer – the three aspects, it might be said, of the ranger's relationship with elephants: lethal, threatened and conservationist. *Elephant Valley* is, quite unusually, actually written by someone else, Elizabeth Balneaves, as if in

Brooks' first-person voice; it is hard to decide how much of the voice is Brooks and how much Balneaves. In other words, despite being presented as factual, the book uses a technique fundamental to fiction – the invention of an implied narrator distinct from either writer or flesh-and-blood subject. As a result, in various passages the style is markedly more lyrical than one is accustomed to in this genre: it evinces a romanticisation of the bush, which the more tough-minded ranger eschews.

Some of Balneaves' (Brooks') observations on the interface of conservation and society are both prescient and of their time, at once holistic and paternalistic.[25] He expresses the wisdom of the day, based on control and fencing – an approach now under serious critique. Indeed, Brooks himself inadvertently hinted at the issue in outlining (from hearsay) the 'career' of one particular elephant, whose migrations exemplify precisely the cross-border dynamics on which the future peace park concept would be based. (In a strong sense, elephants are *responsible* for the peace parks.)

I heard the story of the famous Kolomo elephant called Siachitema, after the old Chief Siachitema in whose area the [tsetse] fence line lies. The Kolomo elephant follows the same course every year, wandering from Kolomo across the Kafue River higher up, through Barotseland, joining the course of the Zambesi to Kasungula, near to Kotombora, where we met the cattle-raiding lion, then roaming back through Kolomo, taking a year for the round trip. With one colossal tusk left (he probably lost the other one in a fight) the elephant has one toe missing on his left near forefoot, which made his spoor easily identifiable. Several Europeans have gone after him with no success, and he is believed to be the killer of one of the Walker brothers, two well-known white hunters working in the Zambesi and Congo area many years ago. The Africans, attributing Siachitema's elusiveness and reputed age of over a hundred to supernatural causes, have long ceased attempting to shoot him. Johnny Uys, a famous Game Ranger in Northern Rhodesia, once followed him, and was probably one of the few people ever to see this legendary creature, for although his spoor had been seen on many occasions seldom has anyone caught up with him, and I cannot help hoping that no one ever will. I like to think of this great, magnificent creature pursing his course invulnerable and unattainable.[26]

The congruence of this quasi-mystical portrayal with those we have already seen in the fiction is evident. If it is not compassion that Balneaves/Brooks expresses here, it is something close to it; but it is also a gesture of defensiveness, surely knowing that this is an ideal rather than a reality. In reality, no elephant is 'invulnerable' to human attack, no matter how magnificent. But the romanticisation of the wild requires such legends.

Brooks found himself embroiled in the progress and aftermath of the building of Kariba Dam in 1958–1960, the flooding famously enforcing the removal of the Tonga people as well as innumerable animals (the rescue of some of which produced one of the great myths of animal compassion in national history, Operation Noah). The effects of the rising waters on elephant territories and migration patterns must have been almost as dramatic as it was for the Tonga – except that the elephants were probably better protected subsequently and better able to adapt to new grounds. In the dam context, and in conjunction with his work as a tsetse-fly control officer (thus primarily in service of agriculture rather than of wildlife per se), Brooks was called upon to deal with elephants marauding human crops. As he notes, a single night's elephant raid on a grain crop could wipe out a family's entire year's work and future food supply. At the same time, Balneaves/Brooks expresses a certain sympathy for the animals, 'who are just as entitled to a square meal as anyone else'. He lists the various 'puny' methods available to the poor Tonga to deter wild raiders, and shows some feeling for those elephants hit by ancient muzzle-loaders or caught in 'a primitive trap of rusty old hawsers which would catch the animal by the leg but could not possibly hold him. Screaming and trumpeting with pain and anger, the elephant would pull himself free, the steel cutting into his leg, and then wander away with a terrible wound to suffer agonies, finally becoming a killer and at last dying of his injuries.'[27]

Compassion in practice takes the form of the lesser evils of cleaner killing and tighter control:

And so there was nothing for it but to say: right, if elephant have to be killed we will do it as quickly, humanely and painlessly as possible . . . I hold no brief for my position as chief executioner. I have had many

adventures and much excitement out of it. There are still plenty of elephants in the valley. There is progressively less crop-raiding although
the number of elephant are on the increase, for they seem to have tacitly
settled for safer areas, and I am hopeful that one day a large tract of the
area will be set aside as a game reserve where they can live and breed
in peace.[28]

These are the distinctive ethical dilemmas or ambivalences attendant on
imperial-style control and self-inflicted responsibility. Such optimism
would not hold for all places and times, however.

Like many rangers, managers and scientists aiming at a non-specialist
readership, Balneaves feels it necessary to include short didactic sec-
tions on elephantine 'natural history', in this case carefully interleaved
with a narrative of tracking a particular elephant. Information over
five pages is divulged about footprint size, bull behaviour, responses
to human attack and, almost inevitably, comparisons with the Indian
variety. The elephants recede from his story thereafter, until Brooks is
called upon once again to deal with a crop raider. This account follows
the now standard trajectory of stalking, confrontation in thick bush,
the botched shots, the charge and the narrator's self-deprecating flight.
The protagonist is a kind of anti-hero, retrospectively slightly amused
at his own terror and rather glad that despatching the several-times
wounded elephant is left to a team of hunters who catch up with it some
days later. There are, too, the standard accoutrements of the African
companion, the recovery of the ivory and the ultimate elephant-flesh
feast of the Tonga residents.[29]

Very different in feel and tone to *Elephant Valley* is a much later
memoir, mostly set on the southern bank of the Zambezi River, Nick
Tredger's *From Rhodesia to Mugabe's Zimbabwe: Chronicles of a Game
Ranger*. (Rangers are nothing if not dull in their choice of titles.) After
an 18-month stint of national service in the Rhodesian security forces,
Tredger joined the Department of National Parks and Wildlife; as a
cadet in 1978 he was posted to Chizarira, in the mountainous country
south-east of Kariba dam. There, by his account, subsistence 'poaching' had escalated to wholesale slaughter during the guerrilla war, and
protection fell to him and a few other hardy rangers 'devoted to the

cause of preserving this wonderful wilderness'.[30] (This is about as lyrical as Tredger gets.) As is conventional, the image of the ranger is set apart from others, especially tourists (who were at that stage nonexistent, in any case). Tredger does provide nuance here, writing for example of the 'sharp, alert and practiced' head ranger at Chizarira, John Ralston, 'a man far from the popular image of a ranger, but in fact a true game ranger with an empathy and love of nature that he seldom spoke about'. Emotions stir, but are quietly concealed from public view.

> From John and a procession of other rangers, I learnt that there was no such thing as a 'tough and rugged' ranger. Some tried to convey that image and I'm sure there are many tourist guides driving visitors around in open game-drive vehicles who have to cultivate that image because it is an expected part of their job. It became a joke between John and me – we bush rangers were T & R (tough and rugged) and the tourist guides were C & B (Coke and buns).[31]

So, with a boyish irony, Tredger preserves the image while denying it. He records that 'most of our time was spent on routine chores. We collected firewood, maintained the accommodation, fixed holes in the airstrip', and so on. Indeed, the definition of a game ranger on the Game Rangers Association of Africa website makes it sound positively bureaucratic: 'ensuring the day to day health and well-being of the game, research and monitoring, game capture and introductions, population management, burning programs, infrastructure and equipment maintenance, public relations, environmental education, and, crucially, local community relations, liaison and involvement. Added to these are the normal day to day financial controls, human resource planning and administration, which must also be carried out.'[32]

But this is not the stuff of entertaining reading, so Tredger emphasises his exposure to animal-related encounters few could hope to emulate, such as a mock-heroic but genuinely compassionate struggle to rescue a baby elephant that had fallen into a steep-sided artificial water trough.[33] Involved in the guerrilla war for his first two or three years – coming under attack, finding landmines, and so on – Tredger can hardly avoid emphasising the uniqueness of his experience. The war also provided a shield for nefarious activities, not just by local poachers, but also by government agencies. In one detailed case a contingent of Internal Affairs people is found to be killing elephants. Tredger's response is interesting, partly for the use of dialogue which, however clearly recalled, must inevitably fictionalise the original situation:

> They [Internal Afffairs] were to 'patrol the limits of our realm', as one of them put it and off they went in a cloud of dust and noise, using Chizarira as a through-route to the remote areas and tribal clans that they claimed to control.
>
> 'They should get off their fat backsides and walk their realm,' said Tore in disgust. 'Maybe they'll do something useful then.'
>
> About a week later the convoy returned, one of the trucks full and covered over with canvas. From this truck came a sweet and cloying smell and, with a flourish, an official untied a corner and showed us two sets of elephant ivory, roughly hewn from a skull with bone and flesh still attached.
>
> 'Nice teeth, hey?' he said.
>
> He pointed to the larger of the two sets, almost trophy size. 'This one had been causing serious problems in the mealie fields, so we did the locals a favour while we were there.'
>
> The rest of the truck was filled with huge chunks of elephant meat, quivering to the touch, long grained, dusty and strong with the odour of elephant blood – once smelt, never forgotten. During the following years of my career I shot and butchered many elephant, particularly during culling, but the sweet smell of elephant meat alway [sic] took my mind back to that first gory encounter.
>
> 'This is state-sponsored poaching,' Trevor muttered. 'I guarantee those tusks will end up on either side of that fat bastard's fireplace – sometimes I despair, I just despair.'[34]

More than ever, perhaps, one can identify with this sentiment. Tredger, later in the book, lambastes the Mugabe government for its wildlife abuses – but he also recalls that the previous government had not been much better; military activity would always be a convenient cover for some renewed 'glorified colonial hunting trip', if not concerted ivory-poaching enterprise.

So we return, with dreadful inevitability, to the other scene of state-sponsored elephant slaughter – the cull, and the essential dilemma as Tredger encapsulates it in a chapter title: 'To Cull or Not to Cull':

> At some stage in my career, it was inevitable that I would have to shoot an elephant. The research section had decided that the population in the [Hwange] park was too high and we were instructed that we would have to take off the odd elephant for rations, instead of the staple buffalo. This ad-hoc cropping of elephant would augment the annual cull, which got into full swing in 1980, the year after my arrival at Robins Camp. This change in rations caused a great deal of consternation among junior staff with the *sibongo* (totem surname) *Ndhlovu* (elephant), who refused to eat the meat.[35]

Objections notwithstanding, Tredger is sent out to shoot an elephant – any elephant – which he duly does, with some blundering:

> The adrenalin was pounding in my ears, but I felt a hollowness in my chest that ached deep down. Somewhere in front of us was a magnificent animal, suffering mightily as a direct result of my actions; I, who had dedicated my life to the preservation of these very animals. I hoped and prayed that we would soon find her and end her suffering. We moved carefully along the spoor, the bright red foam accusingly evident on the leaves and ground as we tracked deeper into the thick bush. The sound of elephant was all around us, a deep growling sound not dissimilar to lion; the sound of disturbed, frightened and very angry elephant . . . I was scared out of my wits.[36]

And having found and killed the wounded cow, being charged repeatedly by another and forced to kill her, too, Tredger ruminates:

> In the bigger scheme of things, our escapade in the thicket was insignificant. A few months later I was seconded to the culling team and we culled another 2 000 elephants in the park over a period of three months. Somehow, though, although I shot many buffalo and antelope of various species during my career, and a large number of elephant for reasons of management, culling and crop raiding, I was never able to escape the emotion that killing elephant aroused in me, each and

every one. Although . . . there was always a deep regret within me that
the end of such huge magnificence could be achieved so clinically – with
a piece of metal no bigger than the end of a thumb.[37]

There is that old hunter's trope – so much achieved with so little –
but laden now with regret rather than triumph. On what is that regret
founded, exactly? Tredger does not go beyond that outworn word,
'magnificent': he seems to take it for granted that his readers will agree
with him, no need to stress intelligence, or sentience, or an emotional
inner life. What does attract mention is elephant family structure,
and the emergent philosophy of culling complete family groups, since
animals 'escaping the shoot would be severely traumatised by the event
itself and by the loss of family support'.[38]

In addressing the question, 'to cull or not to cull', Tredger feels
obliged to marshal the defence not of the sentimentalist, but of the
footsoldier: 'As rangers and employees, ours was not to reason why.
We were given an instruction and a mandate based on the evidence of
scientists, and we did the job in the best way possible, with the least
disturbance and the most efficiency.' (This efficiency, and consideration for family structure, did not extend to numerous calves who were
spared, only to be captured and shipped out to zoos, ostensibly to
relieve gene pools. The trauma of this scenario is somewhat muffled by
Tredger's recounting another quasi-comical attempt to corral a powerful youngster.) Tredger lays out the familiar arguments about culling,
vegetation denudation and impacts on some other species: 'I witnessed
the destruction of the soft, beautiful miombo woodlands in Chizarira,
where the elephants, through being constantly pushed back into the
park by the pressures of poaching, were forced to live in these formerly
transient areas. The devastation is awesome to witness.'[39] The impression of the 'soft, beautiful' woodland reminds us that the response is in
some measure aesthetic, as well as ecological.

Tredger does not presume to adjudicate on the scientific evidence,
though it is the trump card that allows the suppression of emotion-based
objections to culling, but he also remains sceptical of notions of the balance of nature, and uncertain of whether the future would justify this
murderous form of intervention. Without question, part of his doubt is

fuelled by compassion. He is troubled by the muffling of the reality in euphemistic terminology; in the midst of recounting the cull in numbed detail, he returns to the emotional undertows:

> My heart ached for [the elephants], watching and waiting, knowing that at any moment we were going to destroy the whole family. For the first time the work aspect of the culling took a back seat and I became emotional. Usually the hunt was a haze of organized chaos, with no time for introspection, but this view of the doomed family and being privy for a fleeting moment to their emotions and identifying with them, took its toll. A hollow opened up in my chest and I fervently wished that I could be elsewhere. But it was only a momentary lapse on my part . . . There was no time for emotion if efficiency was to be maintained.[40]

It was 'good and honest work,' he finally insists, 'and we just got on with it, leaving the propaganda and the hype to be dealt with by the politicians and by Head Office.' Again, the urges of compassion are suppressed by appeal to greater, apparently irresistible forces. Tredger ultimately puts the problem down to the parks' first intervention, in supplying artificial water sources. 'Once you start to manage, you have to continue.'[41] As he put it when discussing efforts to learn more about these 'intelligent and magnificent' creatures by fitting some individuals with radio collars, so hopefully 'assisting with making informed and *unemotional* decisions concerning their future on this earth': 'With the best of intentions, our predecessors made decisions to start managing the wilderness by interfering with aeons of habits, instincts, and natural cycles that we cannot even begin to comprehend. Combine this with politics and greed, and we have been left with an ecological Frankenstein, always needing to be managed, always needing to be controlled, always on the edge of disaster.'[42]

Chapter 7

Repeatedly Folded Frontier:
The 'field-research memoir'

Google 'elephant + basenji' and you will observe a remarkable event. On the edge of Cecil Kop Nature Reserve, bordering my home town of Mutare, Zimbabwe, one of the reserve's two elephants approaches the fence of a private house. On the house side is a basenji dog. The two animals get as close to one another as the electrified fence permits. They clearly take a great interest in each other. Neither the other elephant nor the household's other dog participate in this exchange. Sometimes, the elephant lies down, and he and the dog continue staring at each other. It is impossible to say what is passing between them, but *something* is going on – more a communing than a communication, perhaps. Curiosity at least, and a measure of trust, tentatively breaches the barrier that humans have erected between them, between wild and domesticated, nature and suburbia. An unpredictable social aggregation, albeit tentative and temporary, has come into being.

Cecil Kop's fences embody other divisions typical of southern Africa's conservation landscape, including land use (the wilderness abuts agricultural and forestry land), class (rich tourists as against excluded poor locals), even nation (the eastern fence is also the border with Mozambique). Also typically, the fences are persistently prone to breaches – by cross-border smugglers, herb gatherers, small-game trappers and benign birdwatchers. Elephant-human confrontation is always possible. Consequently, for years the local wildlife committee, which manages the reserve, debated whether to get rid of the elephants altogether and, if so, whether to shoot or to translocate them. Ecologists maintained that two elephants should not be living alone, divorced from larger family units; the reserve is too small for elephants, too small to be a self-sustaining ecosystem at all. On the other hand, the municipality wanted to keep them for their tourist revenue, but could not afford to renew the fencing that prevents the elephants from wandering. The competing lobbies could never agree; nothing was done.

In mid-2017 the inevitable happened: a policeman in pursuit of smugglers crossing into the reserve from Mozambique was trampled to death. The elephants were immediately shot.

This case echoes dynamics central to the two texts examined in this chapter; both deal with the rifts in southern Africa's fractured, post-colonial conservation arena: rifts between the legally empowered and the impoverished, between ecological science and commercial opportunism, between conflicting visions of resource ownership and use, of animal welfare and human safety, and of local articulations with global economies. Boundaries are repeatedly being erected and breached: the hungry invade formerly sacrosanct lands or steal the fences themselves so that wild animals roam dangerously; legal prohibitions are violated; monies are dishonestly expropriated and ignorant tourists try to pat wild elephants. Material or performative actions intersect with more philosophical and representational debates.

In this fluidity even the most treasured conceptual stabilities – nation, self, place, community – yield to semiotic shifts and ambivalences. We find ourselves dealing not so much with edges or divides, as with 'ecotones' – regions of crossovers, fragmentations, new aggregations assuming multiple reconfigurations and layerings. Elephants have been prominent in the study of these blurrings of animal and human mind worlds. Scientists of various callings – zoologists, neurologists, ethologists, behaviourists and others – have for half a century been building on tentative observations in the field, collating an impression of elephant being that is as complex as the human: emotional, communal, cultural, even wise. Research into elephants' communicative capacities, alongside that of apes and whales in particular, is playing a central part in preservation efforts. Scientists' findings, gleaned as much from non-invasive long-term fieldwork as from either dissection or captive experimentation, continue to couch findings in the deliberately emotion-free language and formulae of 'objectivity'.

However, modern animal studies arguably now unfold within a fundamentally compassionate envelope. Nor are scientists personally bereft of more obvious feelings of empathy or compassion, and increasingly – post Jane Goodall, perhaps – the reading public is learning of these feelings, as well as of the science itself, through what I have termed the 'field-research memoir'. These memoirs, written either by amateur observers who have made the study of elephants in the wild their life's work or by professional scientists bringing their otherwise inaccessibly specialised work to a broader public through personalised narrative, are growing into a distinct genre. The classic such elephant-focused narratives have come from East Africa, beginning with Iain and Oria Douglas-Hamilton's *Among the Elephants* (1978). Cynthia Moss's *Elephant Memories* (1988) inaugurated a series of women researchers' accounts: Joyce Poole's highly personalised *Coming of Age with Elephants* (1996), Katy Payne's sonic researches in *Silent Thunder* (1998) and, in Zimbabwe, Sharon Pincott's chatty trilogy relating her experiences with the so-called 'Presidential Elephants' – *In an Elephant's Rumble* (2004), *The Elephants and I* (2009), and *Battle for the President's Elephants* (2012). While demonstrating some differences in approach (Pincott is neither manager nor scientist, for example), these accounts share their authors' extensive fieldwork and their empathetic passion for elephants. All aim for roughly the same popular or non-specialist target audience. This chapter focuses on two such texts: the late Lawrence Anthony's *The Elephant Whisperer* (2009; written with Graham Spence) and Caitlin O'Connell's *The Elephants' Secret Sense* (2007).

As a scientist exploring elephant communication, O'Connell draws explicitly on previous researchers' work on elephants' subsonic communications, but sets her findings within a highly personalised narrative structure.[1] O'Connell relates, with considerable skill, her experiments with wild elephants in Etosha National Park and the Mushara Collection (a private reserve) in Namibia's Caprivi Strip and captive elephants back in her native United States, showing that elephants respond to ground vibration signals as well as airborne subsonic communications. The story is as much, however, about her own growth and education into the ways of local human communities. Anthony, as a landowning conservationist and wildlife reserve manager, is concerned less with science than with coping with the everyday trials of managing a group of orphaned and wayward elephants, translocated to his private game reserve Thula Thula in KwaZulu-Natal. His account conforms more closely to the game-ranger memoir.

Both texts are centrally concerned with two common themes: communicating with elephants and communicating with other human communities embroiled in the tortuous politics of southern African conservation. The definition of 'community' is highly contested in both human-social and ecological arenas – nowhere more so than in endeavours to extend the notion of community to include the non-human animal. On the one hand, centripetal forces of cooperation, identity and caring persist over time and geographical space to create the sense of community; on the other hand, centrifugal 'otherings' and exclusions also operate to help any community to define itself. In between, however, also occur unpredictable crossovers, new non-binarist communications and cooperative dynamics, mutual learnings and contra-normative rebellions. Such emergent relationships and new codependencies make possible the imagining of new senses of expanded 'community'. I explore here what *literary* expression and imaginativeness, even in these avowedly non-fictional manifestations, contribute to the discussion.

The geopolitics of the national park have been considerably complicated by the burgeoning of privately owned sanctuaries, conservancies, hunting reserves and the like. (Anthony's Thula Thula is one such.) Some 10 000 such reserves in South Africa alone support an important tourist industry as well as a substantial trade network of breeders and buyers of animals marketed as wild species, but in practice handled little differently from cattle or sheep. Each of these private preserves is necessarily restrictive in access, elitist in economics and racially skewed ownership, and selective in its game management and stocking.[2] That any such reserves even constitute coherent ecosystems is, in one view, an 'unfortunate myth'.[3]

As even a casual drive through parts of the Eastern Cape or Limpopo provinces will reveal, huge acreages have to be sealed off from neighbours and highways. This is particularly imperative, obviously, on those relatively few reserves able to accommodate elephants. If there is a single iconic feature governing animal distributions today, it is the *fence*.[4] Both Anthony's and O'Connell's accounts are fundamentally concerned with the fence. In taking responsibility for housing nine elephants, a traumatised and consequently unruly group that would otherwise have been shot, Anthony's immediate task was to erect an electrified temporary boma, designed to replicate the fence around the whole of Thula Thula. By this means, the wild animals could be contained, both for their own safety in an area already vulnerable to poaching, and for the safety of surrounding agricultural communities. The adventure (and *The Elephant Whisperer* is constructed as an action-crammed adventure) begins with the breach of both those fences, first by poachers and then by the elephants. A substantial part of O'Connell's job in the Caprivi, under the aegis of local government authorities and conservation activists, was to devise non-lethal ways of protecting subsistence farmers from elephant incursions, partly by means of electrified fencing.

At one end of a spectrum of suggested responses to this situation are those who continue to advocate for the protection of 'wilderness' (another contested and slippery term). Laura Westra argues that 'while we need to utilise and manipulate some landscapes, wild areas are required to support healthy areas through their natural functions', for the sake of the human healthiness of 'living in integrity'.[5] There are any number of writers in this part of the world who propound some variety of spiritualised – some would say romanticised – love of wilderness, ranging from Laurens van der Post to Ian Player and Ian McCullum. At the other end of the spectrum are those who argue that just such romanticisation is the problem, since it masks the imposition of sundry legalistic, racial and economic exclusions. For at least two decades now – even as national and privately owned parks remain intact – the drive has been towards *greater* democracy and local sensitivity, in the sense of finding ways of incorporating local rural (that is, black, or indigenous) communities into conservation enterprises from which they have been historically excluded. In 1991, for example, Jacklyn Cock and Eddie

Koch, having noted the environmental damages and disempowerments generated by apartheid, argued that greater environmental awareness 'must be part of a wider emphasis on community participation and the democratisation of social and political life. Grassroots democracy is essential to green politics.'[6] Since then, numerous community projects have been attempted in the region, within 'a broader new African [environmental] historiography that is characterised by an innovative interdisciplinary approach, a corrective anti-colonial perspective, an extension of the range of evidence in terms of new archival sources, by oral fieldwork, by incorporating non-human agency and African cultural constructs'.[7] Success has been variable. Sticking points include the continued imposition of alien conservation concepts; the notion that there even *is* a distinct community to receive benefits; that a relatively stable, local environment is available for restoration to some presumed antecedent state; and that 'harmony, equilibrium or balance between community livelihoods and natural resources' is a viable goal.[8] Both O'Connell's and Anthony's texts can be contextualised within this fashionable trajectory towards community engagement, and both evince considerable awareness of the historical provenance, aesthetic underpinnings and societal complexities of their respective involvements.

As she relates it in *The Elephants' Secret Sense*, O'Connell experiences the Caprivi panhandle of Namibia as a characteristic mosaic of government-sanctioned wildlife reserves, private estates and African subsistence communities. All are dominated by a complex history, as O'Connell learns: 'Many elephants in the Caprivi were still reeling from a war-torn past, exposed to landmines, automatic weapons, and poaching, partly to feed the hungry Angolan soldiers for the last twenty years ... Farmers and elephants in the Caprivi were both victims of circumstance, their fates inextricably linked through the competition for land, food, security, and access to water. In desperate times, violence was often seen as the only course.'[9]

On arriving, O'Connell still had everything to learn about both elephant communication and the localised nuances of human-elephant conflict. These were even more entangled than the assertion of one Bukalo leader that 'tradition is quite different here than on the Western side'. O'Connell finds herself not only devising nifty experiments to determine that elephants do indeed communicate through the soles of their feet, but also experimenting with ways of deterring elephants from trampling crops. More broadly, 'the idea was that by placing control of decisions, wildlife management and finances in local hands, the managing of conflict with wildlife would be seen as a community responsibility instead of the government's, elephants no longer being viewed as "Nature Conservation's cattle"'.[10]

She earns a degree of trust from both sides, being highly sensitive to shades of communication, not just sounds and speech, but also gestures, the presence of significant objects and physical settings. What is interesting from a literary perspective is how she uses novelistic techniques of dialogue and description. In this way, she captures the awkward, fraught and incremental progression of negotiation itself – precisely the kinds of action and speech routinely excised from socio-political studies. I return to this point in relation to Anthony; for the moment, I want to go back to her relationship to elephants.

In contrast to the frenetic and intricately conflictual arenas of 'community engagement', O'Connell finds a relative peace and solace in Etosha and the conservancy of Mushara, tuning into the 'slow and contemplative world' of her research subjects, the elephants:

> It was after twilight on a new moon night when I saw three bulls on the northern horizon just before closing into the bunker for the night. I sat on top and waited for them to walk in. In the near darkness, I felt like I was suddenly in the depths of an open ocean, sitting within my little submersible, phosphorescent stars suspended in the distance as the bulls approached. Their gait was so soft and fluid that they seemed to float in the luminescent sea like blue whales in a bottomless expanse, the major and minor Magellanic clouds in the Milky Way looking like the spouting of water through elephantine blowholes in the deep.[11]

In this landlocked situation, O'Connell is inclined to describe this experience in terms of metaphors drawn from (perhaps to her) a more familiar oceanic realm, with its understated parallel with whales. Her bunker – her submersible – is a material sign of her immersion in the local and of her vulnerability to wild predators. The passage signifies an early intimation of the familial connections she will in time develop with both the place and the elephants. In some ways the strangeness itself is the ground for this 'oceanic' development of cross-species 'living in integrity'. She queries this almost involuntarily acquired love and aesthetic: 'How is it that I had come to grieve for this land, for the animals, and for the people? How did I let it consume me?' She recognises the conventional antithesis of science and sentiment, as well as differences between First and Third World norms and attitudes, yet she cannot but accede to the wild's allure – what she interprets, even in the midst of a general struggle for survival, as the 'natural rhythms of the earth':

> The cycle of elephant movements gave the bush a marked rhythm that bound us to its music. The elephants were like silent conductors of a natural orchestra, seeming to summon the frenzied frog calls of the wet season and the raucous hippo bellowing, all of which reverberated up and down the river at sunset. We soaked it in, drunk with a love for the land that ran so deep and strong that it scared us.[12]

This kind of aesthetic love could be all too easily dismissed by the postcolonial sceptic as superficial, even as yet another neocolonial imposition, were it not so complexly meshed with O'Connell's political consciousness. Such aesthetic appreciation, and the literary techniques used to convey it (such as the oceanic metaphors and similes here) is, I think, still undervalued as constituting powerful and viable grounds for a multidimensional compassion, which redounds to the benefit of individual species. In her scientific publications O'Connell rigorously eschews speculation about elephants' emotional states, confining herself to the physiological measurables of seismic transmissions, bone conductivity and so on.[13] The narrative space of the memoir, in contrast, releases her into emotional and imaginative concord: 'Converting scientific concepts into narrative stories helps me see patterns in nature that I hadn't realised were there. It also helps bring a fantastical character to life that has gotten under my skin and won't stop itching until I reveal its true nature to others.'[14] The wild elephant subjects of her study, from which she necessarily maintains a physical distance, take on familial familiarity. Certain individuals are *named*, an act that almost always generates the beginnings of identification in the deeper sense of a certain bond, even if it is only one-way.[15] O'Connell eventually pushes this further, though, until she is – after an imaginative fashion – 'becoming-elephant':

> I went out to the tree, leaned against it with all my weight, and tried to imagine how strong I'd have to be to shake it as the bull had just done. I pushed my hands against the rough bark in vain. The leaves didn't even shiver.
>
> I tiptoed back to the house, imaging myself in platform shoes, rolling my weight forward for the tiptoeing and then back for the more comfortable walking gait. In several instances in Etosha, elephants hadn't seemed concerned about a silent retreat . . . Even then, the soft pad of the heel dispersed the weight so that elephants running never sounded as loud as you would expect.[16]

Hard experimental observation is amplified, even guided, by an intuitive somatic mimicry. And where closer proximity allows, as in the case of a captive elephant 'trained to participate in a vibrotactile threshold study',[17] her expression is even more empathetic:

> During some of the more difficult trials, Donna seemed to transform suddenly from a jolly elephant, happily sucking her treats and making what elephant trainers call 'rasberry' [sic] sounds . . . into a toothless, bearded hag, all hairy and cowardly, tentative trunk lips quivering as she reached towards the 'yes' target, then kicking the heel of her foot into the plate when she got it wrong and didn't get a treat. She blossomed and withered, flourished and soured, depending on her success . . . As we watched her swell and shrink, her suffering made us want her to succeed all the more.[18]

O'Connell's metaphors ('jolly', 'blossomed', 'soured') search for an expression of elephant *Umwelt* that takes her beyond sentimentalised anthropomorphism. She qualifies her reading with the word 'seemed', and notes carefully the outward signs of inner states. Whether or not her interpretation is deemed accurate or credible, O'Connell is using narrative progression, colloquial language, dialogue, metaphor – the poetics of fiction – obviously with her popular target audience in mind. In a crucial sense, the personalised narrative genre *is* the condition for such compassionate companionability.

O'Connell's experiences do recognise a distinction between human-habituated and wild elephants, though her own responses blur it. A progression is achieved from utter strangeness, where O'Connell 'didn't know what to make' of elephant communication, through a mutual habituation whereby she became 'part of the scenery to them' and ultimately 'immersed into their world'. This culminates when, upon losing a traumatised elephant calf, she felt like 'a terrible mother'. As for the calf, she comes to believe it died of 'diarrhea and probably a broken heart'.[19] The anthropomorphic attribution of emotion, obviously, expresses the feeling of familial commonality and compassionate responsibility, predicated on that bodily proximity or '"inter-zone" of somaesthetic conviviality', as Ralph Acampora defines it.[20] It is also, no doubt, O'Connell who suffers in the heart as she leaves, related in a final lyrical, companionable passage:

> [The old bull] came over to me, those wide-splayed mammoth-like tusks all caked in mud. He had a gentle yet robust demeanour, as if he had been around the block so many times that he didn't need to posture. He stood for a few minutes to take me in, playing with the bottom of his trunk, holding it just off the ground, twirling the tip, sniffing in my direction. He looked away as if to pretend that he wasn't really trying to take me in, but he was. He held his head up toward me for one last look and then wandered off, swallowed up by a giant, wavering horizon.[21]

History weighs differently on Anthony, even as he shares some of O'Connell's fundamentally Western aesthetic assumptions. He emphasises his subregional upbringing and bush experience in Malawi, Zambia and Zimbabwe in order to forge an organic 'African' belonging that he can bring to bear on the localised aesthetic of Thula Thula. The reserve is '5 000 acres of primal Africa' with a 'history as exotic as the continent itself'.[22] The primal and exotic – tired tropes of non-European, out-of-time wilderness assailed by academics for decades, but persistent in more popular discourses – are reflected in other passages of aesthetic appreciation in both O'Connell and Anthony.

Anthony's register is less inventive than O'Connell's, more behavioural than lyrical: 'Living rough in the wilderness is salve for the soul. Ancient instincts awaken; forgotten skills are relearned, consciousness is sharpened and life thrums at a richer tempo.'[23] Only once, the writing about this place that Anthony 'fell in love with' borders on the poetic: 'There is nothing more energising than inhaling the tang of wilderness, loamy after rain, pungent with the richness of earth shuddering with life, or taking in the brisk dry cleanness of winter. In the outback, life is lived for the instant. The land thrums with exuberance when everything is green and lush and is stoically resilient when it isn't.'[24]

One need not doubt the feeling to acknowledge that Anthony – or ghostwriter Spence – is no poet: this verges on cliché, and no South African talks of the outback.[25] Otherwise, a rather Nietzschean idea of living roughly, for the instant, dominates the text: the narrative moves swiftly, foregrounding action and verbal interchange, seldom lingering on descriptive detail. The genre demands it.

Anthony purchased Thula Thula in 1998 – so part of the sense of belonging is dependent on a legal-cultural framework of landowner-ship. Thula Thula had been a wildlife reserve since 1911, one of the earliest of its kind, but also, he avers, part of the Zulu founder-king Shaka's 'exclusive hunting grounds' in the early 1800s.[26] In the 1940s, Thula Thula remained a hunter's magnet, owned by a 'retired governor general of Kenya, who used it as an upmarket shooting lodge for the gin and tonic set'.[27] Anthony says nothing about what happened to it between Shaka's death in 1828 and 1911, but this history certainly com-promises Anthony's characterisation of the area as gloriously pristine. But it also provides him with a lever for his assertion that by bringing back elephants he is returning it to a former, Zulu-sanctioned condition of wildness. This is the basis for his whole ethic, as encapsulated during an aerial search for his breakaway elephants:

As we took off, I gazed out over the endless panorama of this charismatic stretch of Africa, so steeped in history. Originally home to all of Africa's once-abundant wildlife – now mostly exterminated – it was where conservationists like us were making a stand. The key was to involve local communities in all of the benefits and profits of conservation and

eco-tourism. It was a hard, frustrating struggle but it had to be fought
and won. Tribal cooperation was the key to Africa's conservation health
and we neglected that at our peril.[28]

The aesthetic is that of the commanding aerial gaze, from which a generalised Africa appears as an 'endless panorama' and as 'charismatic'
(a complex of unspoken attitudes and predilections hovers behind
that word). But the cliché totters; the end of the sentence reveals that
nothing is 'endless'. The tensions between different world views are
palpable here – any one aesthetic or approach is constrained and
channelled by history.

The aesthetic is not some artistic stand-alone concept; it is under-
written by cultural, legislative and, ultimately, race-inflected power.
Anthony is fully aware of the ambivalences and conflicts, writing of
his arrival in the wilderness in terms of an early colonial: 'Initially the
abundant wildlife regarded us as unwelcome colonisers. They wanted
to know who we were, and what we were doing on their turf. Wherever
we went, hundreds of eyes watched. I had that prickly sensation of
being under constant surveillance . . . But soon we too were creatures of
the wild.'[29] Similar dynamics and developments of trust and familiarity
pertain among human communities, too:

> Over the last month I had been taking tribal leaders into the [neigh-
> bouring] Umfolozi reserve and was shocked to discover that most of
> them had never seen a zebra or giraffe – or much of the other indigen-
> ous wildlife so iconic of the continent. This was Africa, their birth-
> right. They lived on the borders of an internationally acclaimed game
> reserve, yet as a direct result of apartheid had never been inside . . . They
> had absolutely no idea what conservation was about, or even why the
> reserve was there. Worst of all, a large chunk of it was traditional tribal
> territory that had been unilaterally annexed and this resentment had
> festered over the generations. It was historically their land and it had
> been wrested from them with no consultation whatsoever.[30]

Despite the consequently necessary and genuine urge to involve tribal
communities, the ideals (and the initiative) of fenced-off conservation areas, funded by international tourism, remain with the white

reserve-owner, beleaguered by a self-inflicted sense of responsibility. The key, it is asserted, is to induct local communities into the existing conservation ethic, rather than adapt the ethic itself: 'It was vital that those rural kids who had been clamouring round the helicopter – kids who lived in the bush but had never seen an elephant – became future eco-warriors *on our side*'.[31] The cohesion of this discourse of warfare with a tiresome essentialising of Africa – 'their birthright' – runs curiously but symptomatically counter to the manifest desire to listen to and record others' views – and potentially to be transformed by them.

Where Anthony uses the term 'the community', it tends to be in the now-conventional, simplified sense of 'relatively poor, rural, tribal, black and uneducated'. Thus Anthony envisages turning an 'unutilised' neighbouring area into a 'Royal Zulu' conservation enterprise, bringing 'benefits such as job creation [that] would go straight back into the struggling local communities'.[32] While Anthony uses 'community' in a fairly positive or neutral sense, a group that wants to use the reserve to graze livestock is termed the decidedly negative 'cattle cabal'. Other intersecting groupings (never called communities) also earn Anthony's disdain: the rich and parasitic 'urban Rambos', the 'brandy and bullets brigade' of local hunters. On the other hand, there are the more formal game rangers, 'honest men of the bush' with their agreed codes and maxims and 'cojones'. Innumerable other human identifications intersect, from the ethnically precise 'Ovambo trackers' to the near-indefinable 'public opinion'.[33]

Such fleeting characterisations court stereotyping, but Anthony shows considerable sensitivity to the realities of community fragmentation or inner contestation. *The Elephant Whisperer*'s narrative style foregrounds aspects of community engagement conventionally excluded from social science studies: its embodied context of corporeal proximities, eye contacts, quotidian objects and the quality of voices. In the following extract, Anthony captures the internal conflicts present in an exchange with one 'community':

> '[The elephants] will eat our crops,' said one, 'and then what will we do?'
>
> 'What about the safety of our women when they fetch water?' another asked . . .

'I heard they taste good,' piped up another. 'An elephant can feed a whole village.'

OK, that was not quite the reaction I wanted. But generally the *amakhosi* seemed well disposed to the project.

Except one.[34]

This is evidently stylised, selective, deliberately rapid-fire. The techniques of dialogue here signal their own 'fictionality', yet they are of the *kind* that occurs in the actual performance of negotiation. Here and elsewhere, the intra-community conflicts are articulated in real-world, moment-by-moment exchanges, in which a phrase or an unwise motion can change everything. Reading between the lines; bringing foreknowledge to bear; capitalising on instinctive and instantaneous realisations; learning to use language itself: among written forms only fiction attempts to articulate these performative actualities of negotiation. To an important degree, indigenous voices and knowledges are aired.[35] That the entanglements and ambiguities are acted out, rather than analytically thought through within the text, is itself an important truth of the situation.

Donna Haraway expresses the fundamental questions in *The Companion Species Manifesto*:

How can people rooted in different knowledge practices 'get on together,' especially when an all-too-easy cultural relativism is not an option, either politically, epistemologically, or morally? How can general knowledge be nurtured in postcolonial worlds committed to taking difference seriously? Answers to these questions can only be put together in emergent practices; i.e., in vulnerable, on-the-ground work that cobbles together non-harmonious agencies and ways of living that are accountable both to their disparate inherited histories and to their barely possible but absolutely necessary joint futures. For me, that is what *significant otherness* signifies.[36]

As Haraway further suggests, such 'emergent ontologies' pertain in human-animal relations, too. The process of forming communion with a elephant is a similarly hard, incremental, somatic accretion of translations, trust and imagination.

Anthony's story of his elephants' progression from aggressive wild-ness to trusting communication is exemplary of Haraway's process of 'vulnerable, on-the-ground work'. Unlike the Indians' centuries-long tradition of taming working elephants, captivity in zoos and circuses, or raising elephant orphans in southern Africa's numerous sanctuaries to bear tourists on their backs, Anthony's group became something in between, transgressing 'the false animal alternatives of herd-like docil-ity or bestial brutality . . . neither fully tame nor entirely wild but rather liminally feral'.[37] Anthony himself calls his herd 'feral', caught between full wildness and what he sees as a necessity to 'trust one human being' – and it takes a certain ferality in that human to connect.[38] Anthony developed a particular relationship with one relocated wild elephant he named Nana. This progressed from potentially murderous hostility on her part, via a breakthrough 'infinitesimal spark of recognition' passing between them, to mutually respectful touch.[39] Here he relates one stage of the developing rapport:

> I was intensely focussed on this magnificent creature standing so close to me. All the while Nana kept glancing across or staring at me. Every now and then she would turn her massive body slightly towards me, or move her ears almost imperceptibly in my direction. Her occasional deep rumblings vibrated through my body.
>
> So this was how she communicated . . . with her eyes, trunk, stomach rumblings, subtle body movements, and of course her attitude. And then suddenly I got it. She was trying get through to me – and like an idiot I hadn't been responding at all!
>
> I looked pointedly at her and said 'Thank you', acknowledging her, testing her reaction. The alien words echoed across the silent veldt. The effect was immediate. She glanced across and held my gaze, drawing me in for several deep seconds.[40]

Recognition of the mere existence of *embodied* communication between one sentient individual and another *is* an act of empathetic imagination, and bears specific ethical consequences. Moreover, the evident diffi-culties of linguistic translation are ultimately transcended by a mode of communication both non-verbal and inexplicable. While cognisant of the scientific research into elephant communications (even obliquely referencing O'Connell's work), Anthony charmingly preserves his sense of wonder at communication that 'defies human comprehension': 'Elephants possess qualities and abilities well beyond the means of science to decipher . . . In some very important ways they are ahead of us.'[41] Aside from a certain mysteriousness, bordering on mysticism, there is nothing esoteric in the process – indeed, Anthony is deeply sceptical of one visitor's efforts to contact the unruly elephants by psychic means.[42] It is rather a matter of patient familiarisation, building trust, reading one another's bodies and sounds. That profound emotional ties develop is unquestionable.

At an early stage of habituating one of the elephant cows to his presence, Anthony confronts her. In a potentially very dangerous situation, Anthony intuits the opposite: 'I remained in a bubble of well-being, completely entranced by the magnificent creature towering over me. I noticed for the first time the thick wiry eyelashes, the thousands of wrinkles criss-crossing her skin and her broken tusk. Her soft eyes pulled me in. Then, almost in slow motion, I saw her gently reach out to me with her trunk. I watched, hypnotised, as if this was the most natural thing in the world.'[43]

The attention to the eyes, the touch of trunk (repeated later in the book, too) are the first manifestations of somatic, non-verbal communication. This deepens over time until man and elephant can commune and feel 'completely content, emanating easy companionship', to the extent that Anthony seems to relinquish his own selfhood. 'This was what intrigued me: the emotions that I experienced when I was with them. For it seemed to be their emotions, not mine. They determined the emotional tone of any encounter.'[44] Alongside this, Anthony surprises himself by apparently becoming subliminally attuned to the elephants' subsonics, making it easier to find them even in concealing bush:

> Somehow I had become aware that elephants project their presence into an area around them, and that they have control over this, because when they didn't want to be found I could be almost on top of them and pick up nothing at all. A little more research and experimentation and it became clear what was happening . . . They were letting everything and everyone know where they were, in their own elephantine way, in their own language.[45]

Communication in the animal kingdom is, as Anthony puts it, 'as natural as the breeze'.[46] Such somatic conceptualisation of language slides easily into viewing an elephant as possessing a psyche closely analogous to the human. Anthony tries to habituate another orphaned elephant, one who 'thought we were going to kill her, just as humans had killed the rest of her family', and so charges at him:

> Her charge, ferocious as it seemed, didn't gel. I could sense that this poor creature, a couple of tons of tusk and flesh that could kill me with a single swipe, had the self-confidence of a mouse. She needed to believe in herself, to know she deserved respect and was a master of the wilderness. She needed to believe that she had won the encounter . . . This sadness bordered on a grief too embedded to penetrate. She was so depressed I feared she might die of a broken heart.[47]

Despite – or because of – an anthropomorphic reach, the development of new sense of community, including both Anthony and other elephants, can begin a calming and healing process. The capacity for such insights to generate feelings of love and companionship, trust and safety, largely *on the elephants' terms*, seems undeniably fruitful. This has limits: human control – the fence, the gun – impose boundaries once more. At another point, Anthony is obliged to shoot one of the group because it has inexplicably started attacking vehicles, even Anthony's own. He is utterly stricken to discover that the cause was merely a rotten tooth that could have been doctored.

Conversely, the elephants develop an attachment, too. When they mysteriously emerge from the distant bush, apparently to greet Anthony at the gate on his return from rescuing zoo animals in Baghdad, he reflects on the lessons they have taught him, among them 'repayment', 'how much family means', 'wise leadership, selfless discipline and tough unconditional love', 'dignity' and 'loyalty to one's group'.[48] Unquestionably, this human and these elephants had in several senses come to constitute a new kind of community, cemented by shared communicability and, above all, trust.

Even more remarkably, when Anthony died and was buried near his house on Thula Thula, an extraordinary thing happened. Two herds of elephants, including those rehabilitated by him, appeared at the house.

According to Anthony's son Dylan: 'They had not visited the house for a year-and-a-half and it must have taken them about twelve hours to make the journey.' The elephants hung about for two more days before slowly moving off – behaviour interpreted as mourning and 'say[ing] goodbye'.[49] Alternative interpretations might be supplied, were the phenomenon unique, but it is not: Dame Daphne Sheldrick recounted how her orphaned elephants, like Anthony's, 'arrived wanting to kill humans but eventually protect their human family out in the bush, confronting a buffalo, or shielding their surrogate human family from wild, less friendly peers'.[50] And there is another southern African case:

> Shortly before Norman Travers was buried on his farm, Imire, in eastern Zimbabwe, two forty-year-old bulls [orphans once rescued by Travers] arrived unbidden, wandered through the crowd of 250 mourners, lumbered up to the coffin and sniffed it long and intently. When the last spadeful of earth had been cast on the grave, they stood together on the heap of ground he lay beneath. Three times in the ensuing week, they returned and stood by the grave. Travers's family is convinced they were mourning.[51]

It is less important whether the interpretation of mourning is accurate to the elephants' inner experience, which we cannot ever know, than that an interpretation assuming commonality has proved possible, that a familial *and* cross-species sense of community has manifested, and that the expression of it necessarily involves an act of the imagination.

'The safest statement we can make about [ecological] community boundaries is probably that they do not exist, but that some communities are more sharply delineated than others.'[52] This is a statement from ecologists dealing with natural dynamics avowedly free of human interference. How much more porous are the boundaries we try to establish between human and non-human entities, especially when one ventures into the realms of representation and the imagination. For in the end, the delineation of a community – as Benedict Anderson recognised long ago – is fundamentally a matter of the imagination.

South African history, in particular, has been dominated by the politics of division, of pitting communities against one another, based on representations of difference; this is true of both intra-human and human-animal relations. But Thembela Kepe, in several studies of the interplay of human communities in South Africa's conservation arena, notes that the definitions of community customarily invoked in developmental and government discourses often mask how 'complex and ambiguous' the term is. Kepe argues that oversimplified applications of 'community' have, for instance, resulted in the marginalisation of less organised groups such as immigrants (and we can add animals), and in idealised notions of community being turned to the advantage of new but counterproductive forms of coercive authority – including highly controlled fortress-conservation areas.[53] Another, subtler form is the insistence on the concept of the uniquely human. Elephants have been adept at breaching both kinds of the 'plural and repeatedly folded frontier'.[54]

Through experiential or phenomenological narratives such as Anthony's and O'Connell's, 'we are asked to be a part of elephant suffering, to own what has happened and is happening to elephants as something that involves us as much as them'.[55] Merely by taking responsibility for his group of 'feral' elephants, Anthony felt himself become 'part of the herd'; ultimately, he says, it was they who whispered to *him*. Nor does he doubt that elephants are 'emotional, caring and deeply intelligent; and that they value good relations with humans'.[56] Among many nowadays, Anthony and Gaye Bradshaw – as indicated by her book's subtitle *What Animals Teach Us about Humanity* – share the belief that elephants can act as 'a model and inspiration' for human behaviour.[57] Attaining such an ideal – a new 'family made up in the belly of the monster of inherited histories that have to be inhabited to be transformed' – is both essential and impossible within the messiness of local conditions.[58] As Alphonso Lingis concludes:

> Before the rational community, there was the encounter with the other, the intruder. The encounter begins with the one who exposes himself to the demands and contestations of the other. Beneath the rational community ... is another community, the community that demands that the one who has his own communal identity, who produces his own nature, expose himself to the one with whom he has nothing in common, the stranger.
> This *other community* is not simply absorbed into the rational community; it recurs, it troubles the rational community, as its double or shadow.[59]

Elephants have become our shadowy double.

Chapter 8

The Cult of the Remnant:
The elephants of Knysna and Addo

'Watch: Elusive Knysna elephant captured on camera', proclaims one of many tourist-orientated website posts that take advantage of the presence of elephants in the dense and rugged Outeniqua forests.[1]

It is ironic that the continent's most intensively and intimately photographed mammal, familiar from hundreds of glossy coffee-table books and films set in Africa's savannahs, should, in this one corner of the subcontinent, attract this kind of attention – an attention derived precisely from its preternatural *un*availability to the tourist gaze. The Knysna elephants always attracted hunters out for ever-greater thrills, and even these rugged forested kloofs did not save them – only a widespread shift in attitude and targeted legislation has done that. Now, however, it is precisely their status as a remnant that draws attention – as a reminder, perhaps, of how close to extinction elephants in South Africa once came and, further north, how much danger they are in once again. On a subcontinent that is now, at least relatively, abundant in elephants, it is the aura of mystique that attracts – as if, in this age of mass extinctions, abundance itself has become dull, almost an embarrassment. To be sure, these elephants are hard to find for all the interested folk tramping around Millwood and Harkerville looking for them – I have done it myself. Yet there is something a little artificial, a little voyeuristic, in the almost cultish generation of mysteriousness that the various literatures have generated around them. They have been, as Melissa Reitz puts it, 'driven into legend'; it has become a matter of 'managing the myths'.[2] One is, as Lyall Watson says, 'beset by the *possibility* of elephants'.[3]

The phantom-like Knysna herd, if it amounts to that, is both a mirror and a counterpoint to the herd in Addo, 150 kilometres to the east. The two populations were once, it is surmised, a single one, migrating across vaster areas, exchanging genes and cementing family ties. They were separated over the course of a century by slaughter and the conversion of land to agriculture. The elephants of the Addo thickets, raiding the nascent citrus farms of the Sundays River Valley, protected by thorny brakes as the Knysna animals were by yellowwood forests and precipitous kloofs, found themselves subjected to the same hunting pressures – at points by the same individuals – and decimated to much the same level of near-extinction. Yet the Addo herd survived, was saved, and thrives. The difference in outcome between the two populations – and between the literatures spawned by them – are instructive. In this chapter, I do not recapitulate in detail the history of these two populations, which is available in any number of places, but try to assess the role of literary works in the unfolding shift in attitude from murderousness to compassionate mystique.

As early as 1775 Anders Sparrman was referring to the Knysna and Tsitskamma forests as an 'asylum' for elephants increasingly harassed by hunters. What may have been a thousand inhabitants – or, more likely, a population moving in and out from more congenial neighbouring countryside depending on food and threats – was probably already down to a few hundred. In the early nineteenth century Henry Lichtenstein wrote from the Langkloof, just north of the Outeniquas:

> Our host [Strydom] and his brothers maintained themselves chiefly by the chase. They roved about the mountains to the south of their habitations, in pursuit of the elephants, buffalos and wild boars, which still inhabit in considerable numbers the vast forests of Sitzikamma. A few months before, they had taken a male elephant fourteen feet high, the tusks of which weighted nearly a hundred and a half. They were sold at the Cape Town [*sic*] for two hundred dollars. He asserted, that

some years before, elephants had been taken here that were eighteen feet high; and experienced hunters, who had travelled through the solitary countries on the other side of Caffraria, assured me afterwards that this was no exaggeration. Strydom celebrated highly the affection of this animal to its young, and insisted that he himself had seen a female elephant take her wounded calf up in her teeth, and run away with it.[4]

Those measurements were, of course, exaggerations – a propensity that would continue to be attached to the Knysna tricksters, mostly by the egotists most desirous of killing them. A persistent notion was that the Knysna elephants constituted a distinct race or subspecies, made taller by adaptation to an elevated forest environment (as opposed to the allegedly smaller Addo group). This manifestation of the 'cult of the remnant', couched in Linnaean biological terms, has been conclusively disproved.[5] It may have begun with Peter Kolb, who fantasised that he had observed a Cape elephant, larger and more powerful 'than the elephants of any other country', being 'yok'd to a ship of no small burthern that was laid on the shore to be careened, and he dragged it fairly along'.[6] The claim of extraordinary size was, in short, a notion built upon fictions perpetuated over centuries, culminating in those of slaughterer-in-chief P.J. Pretorius, of whom more shortly.

Such was the perceived loss over the first half of the nineteenth century that in 1860 the first government protective legislation was drawn up, but nothing was done in practice to protect the elephants. Their number and habitat was further radically reduced by the Great Fire of 1869. Hunting temporarily surged, including most notoriously that of a great bull by the Duke of Edinburgh in 1876. Just nine years later, the first dedicated conservator was appointed, attached to the forestry department – the very outfit largely responsible for the invasion and denudation of the elephants' habitat. Precipitous decline was inevitable, even after additional protection came up for discussion in 1889: 'The preservation and utilisation of elephants have been much discussed throughout the year. Elephants have not yet been placed in charge of the forestry department, but the pernicious system by which they were being wantonly destroyed has been suspended, and when the Knysna forests come under the Forest Act, elephants will fall under the protection of the forest authorities.'[7]

'Pernicious' is an interesting word here, but the undertow is more in the direction of the possible 'catching and training young elephants for forest work' than compassionate conservation of elephants in natural conditions. In any event, it was all too late. Never again would the Knysna elephants exceed a handful in number.

As for the Addo elephants, John Barrow, camped on the banks of the Sundays River in August 1797, encountered a group that 'had intended to quench their thirst near the place where we were encamped; but, finding the ground already occupied, they turned quietly away without molesting us. The following morning we pursued them by the track of their feet into an extensive thick forest of brushwood, among which several made their appearance at a distance; but we were not lucky enough to kill any of them.'[8]

That thick forest of brushwood proved the saving of the Addo herd for another century and more, despite a variety of hunters' incursions. It also ensured a paucity of literary treatments. As the citrus and other farms burgeoned, so the threat from elephants was perceived as intensifying. A couple were killed by trains on the new railroad. In 1920 the farmers called in Major 'Jungle Man' Pretorius.

Pretorius is the hinge between the Addo and the Knysna elephants: he was called in to hunt both groups, bringing both to the edge of extinction, and he wrote about them both. His memoir, *Jungle Man*, is a repellently self-serving work, ranging across an extraordinary and violent career – not least of all as scout to Jan Christian Smuts during his East African campaign in the First World War. Smuts writes the foreword to *Jungle Man*, portraying Pretorius as a man 'of reckless daring and hair-breadth escapes', yet 'gentle, quiet, [and] unassuming'. The next statement can be read in more than one way: 'His very person seemed to be a camouflage.' If Pretorius was a superb military scout among men, he was the 'supreme scout amongst animals'. He possessed 'courage, coolness in facing up to danger, a singular combination of dash and caution, acute observation, and a sense of realities which is beyond analysis and amounts to instinct or genius'.[9] Thus, well into the twentieth century the alleged mystique of the tough but humble hunter is perpetuated; indeed, so alluring is it to the modern hunting set that a new, luxurious edition of Pretorius's memoir has recently been issued.[10]

Its historical interest notwithstanding, *Jungle Man* conceals a cold addiction to violence beneath a style simplified to the verge of bland-ness. Among his wide-ranging adventures, he hunted elephants in the Zambezi Valley. He boasts: 'I shot scores of elephants during my stay there, chiefly with the object of obtaining ivory to barter for supplies and equipment . . . No more enticing hunting fields could be found on earth.' Among the enticing prey whose destruction he economically narrates is an elephant bull he shot, wounded and abandoned, having decided it 'not worth while trailing'. He accidentally found it dead three days later – expressing no compassion whatever for the agonies the animal must have suffered.[11] Such knowledge of elephant behaviour as he gleans is only in the wake, indeed in the service, of slaughter, so echoing his hunter-predecessors, who liked to think of themselves as disproving established myths: 'Here is a case in point showing the foolishness of believing different, tough, dogmatic, hunting stories, such as the one to the effect that the elephant never lies down to sleep. I had shot over two hundred elephants before I observed that they sometimes do lie down to sleep.'[12]

The same cavalier blindness governs the chapter on his hunting in Addo, and the few misleading paragraphs devoted to his elephant encounter in the Knysna forests. He portrays himself as modestly seeking peace and solitude in Natal when he is called upon to deal with the Addo animals, 'a bunch of rogue elephants that had taken a certain toll of life and more of property'. (There is the misnomer 'rogue' again, now applied to a whole population – a disparagement that is a necessary prelude to genocide.) In common with many of the non-fiction texts already encountered, Pretorius couches the call in quasi-fictional dialogue, first with one Major Sillick who claims it is 'impossible to exterminate the beasts', living as they do in a 'hunter's hell' of impenetrable thicket. Moreover, they are 'hardly worth shoot-ing as far as ivory [is] concerned'.[13] In the guise of saving the Sundays River Valley farmers, then, Pretorius takes on what amounts to an egotistical challenge. Despite ferocious difficulties, he sticks to his task for a year, idiosyncratically inventing new methods involving, among other tactics, ladders and a thorn-proof leather suit. Armed with a .475 Jeffries double-barrelled rifle – 'a treasure of a gun' – he killed around 120 elephants in 11 months.

What is revealing is the language of justification. 'The place carried a kind of hoodoo,' he claims. 'The num-num bush . . . is a hideous mess of long and most diabolical thorns.' The elephants, too, are associated with the devilish and evil; when they charge, doubtless terrified by gunfire and noise, they 'came on, squealing like a million scorched fiends'. As for the occasional individual kill he relates, the familiar bland and emotionless details unfold. The postmortem is more important than the death itself:

The elephant spun round like a top – for he had been coming at full speed, and the moment the bullet struck him he was thrown a good two yards off his path – and then almost instantly dropped dead.

The next morning I told the natives to open the elephant's head, for I wanted to see how far the bullet had penetrated. I found that it had gone through the brain after entering the head at the trunk, and had then entered the vertebrae. The missile travelled along the vertebrae for about a foot and then branched off, for we found the bullet in the elephant's liver. The whole of the spine had been neatly cut in two for the length of the bullet's travel. It is difficult to appreciate the striking force of a .475 Jeffries rifle . . . worth every penny of the money, particularly to a man whose very life depends upon the accuracy of his gun.[14]

Damage is the trophy.

Pretorius is not wholly oblivious to the existence of an ethical debate, noting that he was 'severely criticised by the public' for his 'suicidal operations' – though he does not say whether he was being criticised for killing elephants or for being suicidal. In any event, he evinces not a quiver of compassion or remorse – not even for the orphaned baby elephants, which, as discussed in previous chapters, are usually a strong vector for sympathetic feeling. The orphans are, he allows, 'loveable beasts, and in the Addo I captured several', but they seem to evoke amusement rather than empathy. He entirely misunderstands the desperate attachment orphans will form to the very humans who killed their mothers; he gloats how they followed 'tamely as a dog' or 'as meekly as a lamb'.[15] He goes so far as to have elephant milk analysed, in order to obviate the usual rapid decline and death, though only so that he could sell them on to zoos and circuses. One, which was even named 'Addo', he sold to Boswell and his circus for 300 pounds.

In the end when it was, by a series of decisions that Pretorius does not detail, decided to cease the slaughter, he professes himself 'pleased that we had decided to leave a few of the herd – sixteen in fact'.[16] But he does not say why – a caginess about the emotions intrinsic to the professional hunt that remains to this day.

Precisely because the Addo elephants – largely tuskless and placid – have been so successful, so visually available and so unthreatening, they have spawned few literary treatments. What has been written is almost entirely scientific in nature, with a thin spume of genial touristic advertising language, and an occasional poem by a fond local. How different from Pretorius's account is the informative booklet compiled by Anna Whitehouse, long-time student of Addo's family lines and dynamics, and Pat Irwin, professor of Education at Rhodes University.[17] These researchers' admiration for their subject is not in doubt, but how different in register this scientific – almost sociological – outline of the kinship groups and genealogies of the Addo herd, with its diagrams of ear notches and tusk features. As a tourist you can, with a bit of luck and patience, use their guide to identify certain individuals – all named in convenient alphabetical groups, and begin to understand the complexities of the family dynamics unfolding just metres away.

By contrast, the mystique of the Knysna elephants has generated a slew of books, mostly non-fiction, what one might call 'minor search epics'. That the mystique is a recent imaginative invention is indicated by the sober factuality of a report by one E.J. Dommisse, district forest officer in Knysna, published in *African Wildlife* in 1951. The blunt sobriety of language (relieved only by a quiver of wry amusement at legends of elephants attacking hapless woodcutters) is doubtless a product of the author's position and métier, and the tenor of the publication. Dommisse tabulates the decline of elephant numbers from an estimated 400 in 1870 to 30–50 in 1902, plummeting to 7 after Pretorius's hunt (which Dommisse does not overtly condemn, and he uncritically repeats Pretorius's exaggeration of the elephants' size). These are the figures that have been circulated ever since. Dommisse notes the slow uptake of legislative protection, and the countervailing calls by some landowners to eliminate the elephants altogether after the damage they caused to a neighbouring blackwood (wattle) plantation. The only real indication that Dommisse is on the elephants' side is his comment that 'wiser' voices prevailed, and stronger moves towards protection were recommended (the nature of the wisdom remains unspecified). Dommisse's short article was amplified by a brief call by conservator A. Urry for a devoted 'expedition' to conduct a detailed and systematic tracking of now-elusive remaining animals. Urry did facilitate the Bernard Carp survey a year later, which found only four elephants. Unlike the restrained Dommisse, Carp condemned Pretorius's hunt as a 'massacre', which dealt 'a devastating blow from which the herd has never recovered'.[18]

Another expedition was eventually led by Nick Carter, as he related in his 1971 book, *The Elephants of Knysna* – our first 'search-epic'. The account is written novelistically, with some charm and that self-deprecating humour typical of the game-ranger memoir. Carter had indeed been a wildlife warden in Kenya and at Kruger National Park before isolating himself in Natal, attempting to be an 'artistic eccentric' and writing a novel, at which point he was approached by the Wildlife Society to survey the Knysna elephants: 'Having lived in almost monastic seclusion for the past two years I felt agreeably flattered at being "looked for", but kept a poker face, and conveyed to my trusting wife that one of most trying things a game warden has to endure is the positive barrage of pestering from learned bodies and wealthy people wanting him to head expeditions into the unknown.'[19]

Knysna is hardly the great unknown, but the elephants were elusive. Carter notes the conflicting attitudes expressed by locals, a few writing 'sympathetically', but in other accounts he could 'almost hear the drumming of fingertips and catch the glance turned to the nearest firearm'. He heads out, sceptical of the enterprise (previous attempts at surveys having failed spectacularly in the dense forests) and anticipates little gain in knowledge: 'no matter what myth and legend had brewed up over the decades these animals could only be elephants'.[20] Indeed, the questions to be answered seemed anticlimactically fundamental: How many were they? What sex were they? Why did they not breed? Carter is obliged to make much of very little, fluffing up his search step by step, including novel-like conversations with all and sundry. Nevertheless, the difficulty of actually spotting (and, importantly, photographing) the elephants means that even this level-headed, jovially acerbic pursuer succumbs just a little to the 'mystique' factor. He describes his first full sighting:

> He was a bull, and a young one as far as I could tell on that short inspection. He walked away from us leisurely and I had to run to keep up with him. I closed the distance slightly and then he suddenly stopped as though suspicious of something he had heard.
>
> Trying to control my breathing I sighted the camera and snapped the shutter. He stood absolutely still then turned a little towards me. Now it became my turn to stand very still. I could see his tusks and saw that the left one had a distinct upwards curve. They were not very big; about forty pounds of ivory per side. He was fat and in very good shape: I have seldom seen a plumper elephant.
>
> Koffiehoek mealies, I thought, as I pressed the shutter again hoping to get his tusks in the picture, but he was on the move and passed over the open track to surge into the forest darkness from which he had come. A crackle; more swishing, then he was gone like a dream.[21]

Despite the habitual focus on weight of ivory, this is a far cry from Pretorius's gloating. An elephant 'like a dream'.

Though Carter expresses little open feeling *for* the elephants in the course of the narrative, where he ends up is symptomatic, both of his own sympathies and of the socio-political stage at which South African conservation thinking had arrived. Admitting to a rather 'black and white' portrayal of both animals and humans and a somewhat 'fanatical' disdain of 'equivocations', Carter has 'come down firmly in favour of the "goodies", the elephants, instead of the all-too numerous human "baddies"' (these include, oddly, communists, who, he apparently believes, would condemn animals, which breathe valuable fresh air, occupy useful land and so 'must be destroyed, and space made for the spawning of yet more human beings'). More accurate, probably, is his perception that the bulk of 'apathetic' South Africans, including 'complacent' forestry officials, need to be awakened to the value of preserving the wildlife. And 'unless something is done to conserve the Knysna elephants they are doomed'. He asks the perennial question: 'Why, then, bother about a handful of animals who are rarely seen and are not even a distinct species? . . . Shoot the lot and have done with it – as I have heard several quite educated people say. Except that by doing so the world, and South Africa in particular, will be just that little poorer.'[22]

Poorer in what sense? Carter answers in quasi-scientific terms, 'coming to the conclusion that animals must also be included in the incredibly fine, delicate and all-embracing network of relationships on which the ultimate fate of our ecology hangs'. But this seems a somewhat inadequate argument for massive spending on fencing off 40 000 hectares of inaccessible forest for the sake of a handful of elephants, as Carter advocates. The ecological argument, notwithstanding its scientific repute, also functions here as a bolster against too overt an emotional engagement. Like so many in Carter's scientific-managerial field, he suffers 'an amusing cynicism, touched with diabolical truth . . . which makes one suspect one's own emotions'. Even as he claims to eschew a 'more equivocal grey' in his approach, he does equivocate between emotion and utility: 'If a young civilisation, such as South Africa's, cannot learn to live with, and treat compassionately, the other orders of life, less advanced in technology than itself, but perhaps, who knows?, possessing other as yet undiscovered virtues or advantages, then it is doomed to be no better than a race of destructive, and ultimately self-sterilised, ants.'[23] Nevertheless, countering the self-proclaimed eccentricity and touches of misanthropy, compassion emerges as the ultimate recourse and justification.

If scientific language and world views suppress that emotionalism, that of the novel does not – and Carter ends, somewhat amusingly, with a self-consciously novelistic strategy. He notes the turn-of-the-century predilection among novelists 'for telling in considerable detail at the end, exactly what happened, not only to the protagonists, but also to the supporting cast'. He proposes to revive this 'Victorian artifice', though in fact he does not do so at any length. But he does end, tellingly, with a deeply sympathetic speculation *about* the end of an elephant character, his favourite, Adam, or Aftand, the oldest of the group. Carter imagines Aftand's consciousness of imminent death:

> Where will he go then, and what will he do? . . . Has he noted such a haven in the back of his mind for the day when it will be needed, or will he follow his daily round close to the smells and noises of humanity? As pure speculation, I say that I think he will, and that he will ignore the approach of death until it is too close to be of importance. Then, perhaps in the comparative quiet of Harkerville forest, he will be caught, and will sway to and fro for a while in the shelter of some big tree before going down for the last time, never to rise again.
>
> When this happens, somewhere a bell will toll, even if only in the recesses of my mind.[24]

Drawing on Carter, among other sources, is probably the most comprehensive history of the elephants and the region, Margo Mackay's *The Knysna Elephants and Their Forest Home*, a pamphlet produced for the Wildlife Society in 1996, and republished in more lavish format in 2007. It has pretensions to neither literary heights nor comprehensiveness; nevertheless, at 138 pages it is more than a mere pamphlet. Between the conventional snatches of essential 'elephant facts' and some ecological information, couched in non-specialist manner, the bulk of the book relates the history of the management of the dwindling elephant population, its intersections with forestry, mining operations and advances in protective legislation. The language is serviceable if a little dour, leavened with lengthy quotations from books such as Carter's or Knysna residents' letters. It is a kind of poor man's coffee-table book, heavily illustrated with drawings and photographs, many in colour, albeit in small paperback format and on inferior paper. Though Mackay presents less of an obvious 'argument' than some other works, the range of areas of knowledge is also symptomatic of its time. It almost goes without saying, now, that sympathy for the plight of the elephant is the governing impulse. One way of gauging this lies in the portrayal of Pretorius and his nefarious hunt. An extraordinary character he may have been, according to Mackay, but rather than quoting his own few bald paragraphs, she takes a restrained pleasure in showing that his promises of both great tusks and captured elephants proved empty boasts, and in quoting an eyewitness account of the hunt, which shows how brutal and inefficient it had really been. It is, she writes, 'part of a shameful history', and she pays tribute to the 'bravery' of the elephants.[25]

As do many such accounts, the book includes a foreword by a near-obligatory conservation luminary; in this case, the wilderness school and tracking expert Clive Walker:

> There are those who will say that their [the Knysna elephants'] passing will make no difference to the conservation of the African Elephant. They miss the point. The long-term survival of elephant in many, if not most areas in Africa, will ultimately depend upon the co-operation and goodwill of the people who live alongside them. We live in a world where man has stretched out his hand to touch the stars, where he has left his mark upon the dark world of the ocean floor, and where the most inhospitable parts of the earth hold no fears for him. Happily, the pages of this book prove that man does still care, that we are not limited by self-interest alone; that we have the vision to pass this world on to the elephants and to the care of our children in a better condition than we found it . . . The elephant embodies wild Africa as never before.[26]

That last sentence has become so often repeated as to be a banality, if not downright false, a kind of empty signifier for a construct long reduced to a simulacrum of itself. Walker reiterates exactly the same sentence at the end of his memoir, *Dear Elephant, Sir* (1992). In that volume, the respectful, epistolary honorific is amplified in an opening 'letter', reproduced in handwriting for greater visual impact and, one supposes, an air of authenticity. 'I write to you with a feeling of deep guilt and shame,' Walker addresses the elephant:

> In my youth I sought to kill your kind in some misguided belief that this brought me recognition in my world of intellect . . . We have written volumes down the ages about your greatness, and yet we seek to render you a mountain of rotting flesh with blood-filled eyes in the name of science and progress . . . And so, dear Elephant, Sir, I apologise for our indifference and my past pursuits, and hope that you will understand

that I am as guilty as the rest of my kind, for it seems we are jostling ourselves to death in our search for . . . what?

Your devoted friend,

Clive Walker[27]

In his own career, Walker exemplifies a whole era's shift from slaughter to conservation, at least within one portion of the human population. It is not to doubt Walker's dedication to point out the problems with this particular technique. It is charming – if not slightly childlike – to address the elephant as another person, but it is delusory to think the elephant will understand human behaviour, and it is a little unfairly manipulative to use melodramatic gore to lambaste science, which is not the primary source of slaughter. The letter is, of course, really addressed, can only *be* addressed, to other humans, summonsing imaginative empathies.

As it happens, in *Dear Elephant, Sir* Walker barely mentions the Knysna elephants, apart from opining that they are probably doomed.

Almost certainly the best known of the non-fiction accounts of the Knysna elephants is the rather cleverly titled *Elephantoms* – best known because its author, Lyall Watson, was already widely published and read. His sweeping assault on the limits of conventional science, *Supernature*, had garnered something of a cult following, as well as attracting a good deal of scepticism. Watson was unquestionably brilliant, entering the University of the Witwatersrand at 15 and gaining several doctorates in Biology and Ethology, including one under the supervision of Desmond Morris, himself an indefatigable populariser of the biosciences and animal behavioural studies. In valorising such non-scientific notions as intuition and varieties of perception outside the empirically demonstrable, courting 'ESP' and the indefinably spiritual, Watson laid himself open to charges of absurdity and credulity. The preternatural mystique of elephants in general, and of the Knysna elephants in particular, seemed tailor-made for Watson.

Elephantoms is a canny mix: part memoir, part fiction, part popular biology, part quasi-spiritual speculation. It is eminently readable, ranging freely and knowledgeably across South African history and palaeontology, dipping into numerous landscapes and encounters with eminent men such as Nico Tinbergen, Desmond Morris and Raymond Dart – almost always thinkers on the fringes of the conventional. Watson claims that as a youngster roaming in imitation of a *strandloper* on the southern Cape coast, he encountered a Bushman, a kind of avatar of ancient teachings, in conjunction with a solitary 'white elephant' (this was written at a time when the received wisdom was that only one Knysna elephant remained).[28] The Bushman is named !Kamma, meaning, apparently, 'Dream' – this is suspiciously close to Wilhelm Bleek's //Kabbo, and Watson does refer to the Bleek archive. !Kamma seems ageless, having met and all but reincarnated in, decades later, another teacherly elephant-tracker, a latter-day woodcutter/forest-dweller who bears rather strong resemblances to Saul Bernard in Dalene Matthee's novel. Watson's story stretches both coincidence and suggestions of preternatural communication to improbable ends, culminating in his witnessing the white elephant apparently communing from a clifftop with a rare blue whale in the ocean below: 'The Matriarch was here for the whale! The largest animal in the ocean and the largest living land animal were no more than a hundred yards apart, and I was convinced that they were communicating. In infrasound, in concert . . . these rare and lovely great ladies were commiserating.'[29]

Blue whales are very occasionally seen off South Africa's coast, though southern right whales are far more common, breeding close in-shore, and with well-attested communication systems. Evidently, however, it is the rarity factor that has drawn Watson to the blue whale – rarity as an emotive vector, a vector for a kind of pre-emptive nostalgia, and thus a warning of a future denuded of animals.

Though any kind of elephant-whale communication has absolutely no observational evidence to support it, it gathers an aura of oblique possibility in the way Watson draws on the researches of Katy Payne. Payne helped to develop techniques of recording infrasonic communications among southern right whales, technology she then adapted to listening to subsonic elephant rumbles.[30] Of course, other kinds of symbolic connections have been made between elephants and whales, as each the largest mammal in their respective realms – gentle, communal, massively mysterious and threatened alike by human hunters seeking luxury substances.[31] We might have less reason to doubt Watson's claim to have picked up elephant presences by his own heightened sensorium, through all-but-subconscious vibrational and olfactory signals. Watson has much to say about the subtle sensitivities of Jacobson's organ, about which he wrote an additional complete book. Both areas of communication are well-enough attested, even if meanings remain largely obscure.

If at points Watson's narrative stretches credulity to breaking point, perhaps we can shift our generic expectations and accept some things as suggestive fictions, as we would in young adult fantasies. Although Watson admits to courting 'biological heresy', some facets of the text are self-evidently factual and acceptable enough.[32] Watson provides plenty of the usual information about elephant life and physiology, writing as if his readers are entirely ignorant of even the most basic features. He does so, nevertheless, with a verve and a sense of the marvellous that makes even those basics feel like a mystery revealed. This feeds readily into Watson's evocation of the mythic (the Bushman, for example) and the legendary (including the East) – a shift that is contrived at times.

However, it is less important for my purpose to assess what is strictly factual or invented in all this than it is to explore the ethical stance that governs it, and how it is filtered through generic expectations. Watson's respect, essential understanding and compassion towards elephants is indisputable. He is, for example, scathing about Pretorius. He quotes with relish the Eastern Cape resident John Pringle, who met Pretorius and remembered him as an unsmiling 'funny bugger' who could only express himself through the rifle, whose black leather-clad approach was 'creepy', driven by pride and unnecessarily dangerous. By persecuting and killing all but a handful of the Addo herd, he essentially 'created the most dangerous elephants in the world'.[33] Thirty years later, Watson avers, the scars left by Pretorius could still be felt: he claims to have observed a young bull paying homage to the bones of the erstwhile victims.[34]

Regarding Pretorius's egregious excess in Knysna, Watson is equally disparaging. Pretorius not only exceeded his mandate, becoming less hunter than 'executioner' and 'butcher', but he subsequently also lied about his exploits. Watson cites other eyewitness accounts of Pretorius's Knysna hunt, showing how his claims of clean and steel-nerved kills are false, the reality being much more messy, and how he exaggerated the size of the elephant he allegedly measured on the site. Watson tries to cut Pretorius such slack as he can, but there is an audible note of regret in the opening sentence of the following judgement:

> No one shot Philip Jacobus Pretorius. He died aged sixty-two in 1945, a decade before I knew he even existed. He was a child of his time, as I am of mine. Things looked different then, but it is hard to come to terms with a man who had so little affinity for life that he chose to deal in death. And hard to forgive a man who can have himself photographed sitting on top of a heap of dead elephants looking pleased with himself and referring to the corpses as 'Dumbos'.[35]

By contrast, Watson's attitude is profoundly empathetic. Crucially, this stance derives in part from sensory contact with a particular individual – a captive elephant named Delilah at Johannesburg Zoo, where Watson worked for a time: 'She was four years younger than I, a teenager, born in the bush, but having lived most of her life in Johannesburg. She was an orphan, the survivor of a massacre, but despite this background she was one of the sunniest, most consistently good-tempered individuals I have ever met. She was also truly beautiful, with long, thick eyelashes. And I was particularly fond of her trunk.'[36]

Purists will object to the shade of anthropomorphism here, but Watson has no compunction about pushing this a little further:

> I cupped the tip of her trunk in my hand and gently blew into it.
> The result was extraordinary. She entwined my whole arm in her trunk, held it there as she breathed deeply several times, and then put the tip of her trunk in her mouth and sighed. I came a little closer and let her explore my face and neck freely until I could hear a soft growl of pure delight – the elephant equivalent of purring.
> It was love at first sight.[37]

Here, not only are somatic signs interpreted as emotionally cogent, but they can be further interpreted in terms of other species, in this case the more familiar cat. From this point of empathetic contact and mutual understanding, Watson is bold (or unwise) enough to push the materially credible to the edge of the fanciful – in one instance regarding the distribution of skin flakes, which

> elephants are constantly scraping away, losing wheelbarrow loads of dry skin flakes, some small enough to blow away, carrying with them all the olfactory and genetic information necessary to identify, and even clone, a new individual . . . Africa in particular must be liberally dusted with molecules of 'elephantness', readily available for later sampling. The surprise is that more of it doesn't get around and work its strange magic on more people.[38]

It is a sweet thought – elephant-skin molecules partaking in the ecology of the land, as indeed they must – though it is not the most obvious such interconnection. In other ways, too, Watson recognises how elephants are an integral part of the 'stimulating' Eastern Cape landscape of 'staggering biodiversity', and more vaguely or spiritually, part of what 'Jan Smuts called "the ladder of the soul", an awesome interconnectedness of living things, each a small part of something far greater and infinitely surprising'.[39] Not only are elephants wondrous in themselves; they are really superior to humans: 'They would seem to be on their way out, but it is still possible to argue that they represent the most highly evolved form of life on the planet. Compared to them, we are primitive, hanging on to a stubborn, unspecialised five-fingered state, clever but destructive. They are models of refinement, nature's archangels, the oldest and largest land animals, touchstones to the imagination.'[40]

Watson is wise to insert a shade of qualification, as this tendentious argument depends on what criteria one selects as valuable, or how one defines 'refinement'. Interesting here is Watson's resort to metaphor, the religiously validating 'archangels', the not-quite-overt admission that it is in *our* imaginations that elephants exist as 'touchstones' – and it remains a moot point as to what evolutionary value our imaginations might ultimately proffer. It raises the crucial point about whether our compassion is dependent on the animal's capacity to exist as a symbol. For Watson the elephant symbolises 'might and memory, harmony and patience, power and compassion' – those very qualities we so often find lacking in ourselves. Like some of the poets discussed in the next chapter, Watson figures the elephants on an epic, even teleological scale, 'taking obvious delight in one another as they shuffle through our lives, keeping grave appointments at the other end of the world'.[41] Indeed, for all the injection of biological and ecological science, Watson can feel like a latter-day avatar of an almost medieval appeal to the symbolic and the mythic. The sense of mystery must be perpetually renewed.

Watson can write lucidly, accessibly and even charmingly. The same can hardly be said of the last book to trade on the legendary secrecy of the Knysna elephants, Gareth Patterson's *The Secret Elephants* (2009). With its casual style and bitty paragraphs, designed for a popular audience, it reads more as journalism than science, travelogue or story. It does bear some resemblance to the science memoirs examined earlier, not so much the southern African examples (neither Lawrence Anthony nor Caitlin O'Connell are mentioned), as the established canon of East African accounts by Joyce Poole, the Douglas-Hamiltons and Cynthia Moss. Both Pretorius's memoir and Matthee's novel *Circles in a Forest* are cited as influences.

Patterson is better known for his lion studies under George Adamson in Kenya, and had no special qualification to study elephants. Indeed, his justifications take on a particularly esoteric and melodramatic hue. The narration as a whole is framed, in a manner transposed from some fictions, by the disappearance into the Diepwalle forests of a JetRanger helicopter in 1999. In the opening chapter, Patterson offers to help in the search by the occultic method of dangling a pendulum over a map. A semi-circular movement over a certain spot in Diepwalle apparently indicates death. The helicopter is not immediately found and, because the spot is allegedly (on little real evidence) the stamping ground of 'the Matriarch' – alleged at the time to be the last remaining Knysna elephant – Patterson indulges in pure speculation that the helicopter has been buried under branches by death-sensitive elephants. In support, Patterson cites other writers' anecdotes of elephants burying their own and some humans under branches. But a helicopter? Patterson goes on to explain his interest in (to cite the book's subtitle) the 'rediscovery of the world's most southerly elephants' in terms of inexplicable unsettled feelings, coincidences and dreams.

The crashed helicopter *is* eventually found, by chance, in 2006, an event that closes the book. Not far away, the bones of an elephant are found, age unknown, though Patterson hints at some sort of mystic conjunction, something 'very symbolic'.[42] In certain ways, then, Patterson's strategy is not to dispel the mystery, but to amplify it.

At odds with this overt programme, the body of the narrative is concerned with Patterson's efforts to determine how many elephants there really are, by walking 'thousands of kilometres over six years' through the Knysna forests, gathering fleeting photographs, and by sending scats to the United States for DNA analysis.[43] Though in the end the results appear to suggest that at least five individuals exist, a blur of the inconclusive is maintained.[44] This is captured in a number of the chapter headings: 'If Silence Could Speak', 'The Forest of Secret Voices', 'Mingled Destinies', 'The Secret Place of the Elephants' and 'The Soul's Place'. Whatever the biological realities and the routine historical facts about the woodcutters, Pretorius, the failed introduction of Kruger elephants, and so on (to the well-known lineaments of which Patterson adds little) it seems that the mystery itself is as crucial to our feeling for elephants as is knowledge.

Whatever its literary (and even scientific) failings, *The Secret Elephants* is a book symptomatic of its times, and one can hardly demur from its closing appeal:

> Having damaged this earth, having tainted the water, poisoned the air, and changed the climate, the time has now come to protect at all costs all the last remaining wild places in the world. If we do not do this, those who come after us will be spiritually and environmentally impoverished, with mystery gone and secret places no more than a memory. To me, the remarkable existence today of the Secret Elephants represents hope – even for ourselves.[45]

It feels fitting to end this chapter with the most eco-sensitive of all elephant-centred novels, and, within South Africa, one of the most popular and often prescribed in schools: Matthee's *Circles in a Forest*. Originally published in Afrikaans as *Kringe in 'n Bos*, the novel is one of three that Matthee set in the Knysna area. Elephants also inhabit the other two, *Fiela's Child* and *Dream Forest*. The latter's opening paragraph begins: 'As she walked through the forest she [protagonist Karoliena Kapp] suddenly realised that there was an elephant watching her from the thicket. Somewhere above her head in the forest canopy a lourie was gurgling and hissing to warn the elephant that there was a human walking along the sledpath.'[46] However, elephants' presence, if subtly pervasive, is less central here than in *Circles in a Forest*. In some ways the plot of this beautiful yet gritty novel echoes the 'elephant-hunter duel' motif central to so many other elephant pulp novels, but carries the contest onto a superior level.

In Knysna around the turn of the twentieth century, hardy but inbred woodcutters coexisted with substantial numbers of forest elephants. Both are now essentially extinct, and *Circles* is suffused with nostalgia for their more authentic, less commercialised era. The central character, Saul Barnard, sees more clearly than his fellow forest-dwellers the rapid changes induced by ivory hunters, government officialdom and commercial timber merchants on haplessly exploited woodcutters, including his own father. In an attempt to come to terms with those changes, Saul even works for one of those coastal entrepreneurs, and later joins gold panners who invade the forests, half-despairingly appointing himself protector of the elephants and the forest. Through Saul, Matthee powerfully, and with appropriately straightforward diction and conceptualisation, expresses a vision of the necessary symbiosis of nature and humanity, a symbiosis visibly on the verge of collapse. Saul tries to tell his brother Jozef: 'the Forest is dying. Everywhere the sores are standing out like giant pock-marks and they do not heal again! . . . Can't you see that we are killing the Forest and that the Forest is killing us?'[47]

The metaphor of the forest-as-body surfaces repeatedly in the novel: in one important passage, a great kalandar tree, victim of the inexorable axes, is intensely humanised. Conversely, Saul is himself, in his holistic concern for the forest's ecosystem, derisively seen by his fellows as becoming like it: 'Seems to me your Saul's getting bark on his bones now!' jeers his uncle Arno.[48] Matthee wisely refrains from painting even the 'natural', forest-wise woodcutters as living in some kind of pre-commercial idyll: the forest is a dangerous, superstitiously haunted place, and the danger is exemplified by the canny, mysterious, awe-inspiring elephants. The people are also intrinsically damaging, albeit initially on an insignificant scale. The woodcutters' short-sightedness becomes obvious, however, as commerce begins to stimulate a greater scale of irreversible damage; only then can Saul perceive, as the rest of his family cannot, that humans are 'a lot of worms making the apple go rotten from the core'.[49] Saul's realisation is connected with and analogous to his discovery that a local myth that the blue duiker's gall is located in its head, is untrue. Through a crude 'scientific' experiment, essentially, Saul becomes a myth destroyer. This knowledge, however, is not complicit with uncaring exploitation.

Appropriately for her character, Matthee does not express Saul's conception of an 'ecosystem' in scientific terminology, and retains a more mystical element in his relationship with the forest. She does not, cannily, discount the possibility that it might be essentially an *imagined* relationship. This is most true of Saul's bond with the most prominent elephant in the forest, Old Foot. Early in his life, Saul has an encounter with Old Foot in which the terrifying elder of the forest herd spares him from the usual trampling:

> Since that first day when Old Foot stood in the open, he [Saul] had dreamed up an imaginary bond between him and the elephant. When he became a man and his boyhood dreams began to blur, a feeling of respect, of an intense awareness of the old forest patriarch started taking the place of dreams. No, it was more. There was something between him and Old Foot that the most sober thinking could not always staunch. No woodcutter or his child or any other inhabitant of the forest ever underestimated the danger lurking in a bigfoot; hatred built up over ages, lurks within them, hatred for man that carries the hot-lead through their bark-like hides to fester there until pain makes them want to tear the world apart and life slowly passes out of them and chases them down into the deeper kloofs to die in humiliation.[50]

That torrential, empathetic imagining of elephant death foreshadows Saul's later dilemma. Precisely for his ecological defence of the forest's integrity, Saul is spurned by his family – just as Old Foot is accused of killing his brother's child. Matthee links the two: '*they* declared him a traitor in this forest, just as they had declared Old Foot a murderer'.[51] When Saul, aboard a ship and about to leave his homeland in disgust and for good, hears that Old Foot is being hunted down by a disreput-able ivory hunter, Fred Terblans (an echo of Pretorius, one imagines), he makes the awful decision to shoot Old Foot himself, in order to shield the elephant from the indignity of mere commercial exploita-tion: 'Fred Terblans . . . must not find the tusks'.[52] Much later, when he learns that his own brother Jozef is on the elephant's trail, he even comes to contemplate shooting his brother in order to save Old Foot: it comes down, in effect, to a choice of siblings. Matthee avoids the melo-drama of too gauche a denouement: Old Foot is killed by a couple of anonymous gold-diggers, to Saul's grief: 'O God was there ever a more beautiful creature made by thy will? Was there ever a more beautiful creature destroyed by the will of man? Tears stream down his face and blur his vision.'[53]

This final appeal to a certain aesthetic and a biblical rhetoric is underpinned throughout the novel by hints of a subtler, quasi-mystical, inexplicable sense of compatibility, the precise nature of which never-theless remains elusive:

There are times when he gets the feeling, however, that between man and the Forest lies but a thin veil. Like a cobweb. Like an invisible mist through which you would be able to see only if you could open your eyes wide enough. But the next moment he knows it is only a dream. The Forest is like someone you can hear talking, but whose language you cannot understand. You hear him, you see him, you touch him, you see the signs he makes, but you do not know what he says . . . for the Forest, there is no translator.[54]

How often in this volume the issue of *translation* has surfaced – a mat-ter not so much of matching the meanings of one language to those of another, but of finding words that might translate or mediate the material somatic realities of one species or realm (elephant or 'Nature') into somatic responses in the human. For example, Saul's tears, and perhaps an analogous response in the reader of Saul's (Matthee's) story. Empathy, leading to compassion, is a matter, then, of both translation and imagination. This may be less a matter of fully *explaining* feelings within another species – the hopeless quest of the scientific method – than of accepting a sufficient level of commonality, while content to leave a certain amount to mystery, to the unknown. This seems to be precisely what Saul does. A certain unknowability, one might provocatively suggest, is actually essential to compassion, rather than debilitating.

Circles in a Forest is the most 'ecological' of all the fictions explored here, for several reasons. Firstly, it embodies a vision of the workings of nature based on a the notion of a web of integrally cross-influencing (not necessarily friendly) relationships. Secondly, the novel's emplotment and characterisation are fully integrated with the ecological ideas it presents: the relationships between Saul, Old Foot and the surrounding forest pervade the novel. (This is in marked contrast to, for example, Wilbur Smith's *Elephant Song*, explored in chapter 4.) Thirdly, the profundity of Matthee's treatment lies in the recognition that the imagination has a crucial role to play in our relations with the natural world. On the one hand, the operation of our imaginations structures how we deal with other sentient beings and the land we live on; on the other hand, the limitations of our imaginations endow the natural world with certain mysteries, which themselves become integral to our consciousness. *Circles in a Forest* demonstrates mysteriousness translated at times into fear, at others into a reverence, which prevents even the naming of elephants as 'elephants' – a kind of linguistic awe, a primordial taboo. The reverential mystery is contrasted starkly with the exploitative mentality of commerce, which cares neither for mystery nor aesthetically for the thing-in-itself – Old Foot standing with unimpeachable dignity in a clearing. Finally, the novel is ecological also in the sense of embodying a powerful ethical stance against human rapacity. It remains unromantically ethical, moreover, despite the clear hostility to humanity of certain aspects of the natural world. This non-idyllic, dialogical and in some ways unfathomable ethic contains the central paradox of human compassion for the ineffably other – such as the elephant.

Chapter 9

The Elephant Is Unhappy:
Poetry as compassion

I doubt that there exists anywhere a more compactly metaphorical poem describing an elephant than one found in the Bleek-Lloyd Archive. Although it was translated from the Bushman /Xam dialect by Wilhelm Bleek in Cape Town in the 1870s, it may be the most ancient southern African elephant poem we possess:

> Tall-topped acacia, you, full of branches,
> Ebony-tree with the big spreading leaves.[1]

As was seen in the first chapter of this volume, elephants, acacia trees and the Bushmen were together consumed by a wave of hunters, commandos and acquisitive settler-farmers and their stock. Of all the non-human wild creatures whose decimation paralleled that of the Bushmen, none is more poignant, ironic or emotive in its story than the elephant. And no genre is more poignant, more attuned to emotional dimensions, than poetry.

It will hardly be surprising, given the all-too-often gruesome history explored in foregoing chapters, that more recent poems about elephants are dominated by an elegiac tone. A number of poems by southern Africans exhibit the intense confluence of the debates around modern ecological managerialism, racially inflected land use, postcolonial political identities, animal and landscape aesthetics and the validity of anthropomorphic portrayals of animal subjectivity. Hence, the discussion in this chapter will serve to bring to a point strands of argument running throughout this book, as well as to suggest that poetry, as a form, holds a special place and role in expressing empathy and compassion.

On the whole the poems I examine here (there are dozens that I omit) do not make theoretical claims as interventions into these debates. Poems tend towards suggestion rather than philosophical claim – they are *poetry* precisely because they 'cannot be formalised into a set of precepts'.[2] Rather, they fulfil the vital role of what Jonathan Bate calls 'ecopoesis': to 'engage *imaginatively* with the non-human' and so enhance our sense of dwelling within ecosystems.[3] Not only does such poetry elude a straightforward didacticism – of the kinds we have seen as central to scientific language, and even to some aspects of prose narratives – it offers a qualitatively different access to emotional engagement.

There are, of course, a plethora of poems in more popular forums, from nineteenth-century pulp magazines to today's Internet, which do not carry much aesthetic or suggestive complexity or weight, and may be obvious or clichéd, didactic or jokey. While such poems appeal to a wide public, and possibly affect popular attitudes in subtle ways, I will risk a certain elitism by focusing rather on a handful of more dense and conceptually knotty poems. I will touch on just one published example of a more 'popular' form. This is my Zimbabwean contemporary and fellow graduate Gary Albyn's book *Manzovo* (2008). Here, epic poem meets plush coffee-table format: large-print quatrains, one to a page, face vivid and almost photo-accurate paintings by the well-known wildlife artist Craig Bone. 'Manzovo', Albyn explains, is the local-dialect, correct Shona name for what became known as Mazoe (now Mazowe), meaning 'place of the elephants'. Starting from this area, he envisages an epic elephant journey that swings north through Mana Pools on the Zambezi River, past Victoria Falls, southward across 'Matabele' country and east into Gonarezhou, another 'place of the elephants'. Set in the 1960s when, according to Albyn, such a migration could have been achieved without too much human interference, the journey is also meant to evoke something primordially 'African'. As a quote on the book's jacket has it: 'Subtle and compelling, the story weaves in the arcane rhythm that pounds like a tribal drum deep in Africa's chest.' This nativist assertion lies oddly alongside the venerable Western four-line stanza ballad form, with its consistent abcb rhyme scheme, which one might find at times clumsy or forced. The poetry wavers between necessary narrative directions, quasi-scientific explanations of, for example, infrasonic communication and elephants' impact on vegetation, or bright scene setting. With a certain predictability, the elephants are dramatically associated with other giants: baobab trees, Victoria Falls (amusingly, they have a little rub against the statue of David Livingstone) and the great leaders of the Matabele, Mzilikazi and Lobengula. Inevitably, there is a culling scene (the first cull in what was then Wankie National Park occurred in 1965). There is a gesture towards elephant interiority and individuality – as in some of the children's stories, two of the migrating elephants are named Lesedi and Thandi and the latter's career is traced from birth to death. Some exemplary verses:

> Their urge to rove both far and wide
> Is testing the farmers' patience
> Crisp blond grass of the open plains
> Replaced by juicy temptations
> . . .
> With sensitive ears they clearly detect
> Unmistakable mortal pangs
> A distressing herd in a pincer move
> Is surrounded by culling gangs
> . . .
> Thandi has lost her battle with age
> Lesedi must now take the lead
> The matriarch's teeth are worn and flat
> She can no longer browse and feed.[4]

Whatever one might feel about the misfit between lyric verse and didacticism, Albyn touches accessibly on many of the current dilemmas and knowledge of elephant presence: human-settlement constraints on elephant migration, conservationists' culling strategies, subsonic communication, family dynamics, climatic conditions and so on. Albyn and Bone's passion for their subject is self-evident, and Albyn ends with a more sobering and generalised ecological appeal:

Our fragile blue island is withering away
We are rolling the dice on our chances
For each living system we greedily destroy
We collectively lose vital answers.[5]

Elephants here, as in a great deal of popularly disseminated environmental media, are seen as iconic linchpins in the battle to shift human attitudes towards more respectful treatment of our natural heritage as a whole.

Above all, perhaps, Albyn's *Manzovo*, as an artefact, is beautiful. Bone's paintings express an appreciation of elephants themselves as beautiful. Google 'beautiful elephants' and dozens of entries are listed. To pick out one apposite example: a poem with that very title begins with a softly romantic and thoroughly clichéd picture of 'rustling leaves' and 'twinkling starlight' as backdrop to evoking these 'amazing giants . . . moving silently, majestic and grand', with a plea to the public to don 'compassion's cloak' and *do* something. It is not great poetry but, as the comments that follow that post show, people do respond positively, and possibly go on to take some form of action.[6]

'Majestic' and 'grand' are descriptors we have seen applied to elephants from the earliest days of southern African literature, even among those hunters who went on to obliterate them. 'Beautiful' is much rarer, a generally more recent attribution. Evidently, concepts of beauty have shifted, at least for some. It is an important question: how and why are some animals perceived as beautiful and others ugly? How do such concepts of beauty affect the way those animals are actually treated? What role does a reconceptualisation of elephants as beautiful play in the exercise of compassionate action? After all, elephants are *not* conventionally beautiful – baggy, shambling, flapping, even comical beasts, with none of the self-evident grace of a cheetah or springbok. Yet today the adjective is regularly applied.

The question of animal beauty, while pervasive in public discourse, has until recently been 'rarely discussed' philosophically, and almost never in the southern African context.[7] Beauty scarcely appears as a subject in any of the standard texts on animal rights, in the most often cited studies of animal-human boundaries, or even in the extensive online 'Animal Studies Bibliography'.[8] Most older discussions have been in the realm of art, but the transition from appreciating the qualities of an animal painting to appreciating the real thing is a tricky one.[9] Glenn Parsons suggests that this neglect is partly due to the difficult entanglement of the 'aesthetic' with moral and ethical issues, but also that that entanglement is both unavoidable and necessary.[10] He points to the difficulty of relating 'superficial' or 'formal' beauty (line, shape, colour, proportion) to an 'inner' beauty based on more complex and hidden dimensions of animal life and capacity, as well as of 'fitness to function', which might be particularly applicable to elephants. Ned Hettinger argues on a 'fitness' platform that animal beauty *should* play a powerful role in wilderness preservation, whatever the predatory messiness and 'ugliness' of life in the wild.[11] There is clearly a strong case to be made in our context for the aesthetics of elephants, however conceived, playing a crucial role in making wildlife parks attractive, for example. This too is no simple management issue. The beauty of the individual animal has complex and slippery relations with broader conceptions of 'natural beauty' and landscape aesthetics; the two kinds of beauty may even find themselves at odds, as when elephants are culled in order to preserve a putatively 'natural' or 'balanced' ecology and landscape.

Elaine Scarry offers some useful general criteria. In her view, beauty does function to invoke fair and just behaviour in humans towards nature, to raise 'an urge to protect it, to act on its behalf'.[12] Elephants' studied calm, their earth-shifting bulk, their accretion of legends, their capacity to harbour mysteriousness in a way inconceivable in a mosquito, a lizard or even a lion, attracts an attentiveness and desire to do right by their inner worlds closely related to that invoked by more conventional beauties. Scarry outlines a number of other features that echo throughout the discussion below. Among these are, firstly, that the 'beautiful thing seems – is – incomparable, unprecedented'; this very uniqueness 'incite[s] the desire to bring new things into the world: infants, epics, sonnets'. Secondly, then, it 'requir[es] us to break new ground', while obliging us 'also to bridge back . . . to still earlier, even ancient, ground'. In its 'generous sensory availability' (a phrase just made for elephants!), the beautiful object urges a 'radical decentering' – its very difference brings about a 'nonself-interestedness', a ground for compassion. Thirdly, Scarry suggests, an appreciation of beauty, in its innate 'symmetry', redistributes our attention: it 'invites the search for something beyond itself, something larger or something of the same scale with which it needs to be brought into relation'. In short, 'beautiful things give rise to the notion of distribution, to a lifesaving reciprocity, to fairness not just in the sense of loveliness of aspect but in the sense of "a symmetry of everyone's relation to one another"'.[13] It evokes a movement from 'beauty to duty'. in Holmes Rolston III's phrase.[14] Clearly, these ideas are amplified by the recent reimagining of the elephant as complex, cultural, familial, even quasi-human. As this implies, the relationship between attributions of beauty to an animal and anthropomorphism is both unavoidable and complex.

Bate asks the fundamental question in his *The Song of the Earth*: 'What are poets for in our brave new millennium?' His answer: 'To remind the next few generations that it is we who have the power to determine whether the earth will sing or be silent'.[15] In a discussion of her poem 'The Moose', Bate writes that Elizabeth Bishop 'knows that we can only know nature by way of culture'; she knows that 'the ineffability of large mammals' can only be described by way of 'similes out of culture'. But in her wonder at 'the sheer physicality' of the natural, in her willingness to allow for the impenetrability of parts of the natural, she 'squares up to the Janus-like quality of the poet – singer of earth, exile from earth – and remains warily on guard as [s]he crisscrosses between culture and nature'.[16] In what follows I want firstly to explore how the selected poems negotiate this necessary culture/nature crisscrossing; secondly to examine the ethical implications of the congruence of notions of beauty and of anthropomorphic imagining; and thirdly to show how such imagining is dependent on certain instantiations of ambiguity, irony, even mysteriousness.

The development of both animal and landscape aesthetics in southern Africa, and in particular those associated with modern European-
orientated, conservation-minded literary works, may be seen by
comparison with two earlier poems: one indigenous, one settler. The
former is an anonymous traditional Hurutshe praise poem from northern South Africa:

> I'm the big one of the mother of trees,
> The big one eating trees,
> Picker of leaves,
> Big-grain-basket of the hyena's place,
> Worm with the big appetite,
> Digger of trees:
> Let me dig the shepherd's tree and the elandsboontjie.
> I'm the big one of the mother of trees.
> I'm the elephant, kin to mankind,
> Hence I regard mankind's ways with fear;
> And so, when I kill one, I bury him, like people do,
> And I stay unmarried, like people do,
> And I rub on medicine, like people do.
> I'm the big one of the mother of trees,
> Smasher of trees.[17]

Traditional African poetry, as explained in chapter 1 of this volume, is
less given to focused lyrics than to the symbolic, epithet-based spon-
taneity of the praise poem, but this piece, while exhibiting several features of conventional praise poems, lingers interestingly. It invokes a
metaphoric world view similar to that of the Bushmen, one in which
human and animal are intrinsically part of a single realm of consciousness, in which elephant and man are kin. Here, as the editor Jeff Opland
puts it, 'the poet presents the human race as the elephant's totem' – a
reversal of the usual flow of tribal identity, power and reverence –
even as the description embodies finely metaphorical observations of
elephant physiology and behaviour.[18] This kind of first-person imagining of an elephant's inner world is radically at odds with the second
poem, by South Africa's first white poet of any consequence, Thomas
Pringle.

When Pringle arrived with a rather hapless group of British settlers on the Cape Colony's easternmost frontier in 1820, successive swathes of land had been wrested from the resident Xhosa peoples, and warfare simmered continually. Just the year before, a tract of rough but potentially fertile country between the Great Fish and Keiskamma rivers, known then as the Neutral Ground, had been cleansed of Chief Ngqika's Xhosas in a manner that reminded Pringle of the Clearances in his native Scottish Highlands. The ground had not yet been colonised, however, and Xhosa raiding parties had burned the few mission stations. Pringle, gazing over the Neutral Ground, composes a poem entitled 'The Desolate Valley' – desolate because inhabited by no more than a couple of marginalised hunters, but nevertheless rather exuberantly populated by a resurgent wildlife, 'more than the eye may count'.[19] From the point of view of a momentarily quiescent hunter's 'wattled shieling', Pringle expostulates:

> How wildly beautiful it was to hear
> The elephant his shrill *réveillé* pealing,
> Like some far signal-trumpet on the ear!
> While the broad midnight moon was shining clear,
> How fearful to look forth upon the woods,
> And see those stately forest-kings appear,
> Emerging from their shadowy solitudes –
> As if that trump had woken Earth's old gigantic broods![20]

The register and vocabulary, drawn from the more popularised end of the romantic spectrum, is both inappropriate and revealing. The elephant's call is 'wildly beautiful', a characterisation that lies awkwardly against what Pringle earlier calls the 'waste' and 'desolation' of this wilderness. The sight of elephants is, despite their beauty, 'fearful', an almost magical emanation of shadows and solitudes, an atavistic product of a 'gigantic' primeval past. The beauty, evoked by distant sound rather than close sighting, seems to lie largely within the poet-speaker's own emotional response to a generalised thrill of wildness. There is no sense of a functioning independent natural ecosystem; rather, the trope is military, the elephants are an army, royal in stature, but presenting themselves in effect for violent destruction – which, of course, is what happened. Given the recent rededication of substantial swathes of this same territory to wildlife parks, hunting concessions and conservancies of various kinds, the poem feels laden with ironies, if not an inadvertent prescience. Today's aesthetic of conservation is both very different and a descendant of Pringle's display, and is arguably a somewhat artificial recreation of just such a mythic 'wild beauty'.

Subsequent poems are often predicated on growing perceptions of commonality between humans and elephants, but remain striking for the ways in which differences remain inscribed, almost inadvertently evidencing the discomfiture with which they negotiate the borderlands between interspecies subjectivity and exteriorised observation, between an apparent aversion to superficial beautification and an attraction to deeper identification – and between this identification and a residual guilt at their historically exterminatory culture.

Despite elephants being routinely described as 'beautiful' in popular discourse, the word occurs only once more in poems I have found, though with opposite ethical implications to Pringle's. Cape Town writer Mike Cope's Buddhist-orientated poem 'the inner school final knysna elephant tantra' gestures towards the sacralising power of beauty:

> animals including human
> sentient being beyond number
> weep at her passing . . .
> *free paths*
> *no fixed signs*
> *walk on real land.*[21]

These lines suggest a less superficial, non-visual conception of beauty, rather a matrix of longing, elegy, identification and authenticity.

If beauty is to move us towards a sense of responsibility and compassion, we might begin with an elephant *out of* its natural habitat: an 'encultured' elephant. It is one of the more wrenching ironies of human-elephant relations that our compassion has grown out of, and perhaps remains dependent on, captivity. Only in captivity has a fuller understanding of elephant individuality been possible. Only close up have humans been able to gaze into that ruby eye and sense the under-lying intelligence. Almost exclusively, it is in captive situations that ele-phants have been able themselves to trust and develop meaningfully reciprocal relationships with humans and that the full depth and com-plexity of elephant distress and trauma become evident. As we know all too well, however, captivity itself is most often far from compassionate, increasingly provoking the ire of animal-rights groups – witness the furores over the Tuli elephant orphans, and over the selling of elephants to Chinese zoos by Robert Mugabe in 2015–2016.[22] As I write, pressure is mounting to ban elephant-back riding for tourists as an essentially cruel practice, and in 2016, Botswana banned elephant-back riding completely.[23] As elephant habitat has been destroyed, the numbers of elephants in zoos, tourist parks and circuses has increased – but so has pressure to release them from conditions of excessive constraint.

In her poem 'The elephant is unhappy', Arja Salafranca describes a circus scene in its off-hours: defensively shuttered caravans, sparse grass, a 'dog chained to a table', with its tail between its legs. Similarly tethered, equally dispirited elephants attract onlookers, among them a mother holding a baby – an allusion to an ideal of family from which the captive elephants are now excluded. Depicting one female ele-phant, Salafranca compactly inscribes the common process of behavi-oural ascriptions:

An elephant blows sand onto herself,
burrowing a hole into the ground
as she sucks up earth, blows it,
using her trunk to enlarge the hole at her feet.
Her hide is wrinkled grey.
Beyond, cars stream along the wide,
sun-bleached road.
She is tethered by [the] foot,
held by a stake in the ground.
She moves, her ears flap,
her trunk grasps into the air,
she sways, the chain stretches, but just

before she reaches the end of the pull,
she stops, sways, knows she can't go any further.
Her trunk reaches out again,
her big body sways slightly,
a foot moves forward. The elephant is unhappy.[24]

The almost objective description of movement leads to an anthropomorphic attribution of mental states – knowing, unhappiness. Even in the observations, a feeling for the numbing distress of captivity, and perhaps a feminine sense of identification, is enacted in the repetitiousness of phrase and sound, the ponderousness of simple gestures, the poignancy of the self-undermining hole, the trunk 'grasp[ing]' and 'reach[ing] out again'. Salafranca refrains from overstating the identification, from sentimentalising, yet her indictment is clear in the very detachment of the poem's closing lines:

Silently we walk away. The ground is
squelchy underfoot, and the caravans
are inscrutable: you can't see through
their small lace-covered windows.

All too often, the poet suggests, we silently walk away from the distress of creatures, who at least potentially, have as many commonalities with us as they have differences. These last lines depict a fundamental closing off or fragmentation of community: the speaker's sheer recognition of the elephant's subjectivity starkly shows up the deliberate repression of communication by the circus's human denizens. Not only do humans fail to talk to each other enough; most humans do too little, or nothing, to combat abuse or to exert their compassion.

In 'One Elephant', Douglas Livingstone, one of South Africa's most substantial poets, characteristically packages his concern for the elephant in an initially comic guise, mediated by a third person. Livingstone's commitment to promoting the ecological health of his bioregion – indeed, of the planet – saturates his work. A microbiologist who devoted most of his life to monitoring and combating pollution off South Africa's coast, he wrote a number of poems about cruel, unnecessary, or just natural but saddening animal deaths. Characteristic of many of his poems is a self-ironising: a certain suspicion of the sentimental is balanced against a quixotic reaching out to other species, and an almost despairing disgust at human depredation:

> About that time arose one elephant
> from all the herd who stopped and cleared his throat
> and said: I can't for all the world at all
> remember what it was I had to say;
> I only know it was of great importance.
> He shook his ears; looked puzzled; slapped himself
> with gusto on the back and raised the dust;
> shifted capacious businessman's hindquarters
> in their ill-fitting pants; harrumphed and glared
> at the innocent thorn trees – his audience.[25]

While clearly founded on close observation of actual elephant behaviour, the comical humanisation of the elephant suggests that it is the poet himself who is being ironised, unable to find his true subject, trapped between conflicting possibilities and deeply conscious of nature's capacity to puzzle us. The irony becomes more evident, more forbiddingly serious, in the third stanza, in which the grumbling elephant's point of view is used to critique humanity more generally:

> Ah yes! There comes a time when one commits,
> despite oneself, the ultimate! And sick
> of selfish beasts, their egos and their stench,
> their cunning cruelty, destructivity,
> one turns, despite oneself, grimly to Man.

The stanza is fascinatingly ambiguous. In one sense, the elephant/ speaker realises his ultimate dependency on human will, with all its viciousness and failings. In a second possible reading, the elephant is the poet, philosophically divorced from his own species, sick of their selfishness, yet obliged in the end to turn to them for an audience: thorn trees – love of impersonal wilderness – will not suffice. On yet another level,

Livingstone is cleverly inverting a conventional attribution of bestial qualities by humans to animals (stench, unthinking savagery, even the elephants' own infamous ecological impact on 'innocent' thorn trees). Even more subtly, he deftly ironises the kinds of animal epithets used by humans to denigrate other humans. In these involutions, the poet is consciously at odds with himself – alerted to this fact, in a way, by the presence of elephants. The final stanza also involves the refraction of the elephantine consciousness through that of the imagined human listener:

Don't you agree? The thorn trees held their peace.
Injured; his tusks ached in their ivory
tower, he wheeled and shambled off to rejoin
the ambling herd, remembering to avoid
the smoky nests of heedless tingling ants.

There are also poetic gripes here, perhaps, about the irritation of ant-like critics in their 'ivory tower', and an obvious allusion to the dangers posed to the elephant's sheer existence by the ivory trade. In this imagining, then, as Marian Scholtmeijer expresses it: 'As soon as language begins to articulate the vital inner experience of animals, the suspicion arises that culture is learning more about itself than about animals per se.'[26] Nevertheless, these poems strongly imply that the nature-culture dualism requires transgressing. Poems endeavour to take full advantage of the possibilities of language to bridge and embody both anthropocentric and biocentric meanings, without falling into the traps either of self-serving sentimentality or of reductionist propaganda. It is to make a carefully qualified foray towards what Freya Mathews has called 'the ecological self', the 'nesting of a self' within wider 'self-realising' systems whereby 'the logical interaction of the identities of selves both with other selves within the parent system and with the parent system itself' entail 'an effective egalitarianism in respect of intrinsic value'.[27] The ironies and ambivalences, however, embody the intrinsic limitations of that hopeful egalitarianism at every turn.

A second poem of Livingstone's, 'To a Dead Elephant', is again shielded behind another persona, this time that of an indigenous

African man – signified by the praise-poem-like opening line and the Zulu exclamation *'Hau!'*. This speaker looks back on a relationship of near-kinship with an elephant who grew up alongside him:

> Old Python Nose with the wind-rolling ears:
> *Hau!* I remember it well when you came,
> thin, small, grey, twinkle-eyed, stumbling and lame,
> to me, a lone boy with none of the fears
> that stalked the elders. Friend, I had no tears
> for both our young losses: but all the same
> you robbed me of those sweet potatoes!
>   Fame
> walked with us, both motherless, those coupled years.[28]

Not unlike the speaker of the Hurutshe poem, or the protagonists of *A Boy and an Elephant*, this character finds touching commonality between elephant and human in the grief of parental loss. He looks back on a time before fear, to an almost Edenic state of innocence – albeit complicated by the age-old agricultural competition. The 'fame' that stalks them is ambiguous at best: almost certainly such renown lies behind the tragedy of this sonnet's sestet:

> But who can tame the trumpeter, the hill
> who stands invisible with bright old eyes,
> so slow, tree-bulky, dangerous and still?
> Why did you leave me to the elders' lies?
> Both men, we meet again, but not my will
> wrought this antheap with flies and hamstrung thighs.

The reference to eyes in both octave and sestet is interesting; it acknowledges individuated consciousness, the possibility of distinguishing an object of beauty and therefore to move towards non-self-interested ethical valuation. Livingstone's portrayal of the elephant – 'tree-bulky, dangerous' – is scarcely beautiful in any conventional sense, yet it contains the honesty of beauty, to which he opposes the horror of those elders' 'lies' and 'fears', which bring about the poem's shocking denouement. What are those lies? Presumably that no kinship with wild creatures is ultimately possible or necessary and that the elephant, being fearsome, is to be eliminated, and can be exploited for its ivory without moral consequence. That Livingstone places this implication in the mouth of a 'dissenting' African indigene is a move potentially fraught with problems of colonial-style (mis)representation. The poem nevertheless performs a postcolonial gesture, voicing an implicit critique of an entire invasive cultural 'white' mindset.

The internal contradictoriness of such a stance – attempting to critique at least part of one's own culture from within it – is also encapsulated in Noel Brettell's poem 'Elephant'. British-born but resident until his death in both Rhodesia and Zimbabwe, Brettell comes closest of our poets to depicting the elephant as an object of beauty, at first (as in the preceding poems) using metaphors drawn from the elephant's own natural environment, and so expressive of belonging within an ecosystem:

> Slowly the great head turned,
> And the late sunlight slept on massive flanks
> Like the still slabs of riven krantz,
> Immovable, and nonchalantly bearing
> The burden of the old enormous lies,
> The load of legendary centuries,
> The mighty turtle and the seas of milk
> On which the Old World swam;
> And slowly folded back the fluted ears
> Like pterodactyl wings drooping to roost.[29]

Brettell evokes the 'Old World' encrustations of myth – those 'lies' again – through which the elephant has inevitably been perceived, and counters them with the natural imageries of massive primordial rock and of dinosaur antiquity. So it has always been: literary conventions contesting with individuated experiences. The appeal to the primeval is tinged with longing for a slower, more restful, more authentic living, for a more self-confident age imbued with the stillness of the 'immovable'. This longing becomes more obvious in the second part:

> Slowly the great limbs moved:
> The monstrous pistons in the wrinkled sheath,
> Unflurried and unhesitating, lift

The huge façade across the afternoon:
Like a great engine, headed north,
With the deliberation of the six-foot wheels
Slides from the vaulted terminus
Down miles of metal through a continent.

To the white 'Rhodesian,' the phrases 'going north' and 'through a continent' cannot fail to evoke the Great North Road and the Cape-to-Cairo ambition of Cecil John Rhodes, the colonial tycoon and politician after whom Rhodesia was named (and whose stature is slyly evoked too in the first line of the next section, cited below). The description now of the elephant's bulk through metaphors of inexorable mechanical commerce – piston-driven parodies of the old pachydermous migrations – might read as inversely recuperative of the language of machines, but the detrimental ecological consequences for the elephant of such actual machines are obvious. Brettell nevertheless idealises the animal as 'invulnerable,' perpetuating another myth, which is arguably as wistfully hopeful as it is ironic:

Behemoth, baron, lord,
In trigger-fingered world, one creature left unscathed;
Away from us, over the burnt earth, under the prostrate branches,
Casually stripping the green crown from a tree,
Going oblivious, the invulnerable beast.

Another short poem, by the Eastern Cape poet Chris Mann, also treats the presence and effect of the legendary, specifically in the colonial context. In many ways, past and present, the elephant symbolises the mass, the power, the mystery of 'Africa' as conceived by white colonials. In 'The Graveyard of the Elephants', Mann invokes the tale told by 'old time hunters' that 'some place in Africa', in 'a valley strewn with bones', elephants 'would trumpet one last time / then slowly topple over among their kind'. Almost nothing exercises the imagination and the emotional engagement more than the belief that elephants have a preternatural awareness of the death of their own 'tribe' uncannily similar to the human. But now it is the old hunters and idealists who must 'lay their creaking structures down'.[30]

If the decrepit mental structures of old colonials' delusions about elephants, Africa and their own position in it have yet fully to be laid to rest, the idea of the graveyard has taken on new and chilling contexts – on the culling operations. It is a prospect lurking in the background of other poems, too, such as Damian Shaw's satirical squib about the 'white elephant' of lingering apartheid ideologues, slinking off to their own 'White Elephant Graveyards'.[31] John Mateer's poem 'The Elephant Graveyard' is a much fuller, decidedly non-satirical probing of the killing fields of culling operations. Mateer's poem is in five parts, which form something of a template for the concurrent tensions. The first part, 'Uncle', portrays a typical wildlife park scene, in which an American tourist expresses an ignorant and parochial sense of difference from elephants: 'They sure are weird.' The speaker, in contrast, sees one of the elephants as rather humanoid, resembling his uncle. This observation, though jocular, prepares us for a more compassionate response to the culling operation that takes place far from those tourists' eyes. The poem's second part, 'Culling', takes one into the elephants' point of view, outlining what they could hear of their impending doom. It then shifts into what they could not hear, or could not understand, from the anaesthetic drug to the fatal 'worming bullet'. One's feelings of horror at both parts are intensified by their jutaposition. In part three, the general scene is narrowed to one death, that of the matriarch. Here the poem resembles Salafranca's in its indirect, observational style, which nevertheless draws us inevitably into a sympathetic frame of mind:

> They were silent.
> They turned
> to face away from her, their
> trunks hanging limp.
> . . .
> A young cow remained.
> Occasionally with a foot she
> prodded her mother.[32]

There, again, is the appeal to the orphan to generate sympathy, despite the bald expression.

The fourth and fifth parts are also in tension. 'Vultures' records the plundering of the body by scavenging birds 'as haggard as the carcasses they have arrived to strip' – 'nature' in its unfeeling, cyclical brutality. 'Mourning', in contrast, shows elephants as themselves compassionate, grieving creatures, returning to the 'Place-of-the-Slaughter' (as if they themselves have named it, even mythologised it) to 'stand in the family's absence'. Here, then, is the central paradox, one that underlies this whole book, really: how compassionate creatures – ourselves, elephants – can have evolved within an apparently dispassionate nature. In Mateer's poem, as in other texts we have seen, the lamentable passing of that thoughtful, culture-bearing, psychologically sensitive individual elephant stands in symbolically for other wholesale ecocides. At the same time, compassionless nature, including compassionless humanity, continues, and the danger of extinction is far from over. It remains possible that elephants, like dodos and quaggas, may become mere fossil-like words.

Perhaps it is something like this that Harold Farmer means in his line: 'Poems about elephants are better than elephants'.[33] Poems appear, astoundingly and sadly, more likely to survive. Farmer, a Zimbabwean of settler stock, who has been unfairly neglected among southern African poets, has written two poems in which the role of the imagination and writing itself is foregrounded. In 'Dreaming of Elephants' he depicts their ecology and behaviour finely, even as he remythologises it. In the opening section, Farmer, perhaps parodying 'white flight' to South Africa, reverses the northward colonial thrust associated with Rhodes: herds of elephants move 'southward, always southward, as if it were there they were going to make their last stand'. The caution, even humility, lies in that 'as if'. In the second section he captures the essential dilemma of the 'animal other': we are caught between imagining their lives and the scientific or rationalist impulse to 'believe' only in material realities.

None of us have found it yet. The fabulous rumours,
a cemetery of tusks, a mighty stockade of bones,
how could we discount these things,
but how believe in them?

The elephants were like a people who could not perish
in the normal way, but must save up for it,
save themselves for that last expansive gesture.[34]

Farmer's diction has the weightiness of the elephants themselves,
headed for a destiny, which seems on the one hand, inevitable, tragic
and imposed, but on the other hand, heroic and supremely private.
In their sheer bulk, stateliness and silence, in their generous sensory
availability, elephants embody as no other creature apart from the
whale, perhaps, the quintessential mysteriousness of the other, even
as they are, Farmer writes, 'like a people'. In the poem, they are not
undestructive: stripping trees, eroding riverbanks, shoving 'crocodile
and impala, predator and prey, out of the way'. Like people, perhaps,
they too are imperial and imperious; it is 'no joke' to be in their path.
Finally, Farmer imagines a quietly apocalyptic end to the elephants'
journey, a 'fiesta of the dead,' a 'last gathering' sacrosanct in its privacy.
Imagining itself, the poem implies, is powerful and necessary. In their
enormous, epic progress, the elephants seem to be outside the normal
processes even of nature, inviting consideration of something beyond
themselves – another reason for them to be attractive to poets:

The destiny of elephants, their project,
is in their tyrannical mass, and they take it
secretly, as if this is something which occurred
only to the greatest. And perhaps it is.
Perhaps that is why it is hard to resist dreaming
about the fate of the elephants,
and braving that danger.[35]

Even as they march to their apparently unavoidable end, elephants preserve that essential mysteriousness which, Farmer seems to indicate, poetic
imagining must probe, but finally swerve humbly away from: the elephants
must be permitted to preserve their autonomous integrity. In that reticence, the poems enact the 'nonself-interestedness' proposed by Scarry.

Just what Farmer sees as the 'danger' of such imagining may emerge
more clearly from a final poem, Farmer's 'Absence of Elephants'.[36] The
danger is not so much in the imagining per se, but that the poems may

replace the elephants, that human representations might one day be all that remains of nature. In an essential way, in Farmer's view, the poems begin within the elephants, and the elephants' absence would leave only verbal husks. This poem, which begins sardonically, but works its way into a rich sadness, deserves quoting in full:

> Poems about elephants are better than elephants.
> Survival, what's that? The uprooting of trees, who cares?
> The slow, residual thickening of the forest floor
> with the accumulated detritus of elephants,
> the harried, panicky ants staring at logs in their path,
> the abrupt awakening of owls by crashing tusks,
> the collaboration upsetting the repose of the river,
> are only the outward and visible signs of the poem.
>
> The poem in the elephant is the breath of the elephant.
> Do elephants breathe? We never think of it like that,
> of the imperceptible suspiration of lesser beings.
> The elephants march through stanzas, cantos, epics.
> They dash their feet against the glossy, black boards
> of continental circuses. 'Ah!' the crowd cries.
> They take their place in the stone carvings of St Jerome,
> and breathe a soft undertone to the sighs of worshippers.
> The elephant is minister to the soul's grandeur.
>
> Poetry is no more than the breath of elephants.
> In the invisible decline of elephants, the shuddering heap
> from which I turn in embarrassment, the empty waterhole
> which has sent all the animals stamping through
> the cracked, black clay, the dry air falls like a mantle,
> a perfect fury, driving the beasts to madness.
> The absence of elephants is the death of my words.
> Ghostly and grey, in a mute caravan, roll clouds,
> caverns of darkness, the excrescences of the poem.

Farmer, closely echoing Scarry's notions of beauty, might also have been reading Rainer Maria Rilke: 'Yet in the alert, warm animal there lies the pain and burden of an enormous sadness. For it too feels the presence of what often overwhelms us: a memory, as if the element we keep pressing toward was once more intimate, more true, and our communion infinitely tender. Here all is distance; there it was breath.'[37]

In the Blakean imagery of his close, Farmer utters the most moving of all the poetic laments we have examined – and they are all, in their way, elegies to the real and all-too-possible demise of our most fascinating mammal. Above all, poetry is the medium of elegy. In 'Absence of Elephants' we have no better example, I think, of a poem that is so attuned to an ecology of imagining, in which material realities, the ethical implications of independent beauty, a non-impositional anthropomorphism and a humbly sanctifying artistry are so evidently integral. It is a resonant exemplification of one of Livingstone's mantras for a humanity becoming, like the elephants, increasingly embattled within its own ecological destructiveness: 'Symbiosis or death'.[38]

Afterword

This book outlines a heartening historical trajectory, from dispassionate slaughter of elephants to compassionate fellow feeling, even something approaching reverence. Rudi van Aarde, one of South Africa's premier elephant researchers and enthusiasts, writes: 'We have entered a time where animal welfare and compassionate conservation prevails.'[1] But I am not especially sanguine that, on a global scale, it *is* the dominant trajectory; it is certainly not the only one. A purely economic history might offer a very different picture. With the power of crime syndicates allied to corrupt governments, the porosity of international trade controls and a dearth of adequate funding for enforcement, the prospect seems dim, for elephants and for hundreds of other species subject to human delusion and depredation – the 'extinction market', as Vanda Felbab-Brown has called it.[2]

In this book I have asked one central question: what does a reading of our literatures tell us about our (southern Africans') relations with elephants? In a way, this has produced a history of the region from the elephants' perspective, albeit a patchy one. I have tried to see what certain discernible genres of writing – the travelogue, the hunting account, the novel, the memoir and the poem – can offer our 'reading' of elephant being. My choice of genres is not exhaustive – I have barely touched on the short story, for example, let alone the mass media of most recent times, such as coffee-table books, newspaper articles and related journalism, photographic essays, magazines and films, blogs and vlogs and hundreds of clips on YouTube. I have virtually ignored the voluminous scientific writing of recent times – a stylistic study in its own right. Nor has my coverage of each genre been comprehensive. The outline here would be given greater nuance by inclusion of further examples, especially at the popular end of the spectrum. One of the fascinating things has been to find how ostensibly distinct genres have in practice fed into one another in intricate ways – and further into science and actual management. Literature does not exist in a vacuum, nor does it (to recall Megan Biesele's phrase) constitute a simple mirror to society. Some human responses are founded on literary repetitions and symbolic preconceptions, not on empirical evidence or individual experience. Writings on elephants – often internally contradictory, purveying falsehoods and delusions as much as truths – do demonstrably affect actual behaviour towards elephants 'on the ground', whether lethal or redemptive.

A number of subthemes have emerged, all of which I think would reward more focused attention and theorisation in the southern African context: the eating of elephant meat, the role of landscape aesthetics, the impress of modes of masculinity, the precise infiltration of animal rights discourse, visual and typographical layouts across media, elephants in zoos and related captivities, the figure of the 'rogue', the shadowy presence of Indian elephant culture and – most important, perhaps – the southern African specifics of the ivory trade. And there are doubtless more.

I have also posed some subsidiary questions. Can we really know what precolonial attitudes towards elephants were, as they are refracted through multiple, arguably exploitative, modern forms? What impact did early zoological thinking have on the travelogue's portrayal of the elephant? What does the literature, both fictional and non-fictional, tell us about why men hunt elephants? How might we best educate our youth about the value of elephants, and of animals and ecosystems more generally? Can literature help to forge senses of community that breach the conceptual barriers between human and animal, between wildness and domesticity, between the fortress-conservation ethics governing game-ranger memoirs and the self-consciously emotional worlds evoked by our best poets? What is the place of conceptions of animal beauty in our representations of, and actions towards, the animal world?

I do not pretend to have done more than begin to explore these questions; I certainly cannot claim to have answered them. And the major practical question – what will happen to Africa's elephants? – can only be answered in time. Presently they are losing heavily in a one-sided war; they have few defences other than a relatively small number of actively caring (compassionate) people. Possibly there is a growing number of passively caring (sympathetic or empathetic) people, educated through imaginative or textual works. To the extent that 'disengaged caring' (pity, sympathy) can be translated into efficacious action, elephants will survive. There are glimmers of hope – in China's ban on ivory imports at the end of 2017, and in the substantial fall in price of ivory recently. It is no longer just ivory, or even pervasive conflict with human settlements; now the 'fake news' is that elephant-skin products are good for acne, another oriental or just cynically profiteering myth. Sometimes it appears that we are in an inexorable vortex of crazed consumption.

At the same time, efforts to save elephants feel both wonderful and increasingly desperate – such as Malawi's decision in mid-2017 to translocate 500 elephants to a safer zone; or the extraordinary task of providing one landmine-maimed elephant with a prosthetic foot. We can draw some comfort from the knowledge that in southern Africa elephants have been brought back from the brink of extinction before, and they may be brought back again. This will require extraordinary international cooperation, legislative robustness, more efficient crime fighting, wider education and financial resources. And better stories of compassion. In E.N. Anderson's view, rational science, governmental institutions and monetary pragmatics notwithstanding: 'People work on an emotional economy of love and hate, acceptance and rejection, help and hurt. That is not discussed in the ecology texts, but it is actually the wellspring of all our actions . . . Love, including aesthetic delight, is necessary for any broad strategy for environmental management.'[3] And so, perhaps, only love and compassion will do it.

Notes

Introduction

1 Eastwood and Eastwood, *Capturing the Spoor*, 94.
2 Nussbaum, *Compassion: Human and Animal*, 11.
3 Nussbaum, *Compassion: Human and Animal*, 9–10.
4 Snow, 'Compassion for Animals', 61–66.
5 Sunstein and Nussbaum, *Animal Rights*.
6 Armstrong, '*Moby Dick* and Compassion', 20.
7 For excellent discussions, see Daston and Mitman, *Thinking with Animals*.
8 Ahmed, *Cultural Politics of Emotion*, 13.
9 Mitman, 'Pachyderm Personalities'.
10 Rolston III, 'Ethical Responsibilities', 622.
11 On elephant iconographies globally, see Wylie, *Elephant*; Cruise, 'Elephants Are Part'. On Botha, see Thamm, 'When Artists'.
12 Berleant, *Compassion: The Culture and Politics of an Emotion*, 7.

Chapter 1

1 Ramsay et al., '130 000-Year-Old Fossil Elephant'.
2 Forssman and Gutteridge, *Bushman Rock Art*, 174.
3 Vinnicombe, *People of the Eland*, 13.
4 Woodhouse, *When Animals Were People*, 37–39.
5 Vinnicombe, *People of the Eland*, 12.
6 Le Vaillant, *Travels into the Interior*, 80.
7 Woodhouse, *Rain and Its Creatures*, 47–51.
8 Tomaselli, 'Textualizing the San "Past"', 205.
9 Garlake, *Painted Caves*, 58, 56.
10 Eastwood and Eastwood, *Capturing the Spoor*, 94.
11 Deacon, 'Rock Engravings', 241.

12 Guenther, 'Relationship of Bushman Art'.

13 Biesele, *Women Like Meat*, 14.

14 Guenther, 'Relationship of Bushman Art', 165.

15 Finnegan, *Oral and Beyond*, 166, 176.

16 Savory, *Bantu Folk Tales*, 9, 12. This is a selection from numerous previous collections of 'fireside' tales from the Xhosa, Zulu, Sotho, Bechuana and others.

17 Bleek, *Reynard*, xxviii.

18 Bleek, *Mantis*, n.p.

19 Dowson and Lewis-Williams, *Contested Images*, 3.

20 Bleek-Lloyd Archive, BC_151_A2_1_050: pp.3883–3888. The entire archive can be viewed online at http://lloydbleekcollection.cs.uct.ac.za/.

21 http://lloydbleekcollection.cs.uct.ac.za/stories/118/index.html.

22 Bleek, *Mantis*, 41.

23 Van der Post, *Heart of the Hunter*, 170.

24 Van der Post, *Heart of the Hunter*, 12.

25 Bleek, *Reynard*, 61–64.

26 Bleek, *Reynard*, 27–30.

27 Honey, *Folk-Tales*, 112–114. The whole story from Honey is available online at http://www.sacred-texts.com/afr/saft/sft31.htm.

28 Honey, *Folk-Tales*, 5.

29 Honey, *Folk-Tales*, 115–116.

30 Knappert, *Namibia*, 134.

31 Thomas, *Bushman Stories*, 56.

32 Stewart, *Zebra's Stripes*, 74.

33 Biesele, *Women Like Meat*, 23.

34 Biesele, *Women Like Meat*, 149–150.

35 Callaway, *Nursery Tales*, n.p.

36 Callaway, *Nursery Tales*, 281.

37 Callaway, *Nursery Tales*, 331–335.

38 Botumile, *Tlou*, 3.

39 Botumile, *Tlou*, 16.

40 Postel, 'Media, Mediums', 114.

41 Mutwa, *Isilwane*, 12–13.

42 Mutwa, *Isilwane*, 17.

43 Mutwa, *Isilwane*, 107–108.

44 Rycroft and Ngcobo, *Praises of Dingane*, 71, 73, 76, 83, 95, 204.

45 Rycroft and Ngcobo, *Praises of Dingane*, 142.

46 Hamutinyei and Plangger, *Tsumo*, 5, 188, 234, 383.

Chapter 2

1 Le Vaillant, *Travels into the Interior*, 9.
2 Beer, *Open Fields*, 55–56.
3 Pratt, *Imperial Eyes*, 23, 35.
4 Miller, *Empire and the Animal Body*, 55, 61.
5 Le Vaillant, *Travels into the Interior*, 8.
6 Mentzel, *Geographical and Topographical Description*, 2: 338–399. Interestingly, Mentzel also uses the word 'rogue' to describe a lone elephant – or so it is translated from the German.
7 Cited in Skead, *Western and Northern Cape*, 87.
8 Skead, *Western and Northern Cape*, 89.
9 Cited in Skead, *Western and Northern Cape*, 87.
10 Talbot, 'Pathfinders', 4.
11 Talbot, 'Pathfinders', 24.
12 Mentzel, *Geographical and Topographical Description*, 2: 226.
13 Sparrman, *Voyage to the Cape of Good Hope*, 288, 292.
14 Sparrman, *Voyage to the Cape of Good Hope*, 296.
15 Sparrman, *Voyage to the Cape of Good Hope*, 253.
16 Sparrman, *Voyage to the Cape of Good Hope*, 288. He also refers to Buffon at this point.
17 Sparrman, *Voyage to the Cape of Good Hope*, 290–291.
18 Sparrman, *Voyage to the Cape of Good Hope*, 293.
19 Sparrman, *Voyage to the Cape of Good Hope*, 294–295.
20 Le Vaillant, *Travels into the Interior*, 7.
21 Le Vaillant, *Travels into the Interior*, 9.
22 Le Vaillant, *Travels into the Interior*, 101–103.
23 Le Vaillant, *Travels into the Interior*, 107.
24 Le Vaillant, *Travels into the Interior*, 108.
25 Le Vaillant, *Travels into the Interior*, 113.
26 Le Vaillant, *Travels into the Interior*, 120.
27 Hayley, *Designs*, 12.
28 Barrow, *Travels into the Interior of Southern Africa*, 129.
29 Barrow, *Travels into the Interior of Southern Africa*, 129–130.
30 Barrow, *Travels into the Interior of Southern Africa*, viii.
31 Barrow, *Travels into the Interior of Southern Africa*, ix, xi.
32 Barrow, *Travels into the Interior of Southern Africa*, 215.
33 Barrow, *Travels into the Interior of Southern Africa*, 131.
34 Barrow, *Travels into the Interior of Southern Africa*, 163.
35 Barrow, *Travels into the Interior of Southern Africa*, 334.
36 See Wylie, *Savage Delight*, 83–104.

37   Isaacs, *Travels and Adventures*, 1: 49.
38   Isaacs, *Travels and Adventures*, 1: 206. Note that much of Isaacs's 'ivory' was obtained from hippos, more easily hunted than elephants.
39   Gardiner, *Narrative of a Journey*, 291–293.
40   Smith, *Journal of a Journey*, 408.
41   Cited in Milner, *Gallery of Nature*, 585.

Chapter 3
1   Bryden, *Gun and Camera*, 468.
2   Cloete, *How Young They Died*, 157.
3   Cited in Cartmill, *View to a Death*, 157.
4   Harris, *Wild Sports*, xiii.
5   Harris, *Wild Sports*, xv–xvi.
6   Cited in Skead, *Eastern Cape*, 43–62.
7   Selous, *Travel and Adventure*, vii.
8   Cited in Meredith, *Africa's Elephant*, 72.
9   Sanchez-Ariño's *Elephants, Ivory & Hunters* (2004) claims to be the most comprehensive history of elephant hunting thus far, from the hunter's point of view, but it is neither literary nor particular to southern Africa. He boasts of killing 1 300 elephants himself. Haresnape's 1974 compilation, *The Great Hunters*, offers a taste, but not much on elephants specifically. MacKenzie's *The Empire of Nature* (1988) establishes rich ground for a more localised study. Walker's *Ivory's Ghosts* (2009) is a global history of the ivory trade that features southern African hunters only sporadically. Most accounts appear as chapters within larger works, such as Meredith's *Africa's Elephant* (2001), or the chapter by Rothfels, 'Killing Elephants', in *Victorian Animal Dreams* (2007).
10   Carruthers, 'Romance, Reverence'.
11   Gray, *Southern African Literature*, 101–103.
12   Selous, *Travel and Adventure*, 1.
13   Cited in Sanchez-Ariño, *Hunting in Zimbabwe*, 350.
14   Gordon-Cumming, *Five Years*, 6; Gray, *Southern African Literature*, 102.
15   Selous, *Hunter's Wanderings*, ix.
16   Harris, *Wild Sports*, 31.
17   Harris, *Wild Sports*, 264.
18   Stigand, *Hunting the Elephant*, 7–8.
19   Cited in Rothfels, 'Killing Elephants', 57.
20   Delegorgue, *Travels in Southern Africa*, 3–4; Carruthers, 'Romance, Reverence', 2.
21   Bryden, *Gun and Camera*, 281.
22   Cited in Rothfels, 'Killing Elephants', 53–54.

23 Cited in Rothfels, 'Killing Elephants', 58.
24 Cited in Hardin, 'Toward an Ethic', 440.
25 Cited in Hardin, 'Toward an Ethic', 441.
26 Rothfels, 'Killing Elephants', 55.
27 Cited in Hardin, 'Toward an Ethic', 444.
28 Harris, *Portraits*, 97–98.
29 Harris, *Wild Sports*, 168.
30 Harris, *Wild Sports*, 168–169.
31 Harris, *Wild Sports*, 169.
32 Harris, *Wild Sports*, 171.
33 Harris, *Wild Sports*, 173–174.
34 Gray, *Southern African Literature*, 98.
35 Neumann, *Elephant Hunting*, viii.
36 Baker, *Wild Beasts*, vii.
37 Baker, *Wild Beasts*, 58.
38 Baker, *Wild Beasts*, vii.
39 Neumann, *Elephant Hunting*, 325–326.
40 Selous, *Hunter's Wanderings*, 337.
41 Westley, 'Novice's Problem', 12–14.
42 Selous, *Hunter's Wanderings*, 75.
43 Cited in Sanchez-Ariño, *Hunting in Zimbabwe*, 82–83; emphasis added.
44 Selous, *Travel and Adventure*, 476.
45 Bryden, *Gun and Camera*, 300.
46 Gray, *Southern African Literature*, 102.
47 Selous, *Travel and Adventure,* 69.
48 Cartmill, *View to a Death*, 239.
49 Gillmore, *Leaves*, 62.
50 Gillmore, *Leaves*, 63.
51 W. Morrill, 'Conservation and Elephant Hunting', http://www.iwmc.org/elephant/981127.htm.
52 Mathers, *Zambesia*, 51.
53 Ntumi, Ferreira and Van Aarde, 'Review'; Valoi, 'Mozambique Elephants'.
54 But see Hobson, 'Hunting Trip'.
55 It is no coincidence that the first Rowland Ward book of trophy records was published in 1892, just when so much game was in danger of vanishing. The firm republished *Kambaku!* in 1997 despite its assertion that 'it was not and is not there to establish records in the sense of biggest or best, nor to glorify the hunter. It celebrates the animal.' This on a website headed by a photograph of a grinning hunter displaying his trophy bighorn sheep, very rare and perfectly dead (http://www.rowlandward.co.za).

56   Manners, *Kambaku!*, 350–351.
57   Manners, *Kambaku!*, 338.
58   Selous, *Travel and Adventure*, 325.
59   Manners, *Kambaku!*, 351, 352.
60   Manners, *Kambaku!*, 354.
61   Manners, *Kambaku!*, 385, 388, 389.
62   Capstick, *Last Ivory Hunter*, 9.
63   Cloete, 'We Never Fired'.
64   Cloete, 'We Never Fired'.

Chapter 4
1   Bryden, *Tales of South Africa*, 232–233.
2   Katz, *Rider Haggard*, 26.
3   Bryden, *Tales of South Africa*, 266–267.
4   Bryden, *Tales of South Africa*, 238.
5   http://archive.spectator.co.uk/article/29th-november-1856/16/giftbooks-the-approach-of-december-has-produced-as.
6   http://archive.spectator.co.uk/article/27th-october-1883/10/captain-mayne-reid.
7   Reid, *Young Yagers*, 191.
8   Reid, *Bush Boys*, 183.
9   Reid, *Bush Boys*, 149.
10   Reid, *Bush Boys*, 265–287.
11   Reid, *Bush Boys*, 467.
12   For Haggard's (and Smith's) indebtedness to Selous, see Mandingirana and Stapleton, 'Literary Legacy'.
13   Haggard, *King Solomon's Mines*, viii.
14   Haggard, *King Solomon's Mines*, 2.
15   Haggard, *King Solomon's Mines*, 32.
16   Haggard, *King Solomon's Mines*, 35.
17   Haggard, *King Solomon's Mines*, 36–37.
18   Haggard, *King Solomon's Mines*, 34, 38.
19   This is almost repeated exactly in another scene in Haggard's *The Ivory Child*; cf. Selous, *Hunter's Wanderings*, 355.
20   Haggard, *King Solomon's Mines*, 34, 38–40.
21   Haggard, *King Solomon's Mines*, 212–213.
22   Gray, *Southern African Literature*, 121.
23   Haggard, *Ivory Child*, Ch. xii.
24   Haggard, *Ivory Child*, Ch. xii.
25   Haggard, *Ivory Child*, Ch. xiii.

26 As reported by John Collis for *The Spectator* in 1982: 'Van der Post's Inner Voice', http://archive.spectator.co.uk/article/6th-november-1982/23/van-der-posts-inner-voice.
27 Van der Post, *Flamingo Feather*, 115–116.
28 Cloete, *Curve and Tusk*, 114–115.
29 Cloete, *Curve and Tusk*, 114.
30 Cloete, *Curve and Tusk*, 120–121.
31 Cloete, *Curve and Tusk*, 206–207.
32 Cloete, *Curve and Tusk*, 24, 230.
33 Cloete, *Curve and Tusk*, 205–207.
34 Cloete, *Curve and Tusk*, 28–29.
35 Cloete, *Curve and Tusk*, 196.
36 Cloete, *Curve and Tusk*, 216.
37 Cloete, *Curve and Tusk*, 212.
38 Cloete, *Curve and Tusk*, 207.
39 Cloete, *Curve and Tusk*, 222–223.
40 Cloete, *Curve and Tusk*, 232.
41 See Marais and Hadaway, *Great Tuskers*, 84–87. This tusker died of natural causes in 1985, aged about 58. His tusks weighed 65 and 57 kilogrammes. See also Hall-Martin and Bosman, *Magnificent Seven*.
42 See discussion at http://www.pendukasafaris.com/history/who-shot-dhlulamithi-country-life-june-03/.
43 Stevenson-Hamilton, *Wild Life*, 43.
44 See D. Edgcumbe, 'The Life of the Legendary Bvekenya', http://www.africanx-mag.com/the_ivory_trail.htm; http://grahamboynton.com/feature_writing/the-nature-of-the-beast-19/.
45 Bulpin, *Ivory Trail*, 6–7. The book was popular enough that it enjoyed at least six reprintings up to 1981.
46 Bulpin, *Ivory Trail*, 91.
47 Bulpin, *Ivory Trail*, 80.
48 Bulpin, *Ivory Trail*, 204–205.
49 Bulpin, *Ivory Trail*, 219.
50 Bulpin, *Ivory Trail*, 234.
51 Burke, *Elephant across Border*, 120–121.
52 Burke, *Elephant across Border*, 125.
53 Burke, *Elephant across Border*, 192.
54 Burke, *Elephant across Border*, 233.
55 Burke, *Elephant across Border*, 255.
56 Davis, *Taller Than Trees*, 86–87.
57 Davis, *Taller Than Trees*, 116.

58 Davis, *Taller Than Trees*, 116.
59 The ethics of culling have been debated in numerous publications, from every angle; but see, for a start, Whyte and Fayrer-Hoskin, 'Playing Elephant God'; Scholes and Mennell, *Elephant Management*.
60 Smith, *Elephant Song*, 3.
61 Smith, *Elephant Song*, 9.
62 Smith, *Elephant Song*, 21.
63 Hanks, *Struggle for Survival*, 43.
64 Smith, *Elephant Song*, 9.
65 Smith, *Elephant Song*, 9–10.
66 Smith, *Elephant Song*, 11.
67 Smith, *Elephant Song*, 12.
68 Smith, *Elephant Song*, 19.
69 Smith, *Elephant Song*, 25.
70 Smith, *Elephant Song*, 26.
71 Donovan, 'Aestheticizing Animal Cruelty', 208.
72 Midgley, *Beast and Man*, 44.
73 Cawelti, *Adventure, Mystery*.

Chapter 5

1 Almost alone in this area of study to date is the work of Elwyn Jenkins; see 'English South African Children's Literature'.
2 Cited in Westra, *Living in Integrity*, 251.
3 To cite just four relevant discussions bridging these disciplines: Whyte, 'Headaches and Heartaches' (biology and environmental ethics); Lötter, 'Ethical Considerations' (management and philosophy); Pickover, *Animal Rights* (animal rights); Wise, *Drawing the Line* (animal rights, neurology and law).
4 Bradshaw, *Elephants on the Edge*, xix.
5 Hauser, *Wild Minds*.
6 Scholtmeijer, *Animal Victims*, 89.
7 Snowdon, 'Continuing Question', 813–814; Crist, 'Engaging', 832.
8 Midgley, *Beast and Man*, 350.
9 See, for example, Crist, *Images of Animals*.
10 See Kluger, 'What Animals Think', 22–29; Keim, *Inside Animal Minds*.
11 *African Wildlife* 46, no. 3, 106–107.
12 The most comprehensive account is by Czech, *With Rifle and Petticoat*, 67ff.
13 http://www.unz.org/Pub/LiteraryDigest-1917dec08-00052?View=PDFPages.
14 Herbert, *Elephant*, 12, 15.

15   Herbert, *Elephant*, 39.
16   Herbert, *Elephant*, 108.
17   Herbert, *Elephant*, 118.
18   Herbert, *Elephant*, 19.
19   Herbert, *Elephant*, 140, 247.
20   Herbert, *Elephant*, 146–155.
21   Longden, *Goliath*, 3.
22   Longden, *Goliath*, 4.
23   Longden, *Goliath*, 28.
24   Longden, *Goliath*, 74, 77.
25   Kenmuir, *Tusks*, 6.
26   Kenmuir, *Tusks*, 12–13.
27   Kenmuir, *Tusks*, 6.
28   Kenmuir, *Tusks*, 68.
29   Kenmuir, *Tusks*, 36, 33.
30   Kenmuir, *Tusks*, 6.
31   Kenmuir, *Tusks*, i.
32   Kenmuir, *Tusks*, 71.
33   Kenmuir, *Tusks*, 70–71.
34   Kenmuir, *Tusks*, 66.
35   Kenmuir, *Tusks*, 22.
36   Kenmuir, *Tusks*, 32.
37   'Jesse bush' commonly denotes the dense, thorny, mixed-species thickets specific to the Zambezi Valley.
38   Struthers, *Boy and Elephant*, 113, 115.
39   Struthers, *Boy and Elephant*, 113.
40   Struthers, *Boy and Elephant*, 75; Acampora, *Corporal Compassion*, 23.
41   Acampora, *Corporal Compassion*, 119. It is notable, however, that following the work of Judith Butler and others, the body has very recently become a significant focus of philosophical and literary scholarship.
42   Struthers, *Boy and Elephant*, 19.
43   Struthers, *Boy and Elephant*, 71; emphasis added.
44   Struthers, *Boy and Elephant*, 25.
45   Blight, *Elephant Bloodline*, 154.
46   Blight, *Elephant Bloodline*, 52.
47   Paynter, *Elephant, Me*, 13.
48   St John, *Elephant's Tale*, 185.
49   St John, *Elephant's Tale*, 177.
50   St John, *Elephant's Tale*, 209–210.
51   St John, *Elephant's Tale*, 31.

52 St John, *Elephant's Tale*, 123–124.
53 St John, *Elephant's Tale*, 91–92.
54 St John, *Elephant's Tale*, 178.
55 St John, *Elephant's Tale*, 101.
56 St John, *Elephant's Tale*, 191.
57 Anderson, *Ecologies*, 176; original emphasis.

Chapter 6
1   Cairns, 'Replacing Targeted Compassion', 50.
2   Wolhuter, *Memories*, 77.
3   Stokes, *Sanctuary*, 9.
4   Spence, cited in Neumann, 'Nature-State-Territory', 182.
5   For excellent discussions, see Barrett et al., *Changing Face*.
6   Wolhuter, *Memories*, 86.
7   Carruthers, *Kruger*, 1.
8   Bryden, *Game Ranger*, ix–x.
9   Carruthers, introduction to Stevenson-Hamilton, *South African Eden*, 13.
10 Stevenson-Hamilton, *South African Eden*, 250.
11 Stevenson-Hamilton, *South African Eden*, 191–192.
12 Stevenson-Hamilton, *Wild Life*, 37.
13 Stevenson-Hamilton, *Wild Life*, 39–40.
14 Bryden, *Game Ranger*, ix.
15 Bryden, *Game Ranger*, 240.
16 Bryden, *Game Ranger*, 372.
17 Parker and Kuiper, 'Elephants in Africa'. The most recent plans for Kruger are far more nuanced, with culling reserved as last resort; see 'Decoding Kruger's "Elephant Management Plan"', https://africageographic.com/blog/decoding-kruger-elephant-management-plan/.
18 Bryden, *Game Ranger*, 373.
19 Bryden, *Game Ranger*, 72, 61–62.
20 Bryden, *Game Ranger*, 40.
21 Bryden, *Game Ranger*, 42–47.
22 Peirce, *Giant Steps*, 33.
23 See Martin, Craig and Booth, *Elephant Management*.
24 Hulme and Murphree, *African Wildlife*, 1.
25 Balneaves, *Elephant Valley*, 87.
26 Balneaves, *Elephant Valley*, 86.
27 Balneaves, *Elephant Valley*, 29.
28 Balneaves, *Elephant Valley*, 30.
29 Balneaves, *Elephant Valley*, 112–121.

30 Tredger, *From Rhodesia*, 19.

31 Tredger, *From Rhodesia*, 16.

32 See http://www.gameranger.org/. The Game Rangers Association of Africa was founded in 1970.

33 Tredger, *From Rhodesia*, 81–82.

34 Tredger, *From Rhodesia*, 22–23.

35 Tredger, *From Rhodesia*, 96.

36 Tredger, *From Rhodesia*, 113.

37 Tredger, *From Rhodesia*, 114.

38 Tredger, *From Rhodesia*, 160.

39 Tredger, *From Rhodesia*, 159.

40 Tredger, *From Rhodesia*, 164–165.

41 Tredger, *From Rhodesia*, 171.

42 Tredger, *From Rhodesia*, 124.

Chapter 7

1 O'Connell acknowledges both Poole and Douglas-Hamilton – but not, oddly, Payne, whose memoir is generically quite similar, and who pioneered research into elephants' subsonic communications.

2 See Weavind, 'Breeders'.

3 Kepe, Wynberg and Ellis, 'Land Reform', 9. For an excellent discussion in the KwaZulu-Natal context, see Nustad, *Creating Africas*.

4 See Brooks, 'Images'.

5 Westra, *Living in Integrity*, 138, 252.

6 Cock and Koch, *Going Green*, 16.

7 Carruthers, 'Tracking', 809.

8 Leach, Mearns and Scoones, 'Environmental Entitlements', 228–229.

9 O'Connell, *Elephants' Secret Sense*, 3, 26.

10 O'Connell, *Elephants' Secret Sense*, 155.

11 O'Connell, *Elephants' Secret Sense*, 71.

12 O'Connell, *Elephants' Secret Sense*, 117; cf. 120.

13 See O'Connell-Rodwell et al., 'Living with the Modern Conservation Paradigm'.

14 http://www.caitlineoconnell.com/.

15 See also O'Connell's subsequent memoir, *Elephant Don*; she has also written a young adult novel, *Ivory Ghosts*.

16 O'Connell, *Elephants' Secret Sense*, 75.

17 O'Connell-Rodwell, 'Keeping an Ear'.

18 O'Connell, *Elephants' Secret Sense*, 163–164.

19 O'Connell, *Elephants' Secret Sense*, 56, 72, 94.

20   Acampora, *Corporal Compassion*, 84.
21   O'Connell, *Elephants' Secret Sense*, 222.
22   Anthony, *Elephant Whisperer*, 12.
23   Anthony, *Elephant Whisperer*, 80.
24   Anthony, *Elephant Whisperer*, 14.
25   The ghostwriting is important here; though presumably Anthony approved Spence's product, it complicates the 'authenticity' of production. Hence, in what follows, the appellation 'Lawrence Anthony' needs to be read more as a constructed or inferred 'narrative presence' than as the 'real' person.
26   Evidence for such hunting grounds is slender – see Brooks, 'Re-reading the Hluhluwe-Umfolozi'.
27   Anthony, *Elephant Whisperer*, 12–13.
28   Anthony, *Elephant Whisperer*, 41.
29   Anthony, *Elephant Whisperer*, 80.
30   Anthony, *Elephant Whisperer*, 171–172.
31   Anthony, *Elephant Whisperer*, 41; emphasis added.
32   Anthony, *Elephant Whisperer*, 14.
33   Anthony, *Elephant Whisperer*, 212, 34, 53, 49, 74.
34   Anthony, *Elephant Whisperer*, 17–18.
35   This is a dimension until recently inadequately integrated into policy; even in the government's 2007 *Assessment of South African Elephant Management*, including contributions by 57 experts, 'only a few sentences acknowledged indigenous views at all' (Bradshaw, *Elephants on the Edge*, 229).
36   Haraway, *Companion Species Manifesto*, 7.
37   Acampora and Davis Acampora, *Nietzschean Bestiary*, 7.
38   Anthony, *Elephant Whisperer*, 61–62.
39   Anthony, *Elephant Whisperer*, 66. This progression is vividly captured in a television advertisement for Coronation ('Trust is earned'), complete with French-accented female voice-over (Anthony's wife is French). See https://www.youtube.com/watch?v=LJcbi60i1V0&noredirect=1. Pincott, in *The Elephants and I*, similarly relates how a relationship developed with a particular wild elephant, to the point of touch, both results from and generates a particular intensity of compassion.
40   Anthony, *Elephant Whisperer*, 194–195.
41   Anthony, *Elephant Whisperer*, 47.
42   Anthony, *Elephant Whisperer*, 2–3. The title 'Elephant Whisperer' is perhaps ill-chosen, following Nicholas Evans's *The Horse Whisperer*, and sundry further 'whisperers', all implying something more esoteric than is the case here. Some people do seem to have a particular rapport with elephants, one of the best known in southern Africa being the late Rory Hensman.

43 Anthony, *Elephant Whisperer*, 86; emphasis added; cf. 137.
44 Anthony, *Elephant Whisperer*, 151.
45 Anthony, *Elephant Whisperer*, 150.
46 Anthony, *Elephant Whisperer*, 2.
47 Anthony, *Elephant Whisperer*, 220–223.
48 Anthony, *Elephant Whisperer*, 364.
49 'Elephants Say Goodbye to the Whisperer', *IOL News*, 10 March 2012. https://www.iol.co.za/news/south-africa/kwazulu-natal/elephants-say-goodbye-to-the-whisperer-1253463.
50 Cited in Bradshaw, *Elephants on the Edge*, 115.
51 '*Imire: The Life and Times of Normal Travers, as Told to Cathy Buckle*', http://swradioafrica.com/Documents/IMIRE%20-%20Book%20Review%20by%20Mike%20Rook.pdf. As Phillips has noted somewhat sardonically in 'Weeping Elephants', the mourning scene has become 'canonical, even a bit liturgical' in elephant literature (28).
52 Begon, Townsend and Harper, *Ecology*, 478.
53 Kepe, 'Problem', 417.
54 Derrida, 'Animal', 399.
55 Bradshaw, *Elephants on the Edge*, xxi.
56 Anthony, *Elephant Whisperer*, 53, 4.
57 Bradshaw, *Elephants on the Edge*, 137.
58 Haraway, *Companion Species Manifesto*, 97.
59 Cited in Diprose, *Corporeal Generosity*, 168; original emphasis.

Chapter 8
1 http://traveller24.news24.com/Explore/Green/watch-elusive-knysna-elephant-captured-on-camera-20160310.
2 Reitz, 'Managing the Myths'.
3 Watson, *Elephantoms*, 108.
4 Lichtenstein, *Travels in Southern Africa*, 1: 264.
5 Skead, *Eastern Cape*, 41.
6 Cited in Skead, *Western and Northern Cape*, 102.
7 Cited in Skead, *Western and Northern Cape*, 101.
8 Barrow, *Travels into the Interior of Southern Africa*, 164; cited in Skead, *Eastern Cape*, 42.
9 Pretorius, *Jungle Man*, 5–6.
10 Dream Africa Productions & Publishing, 2013.
11 Pretorius, *Jungle Man*, 47.
12 Pretorius, *Jungle Man*, 132.
13 Pretorius, *Jungle Man*, 185, 188.

14   Pretorius, *Jungle Man*, 195.
15   Pretorius, *Jungle Man*, 196, 199.
16   Pretorius, *Jungle Man*, 211.
17   Whitehouse and Irwin, *Guide to Elephants of Addo*.
18   Dommisse, 'Knysna Elephants'; Urry, 'Report on Bernard Carp'.
19   Carter, *Elephants of Knysna*, 3.
20   Carter, *Elephants of Knysna*, 4.
21   Carter, *Elephants of Knysna*, 70.
22   Carter, *Elephants of Knysna*, 213–214.
23   Carter, *Elephants of Knysna*, 214.
24   Carter, *Elephants of Knysna*, 216–217.
25   Mackay, *Knysna Elephants*, 58–59.
26   Mackay, *Knysna Elephants*, 7.
27   Walker, *Dear Elephant*, i–ii.
28   Watson knows perfectly well that there is no such thing as a really *white* elephant – but he is fascinated by the 'idea' of it – and so incorporates it into his story. There is no suggestion anywhere in the literature of a pale elephant in Knysna, nor is it a legendary feature of the African elephant generally.
29   Watson, *Elephantoms*, 191–192.
30   See Payne, *Among Whales*; Payne, *Silent Thunder*.
31   Heathcote Williams wrote parallel poetic/photographic paeans to elephants and to whales. We have already seen how Laurens van der Post fictionally aligned them, and they have been treated alongside one another through the perspective of protective legislation by Ed Couzens in *Whales and Elephants in International Law and Politics*.
32   Watson, *Elephantoms*, 98.
33   Watson, *Elephantoms*, 90–94.
34   Watson, *Elephantoms*, 100.
35   Watson, *Elephantoms*, 108.
36   Watson, *Elephantoms*, 151.
37   Watson, *Elephantoms*, 152.
38   Watson, *Elephantoms*, 166.
39   Watson, *Elephantoms*, 101.
40   Watson, *Elephantoms*, 26.
41   Watson, *Elephantoms*, 26.
42   Patterson, *Secret Elephants*, 201.
43   Most of these photographs had already been collected in Mackay, *Knysna Elephants*.
44   Rangers at the Knysna Elephant Park, not far away, told me they were sceptical of Patterson's efforts, partly because of his lack of expertise, partly

because they said they walked their own elephants through that area at times, so there was potential for real confusion in origin of dung samples. But perhaps there is a bit of comradely territorialism there, too.

45   Patterson, *Secret Elephants*, 201.
46   Matthee, *Dream Forest*, 1.
47   Matthee, *Circles in a Forest*, 70.
48   Matthee, *Circles in a Forest*, 80.
49   Matthee, *Circles in a Forest*, 111.
50   Matthee, *Circles in a Forest*, 71.
51   Matthee, *Circles in a Forest*, 70.
52   Matthee, *Circles in a Forest*, 103.
53   Matthee, *Circles in a Forest*, 354.
54   Matthee, *Circles in a Forest*, 126.

Chapter 9

1   First recorded in the Bleek-Lloyd Archive; reproduced in Chapman, *New Century*, 13.
2   Crist, 'Engaging', 832.
3   Bate, *Song of the Earth*, 199; emphasis in the original.
4   Albyn, *Manzovo*, 49, 120, 179.
5   Albyn, *Manzovo*, 185.
6   http://jennysjumbojargon.com/?page_id=929.
7   Parsons, 'Aesthetic Value'. My colleague Samantha Vice discusses animal beauty only in exploring general hunting ethics in 'Ethics of Animal Beauty'.
8   http://www.animalstudies.msu.edu/bibliography.php. Rolston III's 1987 essay 'Beauty and the Beast' is suggestive but brief, more poetic than philosophical. Aesthetics philosopher Emily Brady has made some forays in this direction, for example 'Aesthetic Value and Wild Animals' (2014).
9   For some discussion, see Adorni, 'Aesthetic Canons'.
10   Parsons, 'Aesthetic Value'.
11   Hettinger, 'Animal Beauty'.
12   Scarry, *On Beauty*, 80.
13   Scarry, *On Beauty*, 23, 46, 117, 29, 95.
14   Rolston III, 'From Beauty'.
15   Bate, *Song of the Earth*, 282.
16   Bate, *Song of the Earth*, 202–203.
17   Hurutshe praise poem: Anonymous, traditional, translated by Jeff Opland from D.F. van der Merwe, 'Hurutshe Poems', *Bantu Studies* 15, no. 4 (1941): 307–337. In Opland, *Words*, 169. Reprinted by kind permission of Jeff Opland.

18   Opland, *Words*, 6.
19   Pringle, *African Sketches*, 21.
20   Pringle, *Poetical Works*, 49.
21   Cope, *back view*, n.p.
22   For discussion of the Tuli debacle, see Pickover, *Animal Rights*, 79–98.
23   See, for example, 'Animal Activists Press Parks to Get Tourists off Elephants' Backs', *Sunday Times*, 26 June 2016. For Botswana, see https://www.iol.co.za/news/africa/botswana-bans-elephant-back-rides-7178715.
24   Salafranca, 'Elephant is unhappy'.
25   Livingstone, *Ruthless Fidelity*, 99.
26   Scholtmeijer, *Animal Victims*, 89.
27   Mathews, *Ecological Self*, 144.
28   Livingstone, *Ruthless Fidelity*, 29.
29   Brettell, *Selected Poems*, 7.
30   Mann, *Kites*, 14.
31   Shaw, *Flora and Fauna*, 18.
32   Mateer, 'Elephant Graveyard'.
33   Farmer, *Absence*, 34.
34   Farmer, *Absence*, 17.
35   Farmer, *Absence*, 17–18.
36   Farmer, *Absence*, 34–35.
37   Cited in Lippit, 'Afterthoughts', 791.
38   Livingstone, *Ruthless Fidelity*, 312.

Afterword

1   Van Aarde, *Elephants*, 51.
2   Felbab-Brown, *Extinction Market*.
3   Anderson, *Ecologies*, 183.

Select Bibliography

Acampora, Ralph. *Corporal Compassion: Animal Ethics and Philosophy of Body*. Pittsburgh: Pittsburgh University Press, 2006.

Acampora, Ralph and Christa Davis Acampora, eds. *A Nietzschean Bestiary: Becoming Animals beyond Docile and Brutal*. New York: Rowman & Littlefield, 2004.

Adorni, Eleonora. 'Aesthetic Canons of Animal Beauty from the Renaissance to Today'. *Antennae Review* (2012). www.antennae.org.uk/download/i/mark.../Beaute%20%20Animale%20 Review.pdf.

Ahmed, Sara. *The Cultural Politics of Emotion*. New York: Routledge, 2004.

Albyn, Gary. *Manzovo: Place of the Elephants*. Illustrations by Craig Bone. Johannesburg: Southbound, 2008.

Anderson, E.N. *Ecologies of the Heart: Emotion, Belief and the Environment*. New York: Oxford University Press, 1996.

Anthony, Lawrence (with Graham Spence). *The Elephant Whisperer*. New York: Sidgwick & Jackson, 2009.

Armstrong, Philip. '*Moby Dick* and Compassion'. *Society & Animals* 12, no. 1 (2004): 19–37.

Baker, Samuel. *Wild Beasts and Their Ways: Reminiscences of Europe, Asia, Africa and America*. London: Macmillan, 1891.

Balneaves, Elizabeth. *Elephant Valley: The Adventures of J. McGregor Brooks, Game and Tsetse Officer, Kariba*. London: Lutterworth Press, 1962.

Barrett, George, Shirley Brooks, Jenny Josefsson and Nqobile Zulu, eds. *The Changing Face of Land and Conservation in Post-colonial Africa: Old Land, New Practices?* London: Routledge, 2015.

Barrow, John. *An Account of Travels into the Interior of Southern Africa, in the Years 1797 and 1798 . . . .* Vol. 1. London: Gadell & Davies, 1806.

Bate, Jonathan. *The Song of the Earth*. London: Picador, 2000.

Beer, Patricia. *Open Fields: Science in Cultural Encounter*. Oxford: Oxford University Press, 1996.

Begon, Michael, Colin R. Townsend and John L. Harper. *Ecology: From Individuals to Ecosystems*. London: Blackwell, 2006.

Berleant, Lauren. *Compassion: The Culture and Politics of an Emotion*. New York: Routledge, 2004.

Biesele, Megan. *Women Like Meat*. Johannesburg: Wits University Press, 1993.

Bleek, Dorothea, ed. *The Mantis and His Friends: Bushman Folklore*. Cape Town: T.M. Miller; London: B. Blackwell, 1924.

Bleek, Wilhelm. *Reynard the Fox in South Africa or, Hottentot Fables and Tales*. London: Trubner, 1864.

Blight, Howard. *An Elephant Bloodline*. Thohoyandou: RRA-Thohoyandou Press, 2007.

Botumile, Bontekanye. *Tlou: The Elephant Story*. Gabarone: Thari-e-Ntsho Storytellers, 2006.

Bradshaw, G.A. *Elephants on the Edge: What Animals Teach Us about Humanity*. New Haven: Yale University Press, 2009.

Brady, Emily. 'Aesthetic Value and Wild Animals'. In *Environmental Aesthetics: Crossing Divides and Breaking Ground*, edited by M. Drenthen and J. Keulartz, 188–200. New York: Fordham University Press, 2014.

Brettell, N.H. *Selected Poems*. Edited by Hugh Finn. Cape Town: Snail Press, 1994.

Brooks, Shirley. 'Images of "Wild Africa": Nature Tourism and the (Re)creation of Hluhluwe Game Reserve, 1930–1945'. *Journal of Historical Geography* 31, no. 2 (2005): 220–240.

Brooks, Shirley. 'Re-reading the Hluhluwe-Umfolozi Game Reserve: Constructions of a "Natural" Space'. *Transformation* 44 (2000): 63–79. http://transformationjournal.org.za/wp-content/uploads/2017/03/tran043006.pdf.

Bryden, Bruce. *A Game Ranger Remembers: Thirty Years in the Kruger National Park*. Johannesburg: Jonathan Ball, 2005.

Bryden, H.A. *Gun and Camera in Southern Africa: A Year of Wanderings in Bechuanaland, the Kalahari Desert, and the Lake River Country, Ngamiland*. London: Stanford, 1893.

Bryden, H.A. *Tales of South Africa*. London: Constable, 1896.

Bulpin, T.V. *The Ivory Trail*. Cape Town: Books of Africa, 1954.

Burke, Colin. *Elephant across Border*. London: Collins, 1968.

Cairns, John. 'Replacing Targeted Compassion with Multidimensional Compassion'. *Speculations in Science and Technology* 21, no. 1 (1998): 45–51.

Callaway, Henry. *Nursery Tales, Traditions, and Histories of the Zulus: In Their Own Words, with a Transl. into Engl. and Notes.* Vol. 1. London: Trubner, 1868 (1970 Kraus reprint).

Capstick, Peter Hathaway. *The Last Ivory Hunter: The Saga of Wally Johnson.* New York: St Martin's Press, 1988.

Carruthers, Jane. *The Kruger National Park: A Social and Political History.* Pietermaritzburg: University of Natal Press, 1995.

Carruthers, Jane. 'Romance, Reverence, Research, Rights: Writing about Elephant Hunting and Management in Southern Africa, *c.*1830s to 2008'. *Koedoe* (2010): 1–6.

Carruthers, Jane. 'Tracking in Game Trails: Looking Afresh at the Politics of Environmental History in South Africa'. *Environmental History* 11 (2006): 804–829.

Carter, Nick, *The Elephants of Knysna.* London: Purnell, 1971.

Cartmill, Matt. *A View to a Death in the Morning: Hunting and Nature through History.* Cambridge, MA: Harvard University Press, 1993.

Cawelti, John G. *Adventure, Mystery, and Romance: Formula Stories as Art and Popular Culture.* Chicago: University of Chicago Press, 1976.

Chapman, Michael, ed. *The New Century of South African Poetry.* Johannesburg: Ad Donker, 2002.

Cloete, Stuart. *The Curve and the Tusk.* London: Collins, 1953 [1952].

Cloete, Stuart. *How Young They Died.* London: Collins, 1969.

Cloete, Stuart. 'We Never Fired a Shot'. *Saturday Evening Post*, 3 September 1949: 28–30.

Cock, Jacklyn and Eddie Koch, eds. *Going Green: People, Politics and the Environment in South Africa.* Oxford: Oxford University Press, 1991.

Cope, Michael. *back view.* Cape Town: Vanity Press, 1996.

Couzens, Ed. *Whales and Elephants in International Law and Politics: A Comparative Study.* New York: Routledge, 2013.

Crist, Eileen. 'Engaging the "Verstehen" Approach: Naturalists' Portrayals of Animal Life'. *Social Studies of Science* 26, no. 4 (1996): 801–835.

Crist, Eileen. *Images of Animals: Anthropomorphism and Animal Mind.* Atlanta: Temple University Press, 2000.

Cruise, A. 'Elephants Are Part of Man's World'. *The Herald*, 10 October 2013: 16.

Czech, Kenneth. *With Rifle and Petticoat: Women as Big Game Hunters, 1880–1940.* Lanham, MD: Derrydale Press, 2002.

Daston, Lorraine and Gregg Mitman, eds. *Thinking with Animals: New Perspectives on Anthropomorphism.* New York: Columbia University Press, 2005.

Davis, John Gordon. *Taller Than Trees.* New York: Joseph, 1975.

Deacon, Janette. 'Rock Engravings and the Folklore'. In *Contested Images: Diversity in Southern African Rock Art Research*, edited by Thomas Dowson and David Lewis-Williams, 229–245. Johannesburg: Wits University Press, 1994.

Delegorgue, Adulphe. *Travels in Southern Africa*. Vol. 1. Translated by F. Webb, with introduction and index by S. J. Alexander and C. de B. Webb. Durban: Killie Campbell Africana Library; Pietermaritzburg: University of Natal Press, 1990 [1847].

Derrida, Jacques. 'The Animal That I Therefore Am (and More to Follow)'. *Critical Inquiry* 28, no. 2 (2002): 369–418.

Diprose, Rosalyn. *Corporeal Generosity: On Giving with Nietzsche, Merleau-Ponty, and Levinas*. New York: SUNY Press, 2002.

Dommisse, E.J. 'The Knysna Elephants'. *African Wildlife* 5, no. 3 (1951): 195–201.

Donovan, Josephine. 'Aestheticizing Animal Cruelty'. *College Literature* 38, no. 4 (2011): 202–217.

Dowson, Thomas and David Lewis-Williams, eds. *Contested Images: Diversity in Southern African Rock Art Research*. Johannesburg: Wits University Press, 1994.

Eastwood, Edward and Cathelijne Eastwood. *Capturing the Spoor: An Exploration of Southern African Rock Art*. Cape Town: David Philip, 2006.

Farmer, Harold. *Absence of Elephants*. Harare: College Press, 1990.

Felbab-Brown, Vanda. *The Extinction Market: Wildlife Trafficking and How to Counter It*. London: Hurst & Co., 2017.

Finnegan, Ruth. *The Oral and Beyond: Doing Things with Words in Africa*. London: James Currey, 2007.

Forssman, Tim and Ken Gutteridge. *Bushman Rock Art: An Interpretive Guide*. Cape Town: Thirty Degrees South, 2013.

Gardiner, A.F. *Narrative of a Journey to the Zoolu Country in South Africa*. Cape Town: Struik, 1966 [1836].

Garlake, Peter. *The Painted Caves: An Introduction to the Prehistoric Art of Zimbabwe*. Harare: Modus Publications, 1987.

Gillmore, Parker. *Leaves from a Sportsman's Diary*. Whitefish, MT: Kessinger, 2009 [1893].

Gordon-Cumming, R.G. *Five Years of a Hunter's Life in the Far Interior of South Africa*. New York: Harper & Brothers, 1850.

Gray, Stephen. *Southern African Literature: An Introduction*. Cape Town: David Philip, 1979.

Guenther, Matthias. 'The Relationship of Bushman Art to Ritual and Folklore'. In *Contested Images: Diversity in Southern African Rock Art Research*, edited by Thomas Dowson and David Lewis-Williams, 160–174. Johannesburg: Wits University Press, 1994.

Haggard, H. Rider. *The Ivory Child*. Originally published in 1916. http://www. gutenberg.org/ebooks/2841.

Haggard, H. Rider. *King Solomon's Mines*. London: Cassell, 1885.

Hall-Martin, Anthony and Paul Bosman. *The Magnificent Seven: And the Other Great Tuskers of the Kruger National Park*. Cape Town: Human & Rousseau, 1994.

Hamutinyei, Mordikai A. and Albert B. Plangger, eds. *Tsumo – Shumo: Shona Proverbial Lore and Wisdom*. Harare: Mambo Press, 1987.

Hanks, John. *A Struggle for Survival: The Elephant Problem*. Cape Town: Struik, 1979.

Haraway, Donna. *The Companion Species Manifesto: Dogs, People, and Significant Otherness*. Chicago: Prickly Paradigm Press, 2003.

Hardin, Rebecca. 'Toward an Ethic of Intimacy: Touring and Trophy Hunting for Elephants in Africa'. In *Elephants and Ethics: Toward a Morality of Coexistence*, edited by Christen Wemmer and Catherine A. Christen, 419–450. Baltimore: Johns Hopkins University Press, 2007.

Haresnape, Geoffrey, ed. *The Great Hunters*. Cape Town: Purnell, 1974.

Harris, William Cornwallis. *Portraits of the Game and Wild Animals of Southern Africa*. Johannesburg: Galago, 1986 [1840].

Harris, William Cornwallis. *The Wild Sports of Southern Africa*. Cape Town: Struik, 1963 [1852].

Hauser, Marc. *Wild Minds: What Animals Really Think*. New York: Henry Holt, 2000.

Hayley, William. *Designs to a Series of Ballads*. Chichester: J. Seagrave, 1802.

Herbert, Agnes. *The Elephant*. London: Hutchinson, 1917.

Hettinger, Ned. 'Animal Beauty, Ethics and Environmental Preservation'. *Environmental Ethics* 32 (Summer 2010): 115–134.

Hobson, Dick, 'A Hunting Trip in Mozambique in 1868'. *The Geographical Journal* 149, no. 2 (1869): 202–210.

Honey, James A. *South-African Folk-Tales*. New York: Baker & Taylor, 1910.

Hulme, David and Marshall Murphree, eds. *African Wildlife and Livelihoods: The Promise and Performance of Community Conservation*. London: Heinemann, 2001.

Isaacs, Nathaniel. *Travels and Adventures in Eastern Africa: Descriptive of the Zoolus, Their Manners & Customs, with a Sketch of Natal*. 2 vols. Cape Town: Van Riebeeck Society, Cape Town, 1936 [1836].

Jenkins, Elwyn. 'English South African Children's Literature and the Environment'. *Literator* 25, no. 3 (2004): 107–123.

Katz, Wendy R. *Rider Haggard and the Fiction of Empire*. Cambridge: Cambridge University Press, 1987.

Keim, Brandon. *Inside Animal Minds: What They Think, Feel and Know*. Washington, DC: National Geographic, 2017.

Kenmuir, Dale. *The Tusks and the Talisman*. Pretoria: De Jager-Haum, 1987.

Kepe, Thembela. 'The Problem of Defining "Community": Challenges for the Land Reform Programme in Rural South Africa'. *Development South Africa* 16, no. 3 (1999): 415–433.

Kepe, Thembela, Rachel Wynberg and William Ellis. 'Land Reform and Biodiversity Conservation in South Africa: Complementary or in Conflict?' *International Journal of Biodiversity Science and Management* 1 (2005): 3–16.

Kluger, Jeffery. 'What Animals Think'. *Time* 176, no. 7 (2010): 22–29.

Knappert, Jan. *Namibia: Land and Peoples, Myths and Fables*. Leiden: E.J. Brill, 1981.

Leach, Melissa, Robin Mearns and Ian Scoones. 'Environmental Entitlements: Dynamics and Institutions in Community-based Natural Resources Management'. *World Development* 27, no. 2 (1999): 225–247.

Le Vaillant, François. *Travels into the Interior of Africa via the Cape of Good Hope*. Vol. 1. Translated and edited by Ian Glenn with Catherine Lauga du Plessis and Ian Farlam. Cape Town: Van Riebeeck Society, 2007 [1796].

Lichtenstein, Henry. *Travels in Southern Africa in the Years 1803, 1804, 1805 and 1806*. 2 vols. Translated by Anne Plumptre. Cape Town: Van Riebeeck Society, 1928 [1807].

Lippit, Akira. 'Afterthoughts on the Animal World'. *Modern Language Notes* 109, no. 5 (1994): 786–830.

Livingstone, Douglas. *A Ruthless Fidelity: The Collected Poems of Douglas Livingstone*. Edited by Malcolm Hacksley and Don Maclennan. Johannesburg: Jonathan Ball, 2004.

Longden, H.W.D. *Goliath: The Tale of a Rogue Elephant*. London: Knox, 1943.

Lötter, Hennie. 'Ethical Considerations in Elephant Management'. In *Elephant Management: A Scientific Assessment for South Africa*, edited by R.J. Scholes and K.G. Mennell, 406–445. Johannesburg: Wits University Press, 2001.

Mackay, Margo. *The Knysna Elephants and Their Forest Home*. Johannesburg: Wildlife and Environment Society, 2007 [1996].

MacKenzie, John M. *The Empire of Nature: Hunting, Conservation, and British Imperialism*. Manchester: Manchester University Press, 1988.

Mandingirana, E. and T.J. Stapleton. 'The Literary Legacy of Frederick Courteney Selous'. *History in Africa* 25 (1998): 199–218.

Mann, Chris. *Kites and Other Poems*. Cape Town: David Philip, 1990.

Manners, Harry. *Kambaku!* London: Rowland Ward, 1986.

Marais, Johan and David Hadaway. *Great Tuskers of Africa: A Celebration of Africa's Large Ivory Carriers*. Johannesburg: Penguin, 2006.

Martin, R.B., G.C. Craig and V.R. Booth, eds. *Elephant Management in Zimbabwe*. Harare: National Parks, 1989.

Mateer, John. 'Elephant Graveyard'. In *The New Century of South African Poetry*, edited by Michael Chapman, 412–414. Johannesburg: Ad Donker, 2002.

Mathers, E.P. *Zambesia: England's El Dorado in Africa, Being a Description of Matabeleland and Mashonaland, and the Less-known Adjacent Territories, and an Account of the Gold Fields of British South Africa*. Bulawayo: Books of Rhodesia, 1971 [1891].

Mathews, Freya. *The Ecological Self*. New York: Routledge, 1994.

Matthee, Dalene. *Circles in a Forest*. Johannesburg: Penguin, 1984.

Matthee, Dalene. *Dream Forest*. Johannesburg: Penguin, 2004.

Mentzel, O.F. *A Geographical and Topographical Description of the Cape of Good Hope*. 3 vols. Translated by G.V. Marais and J. Hoge. Cape Town: Van Riebeeck Society, 1944.

Meredith, Martin. *Africa's Elephant: A Biography*. London: Sceptre, 2001.

Midgley, Mary. *Beast and Man: The Roots of Human Nature*. New York: Methuen, 1978.

Miller, John. *Empire and the Animal Body: Violence, Identity and Ecology in Victorian Adventure Fiction*. London: Anthem Press, 2014.

Milner, Rev. Thomas. *The Gallery of Nature, or Wonders of the Earth and the Heavens*. London: Wm. S. Orr & Co., 1852.

Mitman, Gregg. 'Pachyderm Personalities: The Media of Science, Politics and Conservation'. In *Thinking with Animals: New Perspectives on Anthropomorphism*, edited by Lorraine Daston and Gregg Mitman, 175–195. New York: Columbia University Press, 2005.

Mutwa, Credo. *Isilwane, the Animal: Tales and Fables of Africa*. Cape Town: Struik, 1996.

Neumann, Arthur. *Elephant Hunting in East Equatorial Africa*. Bulawayo: Books of Zimbabwe, 1982 [1898].

Neumann, Roderick P. 'Nature-State-Territory: Toward a Critical Theorization of Conservation Enclosures'. In *Liberation Ecologies: Environment, Development and Social Movements*, edited by Richard Peet and Michael Watts, 179–199. London: Routledge, 1996.

Ntumi, C.P., S.M. Ferreira and R.J. van Aarde. 'A Review of Historical Trends in the Distribution of Elephants in Mozambique'. *Oryx* 43, no. 4 (2009): 568–579.

Nussbaum, Martha. *Compassion: Human and Animal*. Kolkata: Institute of Development Studies, 2008.

Nustad, Knut G. *Creating Africas: Struggles over Nature, Conservation and Land*. Pietermaritzburg: University of KwaZulu-Natal Press, 2015.

O'Connell, Caitlin. *Elephant Don: The Politics of a Pachyderm Posse.* Chicago: University of Chicago Press, 2015.

O'Connell, Caitlin. *The Elephants' Secret Sense: The Hidden Life of the Wild Herds of Africa.* Oxford: One World, 2007.

O'Connell, Caitlin. *Ivory Ghosts.* New York: Random House, 2015.

O'Connell-Rodwell, Caitlin E. 'Keeping an Ear to the Ground: Seismic Communication in Elephants'. *Physiology* 22 (2007): 287–294.

O'Connell-Rodwell, Caitlin E., Timothy Rodwell, Matthew Rice and Lynne Hart. 'Living with the Modern Conservation Paradigm: Can Agricultural Communities Co-exist with Elephants? A Five-Year Case Study in East Caprivi, Namibia'. *Biological Conservation* 93, no. 3 (2000): 381–391.

Opland, Jeff, ed. *Words That Circle Words: A Choice of South African Oral Poetry.* Johannesburg: Ad Donker, 1992.

Parker, Daniel and Timothy Kuiper. 'Elephants in Africa: Big, Grey Biodiversity Thieves?' *South African Journal of Science* 10, no. 3 (2014): 1–3.

Parsons, Glenn. 'The Aesthetic Value of Animals'. *Environmental Ethics* 29, no. 2 (2007): 151–169.

Patterson, Gareth. *The Secret Elephants: The Rediscovery of the World's Most Southerly Elephants.* Johannesburg: Penguin, 2009.

Payne, Katy. *Silent Thunder: In the Presence of Elephants.* Johannesburg: Jonathan Ball, 1998.

Payne, Roger. *Among Whales.* New York: Scribner, 1995.

Paynter, David. *Elephant, Me.* New York: Africa Geographic, 2006.

Peirce, Richard. *Giant Steps.* Cape Town: Struik, 2016.

Phillips, Dana. 'Weeping Elephants, Sensitive Men'. *Safundi* 11, no. 1–2 (2010): 19–47.

Pickover, Michelè. *Animal Rights in South Africa.* Cape Town: Double Storey, 2005.

Pincott, Sharon. *The Elephants and I: Pursuing a Dream in Troubled Zimbabwe.* Johannesburg: Jacana, 2009.

Postel, Gitte. 'Media, Mediums and Metaphors: The Modern South African Sangoma in Various Texts'. *Current Writing* 22, no. 1 (2010): 107–122.

Pratt, Mary Louise. *Imperial Eyes: Travel Writing and Transculturation.* New York: Routledge, 1992.

Pretorius, P.J. *Jungle Man: The Autobiography of Major P.J. Pretorius.* London: George G. Harrap, 1947.

Pringle, Thomas. *African Sketches.* London: Edward Moxon, 1834.

Pringle, Thomas. *The Poetical Works of Thomas Pringle.* London: Edward Moxon, 1838.

Ramsay, P.J., A.M. Smith, J.C. Lee-Thorp, J.C. Vogel, M. Tyldsley and W. Kidwell. '130 000-Year-Old Fossil Elephant Found near Durban, South Africa:

Preliminary Report'. *South African Journal of Science* 89, no. 4 (1993): 165–166. http://researchspace.csir.co.za/dspace/handle/10204/2091.

Reid, Mayne. *The Bush Boys*. Boston, Ticknor and Fields, 1856.

Reid, Mayne. *The Young Yagers, or, a Narrative of Hunting Adventures in Southern Africa*. Boston: Ticknor and Fields, 1857.

Reitz, Melissa. 'Managing the Myths: Knysna Elephant Update'. *Untold Africa*, 5 August 2014. http://untoldafrica.com/managing-the-myths-knysna-elephant-update/#prettyPhoto.

Rolston, Holmes, III. 'Beauty and the Beast: Aesthetic Experience of Wildlife'. In *Valuing Wildlife: Economic and Social Perspectives*, edited by Daniel J. Decker and Gary R. Goff, 187–196. Boulder, CO: Westview Press, 1987.

Rolston, Holmes, III. 'Ethical Responsibilities toward Wildlife'. *Journal of the American Veterinary Association* 200 (1992): 615–622.

Rolston, Holmes, III. 'From Beauty to Duty: Aesthetics of Nature and Environmental Ethics'. In *Environment and the Arts: Perspectives on Environmental Aesthetics*, edited by A. Berleant, 127–141. Aldershot: Ashgate, 2002.

Rothfels, Nigel. 'Killing Elephants: Pathos and Prestige in the Nineteenth Century'. In *Victorian Animal Dreams: Representations of Animals in Victorian Literature and Culture*, edited by Deborah Denenholtz Morse and Martin A. Danahay, 53–63. Aldershot: Ashgate, 2007.

Rycroft, D.K. and A.B. Ngcobo, eds. *The Praises of Dingane*. Pietermaritzburg: University of Natal Press, 1988.

Salafranca, Arja. 'The elephant is unhappy'. http://www.litnet.co.za/the-elephant-is-unhappy/.

Sanchez-Ariño, Tony. *Elephants, Ivory & Hunters*. Huntington Beach: Safari Press, 2004.

Sanchez-Ariño, Tony. *Hunting in Zimbabwe*. Huntington Beach: Safari Press, 1992.

Savory, Phyllis. *Bantu Folk Tales from Southern Africa*. Johannesburg: Howard Timmins, 1974.

Scarry, Elaine. *On Beauty and Being Just*. Princeton: Princeton University Press, 1990.

Scholes, R.J. and K.G. Mennell, eds. *Elephant Management: A Scientific Assessment for South Africa*. Johannesburg: Wits University Press, 2001.

Scholtmeijer, Marian. *Animal Victims in Modern Fiction: From Sanctity to Sacrifice*. Toronto: University of Toronto Press, 1993.

Selous, F.C. *A Hunter's Wanderings in Africa: Being a Narrative of Nine Years Spent amongst the Game of the Far Interior of South Africa*. Bulawayo: Books of Rhodesia, 1970 [1881].

Selous, F.C. *Travel and Adventure in South-East Africa*. Bulawayo: Books of Rhodesia, 1972 [1893].

Shaw, Damian. *South African Flora and Fauna (The Lithic Period)*. Cape Town: Snail Press, 1990.

Skead, C.J. *Historical Incidence of the Larger Land Mammals in the Broader Eastern Cape*. 2nd edition. Port Elizabeth: Nelson Mandela Metropolitan University, 2007.

Skead, C.J. *Historical Incidences of the Larger Land Mammals in the Broader Western and Northern Cape*. 2nd edition. Port Elizabeth: Nelson Mandela Metropolitan University, 2011.

Smith, Andrew. *Journal of a Journey in South Africa*. Cape Town: Balkema, 1975 [1838].

Smith, Wilbur. *Elephant Song*. London: Pan, 1991.

Snow, Nancy C. 'Compassion for Animals'. *Between the Species* 9, no. 2 (Spring 1993): 61–66. http://digitalcommons.calpoly.edu/cgi/viewcontent. cgi?article=1836&context=bts.

Snowdon, Charles T. 'The Continuing Question of Animal Awareness'. *Science* 251, no. 4 995 (1991): 813–814.

Sparrman, Anders. *A Voyage to the Cape of Good Hope towards the Antarctic Polar Circle, and Round the World but Chiefly into the Country of the Hottentots and Caffres, from theYear 1772 to 1776*. Edited by V.S. Forbes. Cape Town: Van Riebeeck Society, 1975 [1785].

Stevenson-Hamilton, James. *South African Eden*. Cape Town: Struik, 1993 [1937].

Stevenson-Hamilton, James. *Wild Life in South Africa*. London: Cassell, 1947.

Stewart, Dianne. *The Zebra's Stripes and Other African Animal Tales*. Cape Town: Struik, 2004.

Stigand, C.H. *Hunting the Elephant in Africa and Other Recollections of Thirteen Years' Wanderings*. New York: Macmillan, 1913.

St John, Lauren. *An Elephant's Tale*. London: Orion, 2009.

Stokes, C.S. *Sanctuary*. Cape Town: Maskew Miller, 1953.

Struthers, John. *A Boy and an Elephant*. Pretoria: Sce, 1998.

Sunstein, Cass R. and Martha C. Nussbaum, eds. *Animal Rights: Current Debates and New Directions*. Oxford: Oxford University Press, 2004.

Talbot, William J. 'Pathfinders and Pioneers, Explorers and Scientists, 1487–1976'. In *A History of Scientific Endeavour in South Africa*, edited by A.C. Brown, 1–32. Johannesburg: Royal Society of South Africa, 1977.

Thamm, M. 'When Artists Are Trampled by the Elephants of Politics'. *Sunday Times*, 31 October 2010.

Thomas, E.W. *Bushman Stories*. Cape Town: Oxford University Press, 1950.

Tomaselli, Keyan. 'Textualizing the San "Past": Dancing with Development'. *Visual Anthropology* 12, no. 2–3 (1999): 197–212.

Tredger, Nick. *From Rhodesia to Mugabe's Zimbabwe Chronicles of a Game Ranger.* Johannesburg: Galago, 2009.

Urry, A. 'Report on the Bernard Carp Knysna Elephant Expedition'. *African Wildlife* 6, no. 1 (1952): 6–7.

Valoi, Estacios. 'Mozambique Elephants Obliterated'. *Mail & Guardian*, 3–9 October 2014: 22.

Van Aarde, Rudi. *Elephants: A Way Forward.* Pretoria: Conservation Ecology Research Unit, 2014.

Van der Post, Laurens. *Flamingo Feather.* London: Hogarth, 1955.

Van der Post, Laurens. *The Heart of the Hunter.* Harmondsworth: Penguin, 1961.

Vice, Samantha. 'The Ethics of Animal Beauty'. *Environmental Ethics* 39, no. 1 (2017): 75–96.

Vinnicombe, Patricia. *People of the Eland: Rock Paintings of the Drakensberg Bushmen as a Reflection of Their Life and Thought.* Johannesburg: Wits University Press, 1976.

Walker, Clive. *Dear Elephant, Sir.* Cape Town: Southern Books, 1992.

Walker, John Frederick. *Ivory's Ghosts: The White Gold of History and the Fate of Elephants.* New York: Atlantic Monthly Press, 2009.

Watson, Lyall. *Elephantoms: Tracking the Elephant.* London: Penguin Viking, 2003.

Weavind, Tina. 'Breeders Sink Teeth into Profits'. *Business Day*, 15 June 2014.

Wemmer, Christen and Catherine A. Christen, eds. *Elephants and Ethics: Toward a Morality of Coexistence.* Baltimore: Johns Hopkins University Press, 2008.

Westley, M.B. 'The Novice's Problem Elephant'. *Magnum* 28, no. 4 (1998): 12–14.

Westra, Laura. *Living in Integrity: A Global Ethic to Restore a Fragmented Earth.* Lanham, MD: Rowman & Littlefield, 1998.

Whitehouse, Anna and Pat Irwin. *A Guide to the Elephants of Addo.* Grahamstown: Self-published, 2002.

Whyte, Ian. 'Headaches and Heartaches: The Elephant Management Dilemma'. In *Environmental Ethics: What Really Matters, What Really Works*, edited by David Schmidtz and Elizabeth Schmidtz, 293–305. New York: Oxford University Press, 2002.

Whyte, Ian and Richard Fayrer-Hoskin. 'Playing Elephant God: Ethics of Managing Wild African Elephant Populations'. In *Elephants and Ethics: Toward a Morality of Coexistence*, edited by Christen Wemmer and Catherine A. Christen, 399–418. Baltimore: Johns Hopkins University Press, 2008.

Wise, Stephen. *Drawing the Line: Science and the Case for Animal Rights.* New York: Basic Books, 2003.

Wolhuter, Henry. *Memories of a Game Ranger*. Johannesburg: Wildlife Protection Society of South Africa, 1948.

Woodhouse, Bert. *The Rain and Its Creatures*. Johannesburg: William Waterman, 1992.

Woodhouse, Bert. *When Animals Were People*. Johannesburg: Chris Rensburg Publications, 1984.

Wylie, Dan. 'The Anthropomorphic Ethic: Fiction and the Animal Mind in Virginia Woolf's *Flush* and Barbara Gowdy's *The White Bone*'. *ISLE: Interdisciplinary Studies in Literature and Environment* 9, no. 2 (2002): 115–132.

Wylie, Dan. *Elephant*. London: Reaktion Books, 2008.

Wylie, Dan. 'Elephants and Compassion: Ecological Criticism and South African Hunting Literature'. *English in Africa* 28, no. 2 (2001): 79–100.

Wylie, Dan. 'Elephants and the Ethics of Ecological Criticism: A Case Study in Recent South African Fiction'. In *Re-imagining Africa: New Critical Perspectives*, edited by Sue Kossew and Dianne Schwerdt, 175–193. New York: Nova Science, 2001.

Wylie, Dan. 'Feral Whispering: Conservation, Community and the Reach of the Literary'. *English in Africa* 41, no. 3 (2014): 119–140.

Wylie, Dan. *Savage Delight: White Myths of Shaka*. Pietermaritzburg: University of Natal Press, 2000.

Wylie, Dan. 'Touching Trunks: Elephants, Ecology and Compassion in Three Southern African Teen Novels'. *Journal of Literary Studies* 30, no. 4 (2014): 25–45.

Wylie, Dan. 'Why Write a Poem about Elephants?' *Mosaic* 39, no. 4 (2006): 27–46.

Index

Printed and bound by CPI Group (UK) Ltd, Croydon, CR0 4YY

09/06/2025

14685798-0002